CHICAGO: CONFIDENTIAL!

Previously Published

by Jack Lait

THE BIG HOUSE

BROADWAY MELODY

BEAST OF THE CITY

PUT ON THE SPOT

GANGSTER GIRL

BEEF, IRON AND WINE (*short stories*)

GUS THE BUS

OUR WILL ROGERS

WILL ROGERS' WIT AND WISDOM

A PRACTICAL GUIDE TO SUCCESSFUL WRITING

by Lee Mortimer

NEW YORK BEHIND THE SCENES

by Jack Lait and Lee Mortimer

NEW YORK: CONFIDENTIAL!

CHICAGO
Confidential

BY JACK LAIT
AND
LEE MORTIMER

CROWN PUBLISHERS
NEW YORK

SECOND PRINTING, MARCH, 1950

Printed in the United States of America
American Book–Stratford Press, Inc., New York

Contents

▼

A WORD WITH YOU

P*-S-S-S-T!*

Lait and Mortimer want to put this up to you—*Confidential!*

Chicago has always been swell "copy." It has been described, deplored, panned, eulogized, analyzed, dissected and diagnosed by travelers and natives.

There have been speculations on what Christ would do if the Second Coming chanced to transpire on Randolph Street. Dickens wept about it, Mark Twain kidded it and Rudyard Kipling found it far from Mandalay. Britishers wrote profound inside stuff about its gangster killings and the Nazi newspapers called its politics outrageous.

Come now two reporters, both of whom live in New York. But Lait was brought to Chicago when he was 12, lived there 25 years during which he started a newspaper career which saw him internationally famous as a Chicago chronicler and commentator before New York called him. Since then he has been back hundreds of times and has made a career in New York writing mostly about Chicago. Mortimer was born in Chicago, trained in New York, then covered Chicago for innumerable columns and news reports on nightlife and underworld topics.

For this book Lait and Mortimer came back to Chicago, again and again, searching and surveying its thoroughfares and its alleys, its beauty-spots and its sordid muck. They think they know Chicago today better than any local, and know some things about it that will amaze the natives. For they have the added advantage of seeing it through objective as well as educated eyes of their craft.

One thing they did not find—and that is a "message." The authors have nothing to sell except books. They have no political prejudices or convictions, feel no mandate to make any place better, hear no call to spare their friends, and know no enemies.

Much of this text will shock the hell out of you. But this is not an exposé. We called 'em as we saw 'em, where we looked.

We didn't look much in the museums, the Art Institute, the lovely parks where we played as children, the homey cottages of the respectable peasants or the busy workshops. This report is not designed to be comprehensive. The bread-and-butter facts and the booster statistics we leave to those who are intrigued by such. It hits the high spots and the low, with no obligations assumed except to set forth the lowdown on such things as interested us and which we think you wouldn't go prowling after, because you are not professional hunters.

We treated New York the same way, and we still live and flourish there. Some important persons no longer speak to us, but others address us with words weird and loud, some of them even new.

It is not our purpose to become beloved. We leave that to the naive and the timid.

The job we undertook led us through crime and slime and dirt and crooked politics; shameful and shameless racketeering on a scale of concentrated and diffused power such as the world had never known before; bums and slums, dope and delinquency, the nation's most flagrant race problems; and a once-rugged metropolis throttled by a super-government of an entirely new degree of organization, might and money that rules the intimate affairs of millions. We caught the Prairie Queen with her slip showing. Before we left we caught her with it off.

That's why we were born—to tell you about it—*Confidential!*

PART ONE

THE PLACES

(*Confidential!*)

1. "OH, WHY DID THEY BUILD THAT LOUSY LAKE SO CLOSE TO THAT BEAUTIFUL BURG?"

—From the assorted poems of
"BATHHOUSE JOHN" COUGHLIN.

'T*WASN'T SO* at all. They built the town close to the Lake, which was and is beautiful.

The vistas of her shore are breathtaking. It is a long line made originally by nature, but largely reconstructed, filled in and distorted but improved through the enterprise of some of the thievingest mayors who had to contrive contracts for the faithful.

Broad boulevards parallel the Lake front and many miles of parks come to the water's edge. There is a plenitude of beauty far beyond that offered by any other American city, but most of it is, like many other of its admirable adjuncts, on the outer fringe. Inland, it is largely ugly and uncouth.

Arriving, the traveler sees a vision of green if by air, black if by rail. From above, the view is colored by trees that strut their heads high. Vegetation seems to grow everywhere—in grimy factory yards, vacant lots and in backyards behind the huts and the hovels.

The railroad passenger enters through a jumble of iron, steel and coal, on a crazy maze of tracks leading to the world's No. 1 junction point. He sees concrete and cement and mills that belch flames at night and ramshackle back-porches hanging precariously onto grimy wooden shanties.

The green for the man who comes out of the sky and the black for the land-locked voyager together symbolize Chicago's story. The green is the green of the village, for Chicago is still a hick town. Vast, rich, mechanized but moribund, it still has the mind and heart, many of the virtues and all of the vices of *ruris Americana.*

The black is the color of its municipal soul, the most corrupt community under all the heavens.

The black, too, is the black of its rails and the soft, choking coal that propels its myriad locomotives. For Chicago is earthbound by its rails. They made it and they ruined it. They brought it people, millions of them. They brought it the wealth of the forests and the plunder of the mines and the loot of all the continents and the spoils of all the ages. Over them rolled in culture and art and civilization, and on them roared in vagabonds and criminals, whores and pimps, deserters and jail-breakers, the scum and the riffraff of the New World. Then came the dispossessed and the impoverished and the unwanted of the Old World, some to become solid citizens but others to import the ancient shady practices which had grown up through the centuries of oppression and intrigue and illiteracy.

Those rails hemmed her in. Like her dream trees, they took root and sprouted wherever there was earth to support them. They begrimed her approaches and transformed her verdant plains into freight yards. They besooted her buildings, befouled her sky and painted all things, living or inanimate, a dead, dun gray. Rails shaped Chicago's destiny and her geography. Even now, in this air age, they are her spine, around which is formed her physical shape.

Until quite recently it was the pride of Chicago that no passenger could ride through it. That meant that thousands every day had to stop there for a considerable time no matter what their ultimate destination. It took an advertising campaign to allow a half-dozen Pullman cars a day to be switched from one station to another; and their occupants are held by timetables so that they must make a considerable stopover.

Into Chicago pour strangers from other cities, and they are jolted by the anachronisms of this comparatively young burg. The first thing that blasts you is the shriek of a crossing-cop's whistle, a shrill nerve-rending toot which ends on a high note. Chicago has automatic traffic signals but it does not trust them. The whistles rend the air from dawn to midnight. In other large places they are used only in emergencies, but the traffic bulls would as soon give up their whistles as their bright, large, tin, six-pointed stars, which would be very uncomfortable if they had to do with them what the hoodlums usually tell a Chicago cop to do with them.

The men with the wheels on their arms pay no heed to anything else. They are intent on de-synchronizing the traffic lights. There is one instance on record where a policeman did step to the side and arrest a murderer: he had parked the corpse in front of a fire-plug.

All this is not because Chicago knows no better. It is the way it is because Chicago has always been unique, strident, obtrusive, pugnacious and self-sufficient. Chicago hangs on to much which has long been wiped out elsewhere, a throwback of its past, on which it built a tremendous city on an uncharted prairie and always did it singularly. That is Chicago, America's last frontier. A city of colossal dimensions in every way, with one of the largest foreign-born populations in the world, drawn from all quarters of the universe, it is more American than any other and its manners and mores have never lost the breath and spirit of the Old West, whence came its cattle, its ore, its timber and many of its founding fathers.

That may explain Chicago's nonchalant attitude toward lawlessness. The frontier was proud of its bad men. New lands are settled by rebels. Blind amorality is slowly going out of fashion in the older and more settled centers. The Eastern cities have toned down through the infiltration of the older cultures. Chicago can take its culture or leave it. It clings to much of the tradition that came in on horseback and by river raft and by covered wagon when it boomed into a bonanza more fabulous than any gold rush.

Dishonesty in the civil service at the higher levels is almost unknown in most European countries, especially in Britain. When our country's cities were swelling with growing pains, corruption was so common that the citizens laughed rather than wept. Political machines and notorious crooked elections and open passing of swag have declined. But not in Chicago. There it has grown and still grows, though the decades have taught the boodlers and the robbers a few niceties of concealment behind more modern practices.

Chicago, the great airport, lake port, river port and above all railroad terminal, is isolated. Surrounded by the richest necklace of nature's bounty and man's handiworks, it is still and alone the capital of an incalculable empire—the Midwest. It is a self-sufficient territory over which Chicago reigns supreme and alone. It is the trading, manufacturing, industrial and financial center for 15,000,000 inhabitants of its domain. And while it rules this hinterland and draws from it its nourishment, it sucks from it too the standards and psychology of the region. To the wheat pit and the stockyards and the rolling-mills come not only the produce of the nation's heartline but also its ideas, customs, flavor and new blood. It is fundamentally a section of farmers. They and their usufruct stream in from Ohio, Indiana, Illinois, Michigan, Wisconsin, Minnesota, the Dakotas, Kansas, Iowa and Missouri and the entire slice south to the Gulf and across to Texas. All that is Chicago's commercial and social suburbs.

Despite the preponderant percentage of foreign immigrants who mingled into the phenomenal growth of the city, the Anglo-Saxon stock has taken over the aliens, who could never throw over the distinctive patterns of far-away life, such as eventuated in New Orleans, St. Louis, Cincinnati, Buffalo and many big New England cities.

Each and every component of Chicago's polyglot and polychrome population strives to hold its own ways, but the Midwest gets them. They have swelled the population and some have risen to altitude and power as among the finest citizens, and the most deadly, but they cannot dent Chicago inwardly or outwardly. As groups they wield tremendous influence for good and evil. But they intermarry, or gradually learn American ways, take on the habits and the dress and coloration of the city and of the sections and leave Chicago still a gigantic village, the heart of thousands of other inland villages, a huge provincial camp-meeting of Americans.

Chicago's provincialism is delightful, refreshing, relaxing, exasperating and smug. Chicagoland flaunts an independence in speech, attire, ethics and human equations that sets it out from what snobs might call the nation's "main current," but which is really only an irritation along the periphery. New York, San Francisco, New Orleans, Miami aren't America; Chicago is. Chicago doesn't give a damn about the rest of the nation nor a thought for the rest of the world. A big football game, a night baseball game, a major boxing-match, a music festival under the stars, a first-class love-nest murder, an aldermanic election—if they happen in Chicago—are the most important things on earth. They are the prime topic of conversation for days before and they flag down business when they transpire. They rub Washington and London and Moscow and Manhattan off the front pages, and they are local phenomena until another comes around.

A famous Chicago editor had a sign hung high over the city room which said:

A DOG-FIGHT ON CLARK STREET
IS MORE IMPORTANT THAN A
WAR IN THE BALKANS

And the Chicago dailies saturate their immediate environs, which formulates the farmers and small-towners into potential Chicagoans conditioned to adopt all that they have envisioned as great.

The city's Western fixation shows not only in its life and its clothes—men wear broader brimmed hats—but in its choice of literature. The Easterner seeks relaxation largely in mystery and detective stories. But when the Chicagoan buys a two-bit reprint it is almost always a Western adventure story. All publishers and distributors recognize that demand.

Chicago's motto was and still is "I Will." That was right, adopted when it was a go-getter town. Its population and its everything spiraled. But something happened within the last two decades. Chicagoans probably don't realize it, but they are nervously aware that somewhere the ball-bearings burned out. The returning expatriate sees it in vivid perspective.

"I Will" has changed to "I Want."

As these pages unfold, you will get a panorama of the gimmies, not in a progress of making and growing, but in one of taking and swiping. There is a price on everything and somebody is getting it.

Chicago was founded by dynamic, hairy individualists who hewed and wrested a new world out of the woods and the mud where only a murky river moved sluggishly—and the wrong way. They fought nature and each other, inexhaustibly, imaginatively and victoriously, against obstacles that now seem incredible. They were the titans of the nineteenth century, which abounded with rugged men and women who built our country without benefit of minimum hours and a sigh for security. Those who created Chicago were of the toughest breed, who battled for riches and not for mere means of existence. The place is so young that we can fix Chicago's decline at about the time its founding fathers went to their Valhalla. When they died, their rich and pampered heirs sought more leisurely and opulent lives. Some moved to the Eastern scenes of society, sport and play. Many of the big enterprises went under management of self-made subordinates. The great industries now are run largely for absentee ownership. The old leaders left few new leaders in their blood-lines. The big brains, the daring and the vision today belong to the comparative newcomers, the intruders who run the underworld.

Almost all the good families that remained turned their backs to the city. They fled from the smoke and the grime and the daily conflict to pleasant suburbs. After them came many from the middle classes and the respectable lower classes, until it may virtually be said that no one lives in Chicago who can get out of it. The influx of Negroes and their wide spread, the overflow of foreign immigrants and the physical decadence of the city which was rebuilt fresh and new after the big fire of 1871 have created and populated subsidiary towns by the dozens north and west of the city limits, whose people come in only to work, to shop, and in a minor degree to get drunk.

They vote, go to school and to church in their own communities, so that Chicago's problems are no longer theirs. Therefore, hundreds of thousands who make their livings in Chicago have no interest in it politically, have abandoned it to those who cannot afford to move, or who will not because conditions, such as they are, are vastly superior to those they have known before.

This shift from the cream to the skim-milk is reflected in every artery of the city's life. Chicago forty years ago was the hub of a virile, vigorous circle of literature, art and, strangely, a center of poetry. It was an important book-publishing producer (the last general publisher gave up his struggle while these lines were being written) and it supported a score of legitimate theaters. Chicago was a booster-burg, with intense activity for civic greatness. Now it hasn't even an almanac. (Brooklyn, Houston and Atlanta have them.) And all attempts at magazines reflecting Chicago have failed. Chicagoans no longer write books about their city, because it has few citizens left who can write and of those even fewer are brave enough to tell the real story.

In 1910 Chicago breezily and confidently expected to surpass New York by 1950; in 1950 it no longer talks of growing bigger than New York—it wonders when it will be smaller than Los Angeles. New York was the target, the rival in a race to dominate America's future. Now New York is hated because it is envied.

With all, Chicago is still rewarding for the few who want to make it a fight. Bustling like an oriental bazaar, its opportunities are boundless for those who seek success and work at it. Life there can be extremely pleasant. The majority of its people are friendly and warm-hearted, not as hard-boiled as those in older communities. There is no established aristocracy. Anybody who is anybody knows everybody who is anybody. The Loop brings them together in a small confine where ways are still democratic and the hand-shake is hearty.

We point out its retrogression, for we see it like older brothers who have come home for the holidays. But we love it, while we sorrow because we have not found it as we left it.

2. THE LOOP AND THE LUPOS

OVER A SALOON on the southeast corner of Clark and Randolph Streets, across from the City Hall and catty-corner from the Hotel Sherman, which in its day was as sporty as any caravansary in the land, is a red neon sign proclaiming it "The World's Busiest Night Life Corner."

It was 10:30 o'clock on a Saturday night. Three stragglers stood at the curb. Here and there someone passed by. Inside, a half-dozen persons sat at the long bar. Two were girls in low-cut evening gowns, dejectedly by themselves, in a corner, drinking cokes.

Yet once that neon sign had justification. Once this storied crossing was one of those where, "if you stood there long enough you would meet everybody in the world." It was the hub of the Rialto, of the humming after-dark activities, of the legitimate stage which lighted twenty theatres played by the most eminent stars and the greatest original casts. It was a lean week when there weren't six Broadway musicals going. There were three big-time and several middle-class vaudeville houses the year around. Burlesque in its best form was played by touring circuit companies. The hotels had magnificent floor-shows which featured top names.

Great crowds still throng past this corner in every direction, daytimes. For here are the municipal and county offices; busy eating-places; the voyagers to and from State Street with its tremendous department stores, and to La Salle Street, the Wall Street of the Midwest; and the teeming office buildings and hotels. For this is the liveliest intersection in the Loop. And the Loop is the heart of Chicago's commercial life, the capital of her civic activities, and the headquarters of her underworld. For crime, like other great enterprises, functions from skyscraper offices and swank hotel suites.

Technically, the Loop is a rectangle of rails on an elevated structure about a half-mile square. In practice, the term has been loosened to include the entire central business district—

Downtown—a larger and still-growing area. This chapter will treat of that portion between the River and Roosevelt Road, formerly 12th Street, and the River and Michigan Avenue, on the Lake front.

The actual circumscribed Loop was once hailed as the diadem in Chicago's golden crown. But it became the stone in her gallbladder. Though it contains the egregious shopping center, the swollen banks, the fantastic wheat pit, the nucleus of its crowded hotels and what is left of its living theatres and all the major movie mansions, it is symbolic of Chicago itself, helplessly hemmed in by a ring of rails.

When a line of cable cars, and then the combination of four elevated roads, first framed these few acres, untold riches came to the landowners and shopkeepers therein. Fierce pride in this concentration put a pall on everything around it and outside it, and if you weren't in the Loop you weren't anywhere.

There was only one way to go and that was up. As the population expanded and the Loop couldn't, a host of tall buildings rose, and so did ground values, up to $20,000 a front foot. Rents got out of hand. The congestion became an impossible problem. While everything inside that small oblong became almost priceless, plots a few blocks away went begging, were permitted to lapse into decay and housed some of the blackest hell-holes known to civilization. On Custom House Place (now Federal Street), on Plymouth Court, along State Street and Wabash Avenue south of Van Buren Street, and on Harrison and Polk Streets from the River to the Lake, were lousy bagnios, assignation coops, barrel-houses and decrepit deadfalls.

Only in comparatively recent years did a few shops and hotels venture past the magic deadline. The unspeakable traffic problems forced the opening of branch and independent stores at outlying points. These were accessible and they became popular and are booming. The very Loop which once brought everybody downtown drove millions out of it, because it could no longer absorb them. Many now say it would be a good thing if the Loop were torn down and subways and modern buses took over the transportation. That would spread business even more and raise values for others, instead of pouring the wealth back into the few old families that own much of the area.

There is still sentiment attached to Downtown, too, for there Chicago became a metropolis and every block created its traditions. Much of that has gone.

The movies, with their continuous grind, can support theatres which no longer could live on eight performances a week at high prices. Many of the fine restaurants could no longer meet the skyrocketing rents. With competition in the air there are fewer fine railroad trains bringing in heavy spenders. The night-places were hit by the same causes that expunged or exiled so many good restaurants.

Nightlife in part feeds on itself. For every ten patrons there is an employe. High-priced actors get money and spend money. Openings of shows, which were frequent, brought trainloads from New York, all people of means. The flight of many wealthy Chicago families before the invasion of immigrants depleted the population of much of the class that supports the arts and the livelier diversions.

Then came the outer drives, the extension of Wacker Drive and the build-up of the single side of Michigan Boulevard open to tenancy, further draining from the Loop some of the flower of its supporters. The Palmer House, with its huge ceilings and its wasteful, delightful dining room, in which served white-haired Negroes, two of whom had waited on Abraham Lincoln, gave way to a commercial chain-operated hotel for tourists and traveling men; the Sherman of a million memories went higher and wider, and the concessions in its lobby now take in more revenue than the whole enterprise did in the days when the beloved manager was Frank Bering, who knew everyone and understood everyone, and Mike O'Brien, a saintly ex-house dick, was night host in the heart of Chicago life; the gemuetlich Bismarck Hotel was turned into a humming and efficient skyscraper; smaller theatrical hotels were torn down.

Now there is a rash of cocktail lounges with big and quick turnover and the usual accessories of B girls and 26 girls and not a few with strippers. These work about as the nabe joints do, which will be set forth as fully hereinafter as our stomachs will allow.

Physically, the Loop and its nearby downtown environs have been metamorphosed considerably during the past 20 years. Decentralization had this effect: Many older office buildings and theatres were unable to pay their way when the demand for Loop space fell off. Some were demolished to save operating expenses and taxes. A few were replaced by one- and two-story taxpayers. Sites of other structures are still vacant or employed as parking lots.

Many visitors remark about the war-torn look of the Loop. If you didn't know better, you might think it had been blitzed and the rubble removed. These empty pockmarks are incongruous amid an otherwise solid mass of granite and concrete. State Street, once the proud thoroughfare of department stores (where they were invented), also feels the pinch as the big houses open suburban branches and decentralize their operations.

Meanwhile, other prime retail locations on the street have been vacated by the old-timers to be taken over by chain stores. Gone are many great names from State Street. Some passed away decades ago, such as Siegel, Cooper's, the Rothschild Store, and Hillman's. Latest casualty is Mollie Netcher's famed Boston Store.

When Chicago was a motion picture production center in the early days of the cinema, before Cecil B. DeMille discovered Hollywood, movie stars commonly hung around the Loop. It was not uncommon to see Charlie Chaplin, when he was the king of Essanay, one of the pioneer companies. Beverly Bayne and Francis X. Bushman, America's Sweetheart and matinee idol respectively, brightened the Loop's night spots. Now the only film stars who are seen in Chicago are in transit.

Likewise, in the early days of radio, Chicago was a production center second only to New York. Many of the big radio names of the 1920's helped lend glamor to the Loop.

Today's theatrical industry is limited to five or six houses, and only infrequently are they all occupied. The drama was once a potent force in Chicago life. Chicago was considered one of the best show towns in the world. Engagements there were usually profitable because of the enthusiasm with which Chicagoans supported the stage. It was one of the few towns where legitimate theatres were allowed to operate seven nights a week by law. This tradition was so strong, even after the inception of Actors Equity, that an exception was made for Chicago. To this day, shows run seven nights a week. Casts are paid an additional one-sixth of a week's salary or skip a matinee.

Proceeding south on State Street, one finds this avenue of merchant princes abruptly changing complexion where the "El" crosses it at Van Buren.

Below this intersection, for a third of a mile, is a Skid Row as low and as lousy as any in the country, with the usual in the way of flop houses, flea circuses, hock shops, tattoo parlors, shooting galleries, poisonous lunch-rooms, and that ever present Chicago phenomenon, the burlesque bar, with strippers and mixers.

Around the corner is the fine old Blackstone Hotel and the world's largest, the Stevens. Unwary guests of both, returning from or going to the Loop, often take State Street as a short cut, and suddenly find themselves in the middle of one of the most vicious areas on earth.

Almost all the better restaurants which were the rendezvous of the sportier sets, the top show people, political prominents, the grand-standers and the box-holders when Chicago had race tracks within its limits, have also been obliterated by rising rentals and declining patronage. Among these were DeJonghe's, Stilson's, Kuntz-Remmler's, Vogelsang's, Billy Boyle's Chop House, Billy Mangler's, the Union, not to mention the world-famed Heinegabubler's, with its collapsing stairs, soap for cheese and many other practical jokes which were considered devilish. Henrici's is among the few standard eating-places left and that has been taken over by a lunch-room chain, though its standards are still high.

There were half-a-hundred more drop-ins, snug beer stubes and dining rooms where newspapermen learned to know more New York celebrities than anyone in New York could know, for the great actors and producers and even the Wall Street nabobs were lonesome away from home, and everybody had to come to Chicago. J. Pierpont Morgan, who reserved all-year quarters at the Chicago Club, lunched at Thibodeaux's on La Salle Street, and there he was as accessible as a clerk. John W. ("Bet-a-Million") Gates, Charles T. Yerkes, the traction magnate and wholesale purchaser of politicians, and Sam Insull, who was to succeed him as the utilities magnate, usually ate at the Auditorium grill. C. K. G. Billings, the gas and coke tycoon and international playboy, had a table in the skylight cafe on top of the Pullman Building, but George M. Pullman, who owned it, could be found in the little exclusive bar which Chapin and Gore maintained, with no street entrance, nearby on Adams Street, for the exclusive trade.

One of the principal theatrical hangouts was the basement table-d'hote under the Brevoort Hotel, adjoining the La Salle Theatre, and it was there the town came to peek at and gasp over Buda Godman, who was called the prettiest girl ever born and raised in the town, and who finished as a prematurely white-haired ex-convict after a unique career as a badger-worker, gem-thief and associate of nabobs, robbers and murderers.

Buda was the daughter of a race track sheet-writer, an only child. Her beauty was so fearsomely fascinating that before maturity she stopped traffic on the streets. She was petite, a wee trifle plumpish, with big steel-blue eyes, a tip-tilted nose, an oval face with a dimpled chin, a peewee mouth and tiny hands and feet.

Her father's calling threw him in with shady people and he decided to guard his growing daughter from such influences. So, when she was 15, he sent her to St. Joseph's Academy, in Adrian, Michigan, a convent school. Adrian was a one-night stand, and when a minstrel show was scheduled there Buda scaled the fence and not only saw the performance, but waited at the stage door for a pint-sized tenor named Tell Taylor, from Findlay, Ohio. Taylor was a small-time ham, but he had written a song of blather and bathos which was to live and become a barbershop quartet favorite, *Down by the Old Millstream.*

He fell in love with the girl, of course, and, since she had passed her sixteenth birthday, he could marry her in Michigan, which he did. To do this he had to blow his company and he brought her to Chicago, where he got a job as the juvenile and got her into the chorus of *The Time, The*

Place and The Girl, which also produced a perennial torch ballad, *I Wonder Who's Kissing Her Now.* The song was delivered by Joe Howard, its composer, and Buda was chosen to sit in a subdued spotlight behind a scrim, as the girl in his memory.

Chicago woke up to the discovery of a new rave, Buda Godman. She was wooed and pursued and she fell. Taylor tried to kill her and fired several shots at her, but missed. He sued her for divorce, got a decree without even finishing his testimony. Buda, now confident of her sex appeal, came to New York. There she met Charles Stoneham, the very rich owner of the New York Giants. He installed her in a plushy apartment on West 55th Street, which became the gathering place of notables, over which Buda reigned, her little hands heavy with diamonds and her eyes bright with wine. At one of these parties she first met "Dapper Don" Collins, an extremely prepossessing international confidence man, who had been in several penitentiaries and was to be in others.

Collins was as well known on the Riviera and in Baden Baden as he was in New York. In Paris a divorced wife of Otto Heyworth, Chicago millionaire, jumped out of a window in an attempt to kill herself because she couldn't hold Collins. He was named as the corespondent when Garnett Patton Inman, wife of an heir to the James B. Duke tobacco fortune, was sued. He was later involved in the shadows of the murder of Dot King (who was kept by the son-in-law of the Philadelphia Morgan partner, Edward T. Stotesbury) a crime with a blackmail background. After the murder of Arnold Rothstein, Collins was the constant companion of the blonde who had been the sweetheart of the gambler-racketeer.

Collins' true name was Robert Arthur Tourbillon.

Buda abandoned Stoneham, with all he had to offer, to become the woman and accomplice of Collins, and in that capacity she and his crew of badger-working crooks carried out one of the boldest jobs in history, the full facts of which are revealed here for the first time.

In New York, stopping at the Claridge Hotel, then fashionable, was a wealthy Chicago importer, who had an estate and a family in Highland Park. He was picked for a plucking. Buda, who was still young enough, was instructed to let down her hair in girlish fashion and make contact with him in the lobby. It wasn't hard for her to meet any man. She began to sob, told him she was a convent girl who had run away (a role she should have known how to play) and she wanted to go home to her mother in Chicago, but had no money. He had a Packard car and he volunteered to drive her back.

They spent the night in Atlantic City, a slight detour from the recommended road. The next morning, while they were both asleep, there came a heavy knock on the door. Since he had registered under a fictitious name and had not ordered breakfast, he refused to open it—until a heavy voice called, "This is the law. United States Department of Justice."

Two men came in. They were George Irwin and Ed Donoghue, conmen. They showed badges and declared him under arrest and Buda held as a witness on a Mann Act charge. They said they had seen them leave the Claridge and, because of the girl's youth and beauty, they had suspected something overt and had trailed them to the seashore resort, across a state line into New Jersey.

He was terrorized. They demanded $25,000 to square the rap. He said he had no way of getting it without exposing his position and they volunteered to ride with him and the girl to Chicago. There, arriving the second morning, they went to his office. But he either stalled or could not immediately get his hands on that amount in cash. They waited until noon and then grabbed him and marched him and the girl into the Federal Building.

Meanwhile they had made telephone arrangements with Doc Brady, Homer French and Jerry Christian, other members of their gang, who had preceded them to Chicago by train. It was the lunch-hour and one courtroom was empty, recessed. With Brady, a scholarly looking swindler, on the bench, and French and Christian acting respectively as clerk and bailiff, they actually started the fantastic farce of "trying" the frightened and guilty merchant, after telling him that this was a preliminary hearing, ex parte, in lieu of a Grand Jury, at which he was not entitled to counsel.

They put Buda on the stand, swore her on a Bible, and she started tearfully to relate that this man had not only taken her to New Jersey for "immoral purposes," the language of the statute, but that he had seduced her. He cried for mercy. He soon managed to obtain $15,000 from a friend and he gave it to Irwin.

The friend was curious and he urged the victim to tell him part of the story. He induced him to make a complaint. Buda and Christian were found together in a room in a hotel and were arrested, and through them the others, still in Chicago, were rounded up. The complete story did not come to light because the six jumped bail, in all $60,000, four times what they had gouged from their victim.

Buda fled to New York, where Stoneham took her back, though she was now intimate with Christian as well, and still working with Collins. She was never brought back to Chicago for prosecution. She remained in the East and was often seen with Rothstein, Owney Madden, New York's boss killer-bootlegger, and Bill Fallon, the "great mouthpiece" of Gene Fowler's classic tale of the shiftiest criminal lawyer New York has known.

Harry Glenby, a rich hairnet manufacturer, who lived in a duplex apartment off Fifth Avenue, was stuck up in his home by three gunmen who got in representing themselves as bootleggers with a delivery for the household. They tied up the butler and Glenby's daughter and got away with $350,000 worth of jewels. The butler identified a Rogues Gallery picture of Sam ("Sammy the Hook") Entratta, alias Ippolletti. He was trailed and good detective work soon tied him up with Joe and Tony Indelicato, brothers, and Buda, who was known to them as Helen Smith and to others as "Sweet Alice" Williams. She was on opium by that time.

She and a blonde with whom she shared an apartment, Ruby Goelet, were shadowed. They had made contact with a "fence" from Philadelphia, to whom they were to turn over the swag for $150,000 in currency. This transaction, for safety, was to be carried out in Central Park. They were watched throughout and detectives with binoculars saw the man pass over the bills and receive a brown paper bag. They arrested the three—and found another, a duplicate bag, containing crushed crockery, beside Buda. Caught with the goods, she not only confessed that she was disposing of the stolen loot, but that she intended after she got the money to make love to the fence and switch bags on him.

The Hook was killed and Tony Indelicato was taken for a ride and rubbed out. Joe Indelicato was poisoned, but survived. Buda got eight to twenty years in Auburn prison, and was paroled at the end of six.

Lait, who had known her when she was a bride, tried to find her. He wanted to buy her story. But the parole officers had closed every avenue of information. They did say, however, that their charge had turned white-haired and fat.

That was sacrilege! No matter what Buda Godman had done, she should never have grown old and never more than chubby, which became her when she was most ravishing.

It brought back to him the priceless scene in the first trial of Harry Thaw, which he covered in New York for his Chicago newspaper. This, too, has never been frankly set forth, because people were stuffy then and even Q and A in a case that shook the world were not printed verbatim.

The theory of the Thaw defense, on a plea of insanity, was that after her marriage Evelyn Thaw had told her bridegroom a story of her seduction by the artist-architect Stanford White in his Madison Square Garden tower studio. Thereafter it mattered nothing whether she was telling the truth, the issue was what she had told Thaw, as a result of which Thaw killed White. And this brutal narrative she related for three days, a little angel-face in a plain blue suit relieved only by a white linen collar.

When William Jerome, the District Attorney, a bulldog, came to cross-examine, he treated the witness gingerly and led her gently, seeking some opening over her long recital. Evelyn had sworn that she told her husband White had given her drugged wine, that she was a 17-year-old virgin when she lost consciousness, and that when she awoke the signs and sensations of having been ravished dawned on her.

The following Lait reports from memory:

"Now, you said that you awoke, that you were nude, that you realized this tragic thing that you say had happened to you, and that White was sitting up in the bed beside you?"

"Yes, sir."

"And did you at that terrible moment say anything to him?"

"No, sir."

"Did he say anything to you?"

"Yes, sir."

"What did he say?"

"He said, 'Little girl, promise me something.' "

The reporters and the courtroom crowd leaned forward, almost falling off their chairs. There was complete silence.

"And what did he ask you to promise?"

"He said, 'Promise me something—promise me you'll never get fat. You're so beautiful!' "

An artist and connoisseur of youthful beauty might well have imposed that pledge on Buda Godman.

3. DOWN ON THE LEVEE

DISTRICTS of sin have mainly become world-famous because their traditional patrons are sailors, and sailors, after brief shore leave, have long days and nights during which they talk over the pleasures of the flesh in the glow of denial and retrospect. Thus, the New York Tenderloin, the Marseilles waterfront, the San Francisco Barbary Coast, the Story Town and the old French Quarter of New Orleans, the dives on the Hook of Baltimore (whence originated the word "hooker"), the brothels of Panama and Port Said and many other harbors became advertised around the globe.

But Chicago is not a port, except for inland Lake traffic. And yet it produced probably the most widely talked-over red light district in history, the Levee.

What seamen are to ports, tourists were to Chicago. And when they spread the word about Chicago it was the last word.

From the very rise of the first wooden huts, Chicago had its scarlet women. By the process of advancing homes and businesses a region was set aside, by law and license, contained principally in the borders of 18th Street, 22nd Street, Armour Avenue and Indiana Avenue. There was considerable slopover, but that parallelogram was the official, recognized, authorized habitat of 50,000 prostitutes in houses that ranged from shambling shanties to the most palatial seraglios known to man.

In that restricted area there was no variation except as to class and price. There were no respectable enterprises, there were no left-over cottages such as were found on the West Side, into which vice moved. This started from scratch to be just what it became, a city within a city dedicated to drinking, dancing and catering to every lechery and lust that man or woman could contrive.

Here was the Taj Mahal of sex-for-sale, the Everleigh Club. It occupied two houses, joined together at 2131 and 2133 Dearborn Street. It outranked anything in Paris for the magnificence of its appointments, the tact and taste of its hostesses, the beauty of its evening-gowned inmates, the vintage of its wines and the quality of its patrons.

Minna and Ada Lester, who became the Everleigh sisters, were small-town Virginia girls. They had both made unfortunate marriages and walked out of them. They read of a fair in Omaha, which would overflow the capacity of that Nebraska burg, and with the few dollars they had they adventured thither, intending to open a rooming house for the grass-roots crowds. They soon found that most of the rooming houses had made more attractive preparations—they had installed in some of the rooms the dames who follow fairs.

The sisters had never engaged in any commercial immorality. Now they saw two possible solutions of their problem of saving their meagre bankroll: sell out for what they could get, or do as the others did. They decided to stay.

It wasn't long before word got around that these two old maids, which they held themselves forth to be though they were still in their thirties, had the coziest rooms, the prettiest girls, and a system of decorum whereby every man got a square deal at a fixed charge, without danger of thieves or brawlers or the annoyance of drunks. The sisters had innate good manners and were too shrewd to be too crabby.

They made more money than they had dreamed they could. But in time the fair closed. They had tasted success and found a profession; now they sought greater scope, and the nearest big city was Chicago.

They brought several of their talented and attractive staff with them and opened up. Soon they were overrun with moneyed customers and with prize-winning beauties seeking admission to their superior establishment. It wasn't long before they added the adjoining building.

There were two parlors, the Indian Room, decked in authentic Oriental furniture, deep rugs, onyx-wainscoted walls hung with damask draperies, and servants from India in native garb; and the Throne Room, which was a Bacchanalian place of regal revel such as one might well fancy a gay, rich potentate would build for frolics with his harem.

In each of these was a concealed orchestra befitting the atmosphere, and in ten other rooms of revelry in the rear of these were art works and music and dancing space.

There was no charge in any of these halls, excepting for drinks, which were ordered by the visiting gentleman or gentlemen, champagne only, at $20 the bottle, when the commercial price was $2.50. No one was asked to buy, but no one who failed to live up to the standards of the Everleigh Club was ever again admitted.

The women, dressed in the latest modes, indistinguishable in appearance from society, asked permission to enter. When they did, no matter how many, one bottle of wine served them all, in dainty glasses known as shells, to accord with the number present. If the man wanted to dance, they danced, and well; if he wanted to talk, he got conversation, intelligent and always comparatively decent. If he chose to go further, he invited the woman of his selection—they never solicited him.

If a gentleman occupied as much as an hour of an inmate's time upstairs, the fee was $50. Those who made a quick selection and did not choose to tarry midway paid a minimum of $20. Those who remained all night and all the next day were expected to contribute $200. That was not unusual.

A gentleman was expected to give a lady a gratuity, but this was never asked, and that was the only money the girls in the Everleigh ever handled openly.

When a patron emerged, a maid helped him with his hat and cane. He wore freshly pressed clothes, which had been cared for by a valet. As he came to the outer corridor, a polite mulatto maid quietly advised him of the charge, for everything. His check was good. Men whose checks weren't never had a chance to be asked for them. And when the checks came back from the bank they were endorsed by the Utopia Novelty Company, Inc., with a rubber stamp, and no other form of identification of the payee, who was always "bearer." After one visit the man had credit. He would receive a bill from the company, on the letterhead of an office in a downtown bank building.

The sisters lived in two suites, one in 2131 and one in 2133, which expressed their widely differing temperaments. Minna, who was dark and slender, volatile and effusive, had marble walls, Persian floor-pieces and a huge bed dressed in pink silk with a canopy which was a mirror, some eight by twelve feet. She had a library with books in fine uniform bindings, and she not only had read them, but she was writing one.

Ada was blonde, tall, cold, the executive, rarely seen downstairs, operator of the enterprise. Minna was a mixer, though not an intruder, and was inclined to be gaudy, with too many bracelets and rings and pins and brooches all over her bodice, of emeralds and rubies forming lizards and other strange jewelers' compositions.

It was Ada who wrung her hands, but Minna who bought a gold-plated piano costing $15,000, a big bronze statue of Cupid and Psyche, and innumerable other art works. She contrived the Gold Room, the Copper Room, the Blue Room, and the basement chamber known as the Pullman Room, where breakfasts were served a la dining car for late-departing guests.

There were no very young girls in the Everleigh Club. With their choice waiting list, they took on only experienced courtesans who had reputations and followings. It was nothing spectacular for a man to travel a thousand miles to spend an hour or two or a night with a designated one, having engaged her by correspondence, and then return to his business and probably his family.

The Everleighs paid off. This, too, by check. The collectors —for the Levee ran long after it was licensed and legal—took about $75,000 from them, but never as a direct pay-off. They refused to be earmarked for set amounts. They contributed on special pleas of the need of campaign funds to fight reformers, and such as that. But no dick came around for an envelope on a certain day. When Mayor Carter H. Harrison threatened and finally doomed this "last sanctuary of pleasure," Ike Bloom, then the official extortioner, said he thought he could let them run a while for $20,000. They refused.

There was one final night of unconfined revelry, and then they closed up.

They made a tour of Europe, then bought an unpretentious brownstone residence on West 71st Street, in New York City, lived for years like retired gentlewomen, were driven about by an aged chauffeur in a black imported limousine, and were seldom seen except at opening nights, when they engaged an entire box.

Minna died in 1949 in a hospital, past 80, of senile exhaustion. Ada was at her bedside and had to be carried away, apparently not long for this world.

There were other houses of quality, though none could compare with the Everleigh Club. Among the best-known madames were Georgie Spencer, Frances, Irene Woods, Zoe Willard, French Emma (inventor of the all-mirror rooms), and Vic Shaw, who ranked second, and who, as this is written, is living at 2906 Prairie Avenue, supposed to be in her nineties. Theirs and the Library (Frankie Wright's) and the House of All Nations and Aimee Leslie's were all conducted on a superior scale, with a $10 minimum for services.

We will not attempt to name and classify the hundreds of cheaper and cruder parlor dives and backroom dance places where girls in short skirts hustled men to their rooms upstairs. Among the owners who had political drag were Roy Jones, Harry Guzik, George Little—at one time manager for Jack Johnson, the Negro heavyweight champion; Duffy (the Goat) and Leather's, Ed Weiss', the Bucket of Blood, Black Mag's, the Silver Dollar and one enticingly named Why Not?

On 22nd Street, strung along the north walk, were combinations, deadfalls with big dancing and drinking halls on the street level and assignation rooms above. One was Freiberg's, named for the orchestra leader by the owners, Bloom and his partner, Sol Friedman, who at the end were the taxers, collectors and immediate contacts for the perennial aldermen, Bathhouse John Coughlin and Hinky Dink Mike Kenna. Friedman was given the monopoly on the sale of whiskey and no one could operate unless. There were regular protection scales, as follows:

> Massage parlors and assignation houses, $25 weekly; larger houses of ill-fame, $50 to $100 weekly, plus $25 if drinks were sold; saloons allowed to stay open past the legal closing hours, $50 a month; sale of liquor in flats without licenses, $15 a month; gambling, $25 a week for each table.

It has been authoritatively stated that such graft brought a total of $15,000,000, which was cut up in various ways. When ex-Mayor Bill Thompson died, something like $2,000,000 in currency, some of it in the old blanket-sized bills, was found. Kenna died with $1,500,000 in cash and large real estate holdings. Coughlin died practically broke, as he was a crazy spender who owned stables of race horses and built a fantastic amusement park, with a private railroad, in Colorado, which he had to abandon completely when the county went dry on him and all the good mountaineers went to Denver for their amusement.

Principal competition to Freiberg's was Buxbaum's, at State and 22nd Street, with two floors of boozing and the malodorous Marlboro Hotel above as the next port of call. Ferdinand J. Buxbaum, who was a whoremaster, proprietor and manager of as vicious a place as ever ran for robbery and jackrolling and every department of vice, had a wife and two children and a respectable home, lived there as a decent citizen, had no affairs with trollops and said he had never tasted liquor.

We went through the district in the winter of '49. We had no regrets over finding it a graveyard of what had been an unbridled compound of all that was evil. But maybe even such corpses, so long dead, might have had a merciful burial.

Here is where the buildings of the Everleigh Club were—right there. They could have become rooming roosts for Negroes and Chinamen, who did take over many of the old dens of joy. But time had dealt the Everleigh Club the supreme indignity: 2131 is not just a vacant lot—it is a junkyard, with rusty worn-out auto parts and bedsprings (a poetic touch) heaped in a confusion of worthless litter, where rang the soft gongs of the Indian Room, where beautiful women laughed and rich men raised their glasses; 2133, what is left standing of the Everleigh Club, is a Negro short-order restaurant where once was the Throne Room. Across its front, in home-made lettering, is this sign:

Hot Fish, 25 Cents; Hamburgers, 15

Vic Shaw's is an empty lot, overgrown with weeds. The Library is a ramshackle house for "Photo Equipment Supplies." And Colosimo's, which is treated at some length in another chapter, had been a colored cafeteria and was recently reopened as a burlesque bar, as dowdy as many others described in this treatise. It is closed again.

At its peak, the Levee had a population of about 55,000, of which roughly 40,000 were females, which was rough enough. That was before equal suffrage and there were some 7,000 votes, of which Coughlin or Kenna, whoever ran that year, got about 11 to 1 against all other contenders, and that might be one, two or three. Harold Ickes, later to be Secretary of the Interior, made a part-time career of running reform candidates to dislodge the "gray wolves." He even entered a pretty woman. The Hink and the Bath treated her courteously, gave her campaign headquarters in a building Kenna owned, serenaded her with the Cook County Marching Club Band, piled cases of free beer all around the store (she was on a dry ticket) and she finished with something like 400 votes.

Books have been written about the two aldermen, one, *Lords of the Levee,* by Lloyd Wendt and Herman Kogan, a comprehensive and understanding dual biography. But the authors were too young to have known their subjects in their prime. Lait was an intimate of both men, if anyone was ever intimate with Kenna, who rarely said more than "yes" or "no," and whichever he said and whenever he said it, it went. Kenna weighed 100 pounds and came up to the armpits of Coughlin, who was a giant up and down and all around.

Kenna kept the Workingmen's Exchange, the crummiest flophouse on South Clark Street, with a deep, wide groggery beneath which advertised "Beer, 5¢, the Largest and the Coolest in the City."

The schooners a man couldn't lift with one hand. When Prohibition came, Kenna presented one to the W.C.T.U. for its museum. Over the Exchange were sleeping accommodations for 600 of the scum and 200 more reposed on the floor of the barroom around election periods, when they were recruited to vote and vote again and again, which they did despite bloodshed and gunplay and riots. Kenna also had a little refined mahogany-and-glass saloon further north on Clark, where he made his office, so constructed that to enter it or leave it he had to cross behind the bar; he refused to walk in front of it ever, for he called it "the sucker side."

Coughlin was vain, flamboyant, ridiculous. He had started as a rubber in a bathhouse and later owned several. His clothes were in all the combined colors of the rainbow, including full evening dress. It was not out of his character to appear with purple pants, yellow vest and green coat. His apparel made news all over the country and New York sent feature writers to describe it. He wrote a poem, "Dear Midnight of Love," which was sung at his command in the Chicago Opera House by Mae de Sousa, who was the daughter of a detective, whom Coughlin drafted for an indescribable performance at which the entire Levee and all 70 aldermen and the other city officials attended. Here are the first verse and the chorus:

When silence reigns supreme and midnight love foretells
  If heart's love could be seen, there kindest thoughts do
      dwell.
In darkness fancies gleam, true loving hearts do swell;
  So far beyond a dream, true friendship never sell.

Dear Midnight of Love,
  Why did we meet?
Dear Midnight of Love,
  Your face is so sweet.
Pure as the angels above,
  Surely again we shall speak,
Loving only as doves,
  Dear Midnight of Love.

The newspapers kidded the mauve pants off Coughlin, but he smirked and smiled and said they knew nothing about literature. John Kelley, then on the *Tribune,* and Lait, on the *Examiner,* badgered Coughlin to turn out more "poetry." He never quite came up to his maiden masterpiece, but whatever ran under his by-line was page 1 copy, and when he didn't produce, Kelley and Lait—mostly Kelley, who was an Irish immigrant with rare gifts of humor—cooked it up. Most of the thirty or forty effusions credited to Coughlin, including the following dedication when he handed Kenna's half-gallon beer-tub to Miss Emma A. Jordan, president of the W.C.T.U., were written by Kelley:

Dear, gentle, gracious, efficient president of the WCTU,
This souvenir of pre-Volsteadian days I beg to present to you.
My sentiments go with it, and as you gaze upon it filled with flowers sweet
I prithee remember that it oft contained Manhattan suds on Clark Street.

The Hink and the Bath were the sponsors of the infamous annual First Ward Ball, at the Coliseum, when everybody had to buy tickets by the bale. Here every madame had to bring all her women, every thief and pimp and grafter and bouncer had to be there. Orgies in which as many as 15,000 engaged followed the grand march, on the stroke of midnight, led by Coughlin between the two Everleigh sisters.

They waded in whiskey up to their ankles. Drunks grabbed for the gowned whores and tore their clothes off, though each contingent was guarded by its own police squad. The Chicago *Tribune* finally choked it off by pledging it would print the name of every man and woman in the hall. This event usually made a personal profit of $70,000 for the aldermen.

Yet these two strangely mismated creatures ran with iron hands not only a dirty district beyond the proportions of New York's Tenderloin, but they held sway over the Loop, with its incalculable Golconda of graft from permits, tax-juggling and public contracts. They at times, and years at a time, virtually ran the city, made and unmade judges, mayors and even governors.

Eventually the aldermanic system was revised to 50 wards with one alderman each, and they took turns until Coughlin died and Kenna, old and weary and rich, retired to his quarters in the Auditorium Hotel, and when that was closed, to the Blackstone Hotel, where he passed away recently, at the age of 90, in the ward in which both men were born.

In the First Ward now the election and re-election tactics are still reminiscent of the original, though there is no Levee. And the Syndicate is so solidly entrenched that the mighty First, like almost all of the wards, is under its domination.

The style of vice and contempt of the law have changed. But the spirit is the same. It is the same except that it is furtive and hypocritical, where once it was loud and lewd, boisterous and open, with a strut of pride and braggadocio over iniquity and lechery and larceny. Consider the case of Duffy the Goat:

Duffy was a Frenchman, right name Dufay, on the lam from the Montreal docks. In Chicago he was arrested for a stick-up murder in Indiana. He was extradited, convicted and sent up for life. But he was out in a few years and he returned to the Levee.

He went into the barber shop of the Cadillac Hotel, next door to Colosimo's, got a shave, a shine and a haircut, and then said to the barber: "You're new here, aren't you?" The barber nodded. "Last time I was here I stashed a gat in that cash register, a Smith & Wesson .38." "Oh yes," said the barber, "it's still there." He handed Duffy the gun—which the Goat promptly stuck into his belly and held him up for all the cash on hand.

That called for a drink. So the Goat saw a saloon across the street, owned and run by another ex-con, Jimmy Leather. Leather was behind the bar. Duffy bought a shot, looked the premises over and said: "Nice place you have here. What you need is a partner." Leather hadn't felt the need of one. But Duffy leaped over the bar, ran his muzzle into Leather's midriff, and said: "You definitely need a partner. And, brother, you've got yourself one." Next morning the lettering on the window read "Duffy & Leather."

Back of the saloon was a room where some 20 or 30 tough hustlers, under direction of a French brunette named Black Marie, solicited drinks and took men upstairs, where they were usually rolled and sometimes stabbed and stripped.

The Goat was in trouble almost every night. He was a hard drinker and a belligerent rowdy as well as every kind of known crook. On one occasion, acting as greeter, in hospitable proximity to a North Dakota cattleman, he bit a two-carat diamond out of his guest's tie and swallowed it. He followed his own customers into the street or the alley, if they had anything left, and he took it away from them.

One afternoon, when the upstairs room was empty, a San Francisco madame known as Frisco Kate, who was en route to New York on a bender, came in there accompanied by a young pug she had picked up. As Duffy served them he noticed that she was ablaze with rocks, and when she reached for money to pay, that she had a roll.

Duffy thought he ought to have that red-head for himself, and, forgetting his manners as host, he ordered the other man to scram. Instead, he got a wallop on the jaw that knocked him down. Duffy got his nickname because he was bull-necked and muscle-bound, had short arms and chunky legs, but was a wicked man in a fight, as he would put his head down and charge like a billy-goat to the stomach. He tried it this time, but he was sidestepped and he ran his skull into the wall. Seeing he was up against a boxer, he calmly pulled out the same pearl-handled .38 and shot the man six times.

This was too much, and Duffy got life in Joliet, where he died.

Thousands of people knew Duffy the Goat, knew his ways and his deeds. But he was a precinct-worker, handy at rounding up votes and dragging in voters. He marched with the First Ward Democratic Club to conventions and he was part of the Kenna-Coughlin-Colosimo "organization." This side of daylight murder in the first degree in his own licensed premises, he was immune.

The higher echelons of the outfit were bruisers, sluggers and killers, who lived off prostitutes and prostitution, gambling and graft. Everybody knew it. The newspapers published it. Nothing much was done about it. They controlled the police and the courts and often the state legislature.

Though this system still prevails, except for a few tough handymen required in emergencies for coarse work, the emperors of the underworld, with far wider sway, eschew violence and give orders in fine offices with corporate names on the windows. They are seldom mentioned in the press, and when they are it is more often in kindness and admiration than in criticism, let alone exposure. They are sensitive on "public relations," engage costly men to influence publicity, and go to enormous lengths and tremendous expense to try to keep their names "clean," where their predecessors swaggered and boasted and filed in their scrap-books with gusto the tales of their criminal derring-do.

4. BLACK PARADISE

THE LARGEST concentration of Negroes on earth is in Chicago.

We have scoured a score of sources for figures and found none definitive. Apparently, authoritative estimates range from 450,000 to 900,000. The Negroes for some reason known to themselves press for minimum figures. The last census of record at this time is no guide, as at least half the colored residents have come since it was made. There is a precious pressure against putting anyone on almost any piece of paper as a Negro. The new census is expected to be as inconclusive. We judge that there are at least 750,000 in Chicago, about 100,000 more than there are in New York.

Here a remarkable picture presents itself. Instead of being bound into black ghettos as they are in most other cities, they have preempted many sections, including what was once the residential area of multi-millionaires. They have swept south, where about three-quarters of the race live, spread over wide and vernal boulevards, in splendid apartment buildings and luxurious private homes with ball-rooms and greeneries, in the mansions which a few years ago housed the exclusive and the snobbish.

The Negroes have taken over mile upon mile, lineally and laterally, whole public parks where no Caucasian is seen, entire business streets, churches of all faiths, synagogues, hotels and what were the first of the big movie palaces, and perhaps a third of the twenty-six miles of lake shore.

They have inundated other sections, particularly the West Side. That will be taken up in another chapter. This one concerns chiefly the South Side major settlement, which its residents euphemistically call "Bronzeville." Within its precincts live, by our best estimate, 400,000 Afro-Americans. This is the nerve-center of Chicago's Negro life and by it is set the pattern for all the smaller ones, scattered south, west and north. Bronzeville dominates the Negro element politically, financially, socially and criminally.

Bronzeville begins about a mile south of the Loop and extends seven miles along a belt two miles wide. As you step across its borders you are virtually in a different country. From the lousiest shanties and the lowest reaches of human existence, you gradually enter a seemingly endless city of fine homes and lawns, but overrun and overcrowded by a dusky multitude with its own ways and in many instances with its own laws. Many of these people have made a quick metamorphosis, the humble share-cropper and slave-wage toiler of the deep central South to cocky and overbearing characters who know their strength, for they are the undisputed balance of power in Chicago politics. In New York the Negroes have learned that, en masse, they swing influence. But they can be absorbed. In Chicago, however, they are preponderant, and they vote as a bloc under dictation of their boss, who switched his own allegiance from the Republican Party to become a Democratic Congressman and took his people with him. The Negroes made the Kelly-Nash-Cermak-Arvey machines impregnable. Don't they know it!

New York's Negroes were there as soon as its whites—some fought in the Revolutionary War. And when the substantial influx came it was mostly from the Carolinas, Maryland, Virginia and the sea-faring Atlantic zones, where Negroes were not drastically oppressed and were largely literate in days of slavery. But the principal Chicago migration came right up the Illinois Central Railroad, from the Mississippi Delta and from Tennessee and Arkansas and western Kentucky, where the Uncle Toms and their children's children scarcely knew of the Emancipation Proclamation.

One of the greatest mass movements of humanity in the history of our country took place during the last war, when some 2,000,000 rural Negroes left the South to glean the swollen wages of the war plants in the industrial North. Chicago was the nearest Golconda, easiest to reach. It got the biggest share in the scramble. How many is not known and may never be known.

That many of these were proselyted, much like the Puerto Ricans were induced to flock to Manhattan, is definite. Democrats below the Mason and Dixon Line were a dime a dozen. Chicago often went Republican and Illinois generally did. The New Deal needed Illinois. It turned the tide in Chicago with new Negro votes and in time Chicago turned the state, took it away from the GOP.

The payoff for voting right has been impressive. The city has one Negro state senator, one state representative, two councilmen, two judges, three assistant attorney-generals, a county commissioner, a planning commissioner, a commerce commissioner, a boxing commissioner, two industrial arbitrators and thousands on the city, county, state and federal payrolls in posts running up to high degrees of importance. These elective and appointive offices are now allocated to the race in perpetuity, with more to come. The political factotum through whose itching palms all this flows is Congressman William Dawson, now vice-chairman of the Democratic National Committee, a lawyer who has amassed wealth and without whose nod almost nothing of public importance can be closed. He is the turncoat who left the traditional Chicago Negro Republican party to hook on with the machine Democrats. He is the King of Bronzeville.

The most squalid portion of his domain is from 35th Street north, along State and parallel streets, the original Chicago "Black and Tan Belt." This was the overflow of the old Levee, the restricted vice district where many of the colored women were employed as maids, and they kept the men. When those conditions were rampant, that area became a popular slumming retreat for the rich whites and there flourished the new musical improvisations, known successively as ragtime and jazz, brought up from New Orleans. The boss then was Bob Motts, a reliable Republican with no assumptions beyond his own borders. The Negro was an inconsequential element and every inch he sought was contested, leading to bloody race riots. There is an occasional flare-up now, but the Negroes are powerful and command enough propaganda and police influence so that they spread with little open opposition.

Here is one for the sociologists who have long proclaimed it an axiom that crime is a concomitant of poverty, ill-housing and underprivilege:

Chicago's sore spot of malefactions is not north of 35th Street, where the poorest Negroes live, but south of it—the infamous Fifth Police District, which runs from 39th to 60th Streets, between Cottage Grove Avenue and the Rock Island right-of-way. This police division, less than three square miles, contains some of the finest housing in America, recently occupied by rich whites. Now it is almost 100 per cent black—and it produces about twice as much recorded crime as the Negro Third and Fourth Districts combined, immediately north, somewhat smaller in area, but many times more congested.

The Fifth Police District of Chicago has attained world-wide eminence. It is known to law-enforcement students around the globe. For it has, consistently year after year, the highest crime per capita known to man, having passed Casablanca's diabolical Casbah, about which a library of literature has been written and staged, in wonderment of its wickedness.

The startling figures may not be ascribed to the Negro as such, or even to the Negro in the North. We have already observed that the neighbors, of the same race, commit fewer offenses. But in Chicago, never forget this—law-breaking is the handmaiden of the political tieup, and nowhere is there any as insidious as that which swaddles, nurses and protects Bronzeville. And even its record is far from disclosing it all. There is an unwritten understanding that minor fracases, knifings, prostitution and often capital felonies are to be kept off the blotter, especially if there is no complaint from a white person. Detectives throw up their hands at beefs coming directly to headquarters if they allege misdeeds in Bronzeville. The Negro politicians immediately go over their heads with yelps of race prejudice and interference with things that are no white man's business. In fact, it is a standing policy to keep this most sinful of all sections under-policed.

Almost all you will find in the book has been personally investigated by Lait and Mortimer, proven and copper-riveted. There will be few "authorities," because we have found most public officials either uninformed or untrustworthy. But we will here sum up blunt conclusions given us by Virgil W. Peterson. He is the Operating Director of the Chicago Crime Commission, a nonpartisan group supported by leading citizens alarmed over Chicago conditions, who could get nothing from the police and prosecutors except a runaround and a laugh. Mr. Peterson was drafted from the F.B.I. He is an attorney and a criminologist of note. He has been on the job for years, with a large and meticulously selected staff. His research is so accurate that law-enforcement bodies throughout the nation come to Peterson for aid and advice.

This is a summation which Mr. Peterson will have checked for accuracy before publication of his findings about the Fifth Police District:

> There is little respect for law and order there or for those assigned to enforce law and order. Police personnel is inadequate. Carrying concealed weapons is commonplace. Robberies and other acts of criminal violence occur during daytime and nighttime and little has been done to effectively curb them. Numerous gangs of boys, some this side of their teens, simulating the methods of adult gangs, infest the district. Complaints of shakedowns by police are frequent. The attitude of the courts is not conducive to building up a proper respect for law and order. Serious offenses are too often treated as innocuous childish pranks by Municipal Court judges sitting in the district. The policy (numbers) racket is and has been permitted to flourish. Common knowledge that it has been officially protected adds to the general disrespect for law-enforcement officers there. Guns and knives are carried promiscuously. Many shootings and cuttings result from trivial disputes. Dangerous knives can be bought across the counter of almost any drugstore, and in many other establishments. Almost everyone arrested has a knife on his person. Some of the knives confiscated have blades several inches long and are constructed like daggers. They can be opened by pressing a button ("switch-blade pig-stickers" is the slang appellation for them). Citizens complain that a police officer is seldom seen on the streets.

There is virtually no restriction in Chicago on the purchase of firearms. There is a law against carrying them concealed, but none against having them in the home or automobile, and, therefore, they are loosely supervised. The state's highest court time and again has ruled that an illegally carried gun cannot be placed in evidence unless the arresting officer had a warrant to search the law-breaker's person. This makes enforcement virtually impossible. They are used in countless stickups and brawls. The boys make their own, with tubing into which bullets fit, which are fired by pins propelled by powerful rubber bands.

Purse-snatching takes place almost by the minute. Whoring in every phase and form is prevalent. Mugging (attacking a victim from behind by strangling with a bent arm about the neck) is a typical form of robbery, executed by women as well as men. Crimes are so customary that there is no attempt at concealment and they are pulled off without embarrassment before the eyes of passing throngs. It seems everybody in Bronzeville sees such things except the police. They are always the last to arrive on the scene and never seem to get any information that leads to punishment. They always get there too late to do anything except block traffic. People walk around the wounded and the dead on the sidewalks, take a fleeting glance and move on.

Not only are there too few police, but those who try to do their duty run into official obstacles. Politicians spend more time getting criminals "sprung" than they do in all their other activities combined. A cop who gets too obtrusive finds himself picking stickers out of his harness in the distant wilds.

The attitude toward the policy racket is an open scandal. A few manipulators have made fortunes out of it. Thousands of others become more impoverished. It is a monopoly of big shots. Under the wide-open Kelly regime, police officers took up stations at each policy drawing-place to protect the money on hand for the payoffs. These policemen were on the payrolls of the operators and worked in full uniform. Such a sight engendered contempt of police and all they stood for, which was amplified when decent citizens attempted to appear as witnesses against criminals and found that a definite or general "fix" was in and their evidence was useless.

While the Negroes have their full quota on the police

force, not enough Negro officers are assigned to the Negro district, especially in Bronzeville. Negroes in police work have proven themselves as honest, as conscientious and able as the police of any other race. Among their own people they are far more efficient because they know their ways and they command confidence where white officers are resented.

A typical case was that in which two white officers, passing in a squad car, saw a Negro man dragging a Negro woman into an alley intent on rape. They jumped out and grabbed the attacker. They were immediately encircled by a group of hostile Negroes. The prisoner struck one of the white officers and others surrounded him menacingly. Just then a Negro merchant patrolman arrived. He elbowed his way through the crowd, knocked down the Negro offender, threw him into the squad car and saw it safely off. None of the Negroes objected to his action, though he had no official status as a police officer.

The Crime Commission suggested that in police cars patrolling or cruising districts with large Negro population one officer be a Negro and the other a white man. This procedure was followed by the Military Police in such localities and the results were satisfactory.

Now for some figures about Bronzeville: about 200,000 people live in its Fifth Police District. This is less than 6 per cent of the city's population. There are 39 Police Districts. The Fifth produced 21 per cent of all murders, 11.2 per cent of all robberies, 29 per cent of all rapes and 18.4 per cent of aggravated assaults committed in Chicago in 1947, the latest official statistics available. This despite the obvious leniency and difficulty as to arrests and a definite inclination of the people to protect rather than to prosecute.

It is not the purpose here to impugn or condone. But those who knew these neighborhoods twenty years ago are appalled at the change. Filth and overcrowding, a general spirit of roughhouse, a superfluity of saloons and pool-halls and dance-halls, garbage in the streets and in the alleys, the unmistakable odor of marijuana, are surface indications of the terrific transformation. When you venture beyond these you find dingy dens, depraved homosexual exhibitionism, lumber-camp licentiousness, drunkenness, dope and every sinister sign of virtually uncontrolled abandon.

Of course, this discounts the many thousands of respectable Negroes who not only take no part in such places and practices, but who have only a vague idea of their existence. We cannot stop with every paragraph to make such observations. This book is not intended to be all-inclusive and there is nothing "confidential" about the fact that the majority of Americans are decent, or reasonably so, and we proceed with that premise.

The main drag of Bronzeville is 47th Street, with high-grade shops, theatres and chain-stores, for it is the principal highway of the richer Negroes, no matter how they got it. This was a fine old street which cut through the residential zone of one of the older portions of the city. Geography was on the side of the Negroes as they spread south and then east and west. They were not hemmed in like their people are in Harlem, by rivers, heights, Central Park and Columbia University, which form deadlines that confine more than 600,000 in a space inadequate for one-third that number. Bronzeville expanded as the Negroes poured in and the Caucasians moved out. In the vacated quarters twenty families often live where one did before—a case of record shows a five-flat building remodeled into 65 flats! Instead of fighting the dark advance, many owners, especially of private homes, found they could get rent from several in the space intended for one, and overcharge them all, so many quenched their qualms and greedily accelerated the movement.

Into mansions and terrace apartment buildings, on boulevards, parkways and leafy avenues, flooded the thousands whose backs were weary of picking cotton and herding hogs, of being an inferior people often by law as well as social and financial opportunity. Bronzeville became a Negro heaven. Nowhere in the nation were Negroes so well off, so well treated and so well housed. Hundreds of thousands of whites still live in Chicago slums and lebensraum problems are as drastic throughout as they are anywhere. But Negroes, with full right to do so and virtually with none to hold otherwise, are entrenched as far south as 90th Street and are approaching Hyde Park, along the south shore of the Lake, not too long ago a seat of white society. Most of Chicago's blighted areas are occupied by Negroes. But most Negroes in Chicago do not live in blighted areas. In truth, an amazing American anti-climax emerges: instead of being hemmed in by whites, the Negroes are hemming in the whites.

Of the 94 square miles of Chicago's 200 and some area, between 4,000 West and the Lake, from Devon Ave. on the north to 71st Street on the south, approximately 60 square miles are utilized for living. Of the 60, more than 20 have in excess of 90 per cent Negro population. In these 60, where dwell 3,000,000 of the 3,600,000 in Chicago, are the choicest locations because of proximity to the central business section, to the Lake, parks and public services. Calculating that there are 750,000 Negroes, less than 25 per cent of the inhabitants, we find that they occupy 33 per cent of its land. The white citizens are concentrated into more constricted space or leave their first choice of locations and settle in the suburbs. This situation will be dealt with in a later chapter not devoted to Bronzeville, where it should be pointed out again, most of the Negroes came from the central deep South, where their living and literacy standards are the lowest in the country. There was (and is) a rigid caste-system among Negroes and the new arrivals were met with hostility by the older Negro residents, much as the Sugar Hill snobs in Harlem look down on the "lower classes" of their race. There was no attempt to absorb them, to lead them toward churches and social activities, to mingle with them and advise them of things all new, all marvelous, and many dangerous. The non-native Negroes went dizzy with the conveniences and opportunities of the great city. Most of them had never seen a toilet before.

During the war, when the Chicago labor shortage was more severe than in most places because of the diversity of her plants and her unequaled transportation setup, it was not unique for a farmhand who had never owned $10 at one time to earn $200 a week with overtime. This started the Bronzeville boom, with its drinking and doping and the resultant laxities that blossomed into flagrant vice.

Most of these people had left behind them the influences

which they had come to respect, in entirely different conditions. The problems attending migration from rural areas proved particularly acute with the youth. To get the swollen wages, the parents left their children largely to themselves, and they went wild. When the layoffs came the children had been up North long enough to refuse to accept the conditions of ordinary living, such as most Negroes in this country are accustomed to. Vice and crime were easy money. Politicians had discovered that they could remain in office indefinitely by buying the votes of entire large segments of the population. Newly-arrived Negroes, not allowed to vote where they were born and raised, were easily organized by astute professionals, black and white, and bribed with money and immunity, to ballot in blocs. They were encouraged to send for more of their people and special cheap rates were procured to bring them on. As the voters began to realize what was being done with them, they held out somewhat and new consideration was flaunted to hold them: jobs. Government, state, county, city jobs, and when these began to run out, private jobs. Whereas in New York the social do-gooders and the radical newspapers have fought long and with little effect to open the doors for other than menial work to Negroes, in Chicago the politicians themselves took up the cause, and they didn't plead, they demanded.

Employers need licenses, signs, porticos, immunity for petty violations, and what not, for which they must get their alderman's sayso. They can be ruined with high assessments (in Illinois there is a personal property as well as real estate and business tax, which is juggled and is brought very close to individuals) and these aldermen deal with and get appointments for the estimators and assessors. Word was brought impressively to employers in wholesale, retail, public utility and other institutions of trade that they had better take on Negroes, and not only as porters and elevator operators. This was exercised not only by the Negro politicians. They had become a major factor in the election of the higher white candidates. These orders came from up above.

The economic need for more Negroes in Chicago had passed. The stockyards, common labor, house servants and restaurant workers were in competitive fields. But there was a desperate political need. As more Negroes were colonized from the South, more were placed on relief immediately—often illegally—and the trickle of employment by persuasive blackmail never stopped. The Negroes began to enter the real underworld life, not in a spirit of mischief and high binges, but for direct financial results. They became shake-down specialists and they dealt in women and narcotics and the proceeds of bold payroll robberies. The happy-go-lucky darkie of the Bilbo times and regions was being educated—in a field not fertile to him for the product of the sweat of his brow.

On 47th Street you can buy anything: reefers, "hard" dope, policy slips, guns, brass knuckles, knockout drops, trick knives, and women. In Harlem the price of a good-looking high-yaller is now $20. Older and darker ones wouldn't spit at you for less than $10. But in Bronzeville they solicit you for $2. Some of these jezebels are in their early teens and contact with them is a statutory felony. This is the easiest touch for the badger-game, as most of the prostitutes are followed and observed at all times by their male owners.

Going to a room with the older ones is almost as perilous, because the man frequently enters with his key and puts on the ancient act of claiming the woman is his wife, and demanding money on threats of arrest or armed violence on the spot. Other systems are used, including the panel game. In this the girl puts the man's clothes over a chair which can be reached through an opening in the wall from the next room, and while his thoughts are on other things, his pockets are cleaned. If he does not remove his clothes, the girl goes through them while he is preoccupied, a specialty delicately known as "cold-finger work." In instances where amorous unsophisticates are lured into dark alleys or up on roofs, they are often hit on the head by the men and stripped of everything, down to their shoes.

There is no item of property so valueless that it cannot be "fenced" in Bronzeville or further north. Hundreds of second-hand hole-in-the-wall stores offer any used articles and the myriad pawnshops, which are a perennial outcropping of such localities, will lend from a dime up. There is no age minimum in these hockshops and much of what goes over their counters is from the hands of juveniles. Under-age delinquency is a blot which seems to foretell even worse conditions. Youth gangs, male and female, have gotten beyond control. In groups ranging from ages of 11 to 18, and often in numbers up to 200, they terrorize the entire Black Belt and frequently invade white neighborhoods to pillage, rob, rape or beat up people of any race for the sheer pleasure of it, which is called "going on a rumble." Inter-gang wars are ferocious and often fatal.

One young gang is known as the "Blue Demons," with headquarters around 39th and Dearborn Streets, but not confined there. An adjoining gang calls itself the "Iron Men." Members of these have frequently killed their rivals, though at times their presidents (that is the title of every gang head) or representatives meet, declare a truce or combine an alliance against a third gang, such as the "Blue Rockets." It is not unusual for 15 or more to be shooting at as many others simultaneously.

The "Corsairs," out of 41st Street and Calumet Avenue, was one of the strongest gangs, which bullied and terrorized for miles around. The "Deacons" are controlled by five brothers. The "Spiders," one of the youngest mobs, operates around the Burke School. Other youthful Negro gangs are the "Counts," the "Jokers," the "Little Foxes," the "Tornadoes," the "Bullets" and the "Sharks."

Each of these has its female contingent, known as "Debs." The girls are intimate with the members, are often deflowered by them as a passport into gangsterhood. They carry weapons, act as lookouts, appear in groups as alibi witnesses, and at times wade in with fists, knives and shooting irons with their "men." As they graduate from adolescence into early maturity the males become full-time gangsters, policy runners, dope and marijuana pushers and pimps for the girls, who in turn develop into thieves and hookers. Through the whole process runs a spine of dope.

That commerce is closely controlled from the top by the white wholesalers, one branch of the over-all white downtown Syndicate. Street peddlers and neighborhood jobbers are independent operators, buying for cash from the central source at set prices. Sometimes the rates are cut by the main dealers to stimulate the traffic. That was in process at the time of our investigations on the ground and the retail market was pegged as follows:

> Heroin, reduced from $2.50 to $1.50 per capsule.
>
> Reefers, 50-cent grade, now three for $1.
>
> Cheaper reefers, mostly bought by school-children, ranged down to 25 cents per cigarette, but these are diluted with tobacco and, instead of a binge, produce a beep.

As a rule the peddlers are users. We presume that most of our readers have an idea of the effects of habit-forming drugs and we will not go into detailed descriptions of the physical, mental and moral disintegration, the reefer parties with their dark, crowded rooms where the mixed sexes reach orgiastic stimulation after "kicking the gong around"—which is where that phrase originated. These are not individual to Chicago and were rather fully detailed in the Harlem chapter of *New York Confidential.*

Before the Negro avalanche, whites and Negroes did business together. But that is past. Now it is dangerous and sometimes lethal for a white stranger to enter the section after dark and few venture there alone by the light of day. Rent-collectors usually demand police escort. Even respectable Negroes tremble if they are well-dressed or display valuables. Muggers draw no color lines. White women are unsafe thereabouts at all times, even if escorted. But many Caucasians must pass through and they are in danger when they stop for crossing signals. Most of the "carhops" who slide in and rob motorists are women.

As in all Northern cities, the lowest of the races get together. This is most common among the degenerates in the twilight zones of sex. They meet everywhere, but their principal point of congregation is around Drexel Avenue and 39th Street.

White prostitutes are luxury merchandise in Bronzeville. Many of them have black lovers and exploiters. They work the Loop hotel lobbies during days and early evenings, and are on call, with bellboys the usual procurers. Later, their

Negro apaches pick them up, usually in shiny Cadillacs bought with their earnings, and drive them to flats in Bronzeville, where they are sold to Negroes.

There is comparatively little demand by white men for colored girls, though that was a Chicago fad a quarter of a century ago. Those who now "deal in coal" are predominantly white women with a yen for dark men. This holds true not only on the levels of depraved professionals, but has seeped into the other circles of extreme "liberalism" and academic life. Communist women accept, when it is a party-line policy, intimacy with Negroes, who are regarded as soft converts and must be imbued by practical demonstration with the complete equality of all comrades. The tremendous intermixture in grade schools, high schools, business schools, colleges and universities inevitably leads to a certain amount of extra-curricular intermingling. Propinquity of the races in their home and business zones creates added opportunities.

Inter-racial marriages are on the increase in Chicago and Cook County. They are now recorded at about 200 a year, about four a week. Before the war such unions were virtually unheard-of. In almost every instance it is a Negro man marrying a white woman. Some are ex-servicemen who have sent for white girls they met abroad, but most such unions follow street or school or saloon attachments.

There is no clearer picture anywhere of the tieup between vice, crime and politics than that which is luridly and brazenly painted in Chicago's Negro districts. There all profit-making lawlessness which can be humanly organized is controlled by the white Syndicate, which will rate considerable space further on in this book. The Negroes, even their political padrones, are only lieutenants of, directed by and accountable to those master-racketeers. Bronzeville is a province of a great empire inherited from Al Capone, run by his surviving kinsmen and department heads, and expanded since his death to an extent of which even he never dared to dream.

Among the principals of the Negro underworld are Dan Gaines, Ted Roe, the Jones Brothers and Jim Knight. Winston Howard, the policy king and close friend of Marva Louis, ex-wife of the retired heavyweight champion, was one of the bosses until he was murdered in 1949 by a partner in the cocktail lounge of the Pershing Hotel, the swankiest Negro rendezvous in the country, in which Howard owned an interest. Congressman William L. Dawson, political tycoon of the Second Ward, is the leader, ruler and spokesman for all Chicago's colored population. In Washington he is the Chairman of the mighty House Committee on Executive Expenditures. He is a patronage dispenser for the Cook County Democratic Central Committee. As a lawyer he was a foremost defender of gamblers and other unsavory characters of his race. "Shotgun" Alex, the Greek bodyguard of Jake Guzik, who is the executive head of the Syndicate's entire vice setup is a frequent visitor to Dawson's office, which is next door to a gambling house on South State Street.

Dawson, in 1948, was charged before a Congressional Committee, of having defended "the racketeers out there in Chicago—the policy racket, in the district he represents—to the tune of millions of dollars every year."

To the repeated assertion that "you defended all of those rackets," Congressman Dawson answered, "I would defend any man."

Clifford C. H. Tavernier, close to Dawson, is the present Bronzeville mouthpiece.

Bronzeville, while it knows it is exploited, also knows it is protected. A goodly percentage of the profits of degrading traffic is siphoned off to go into the hands of men the Negroes never see. But they are almost immune against penalties for what they can keep from dirty sources—safe from almost every consequence except the tremendous ravages of venereal disease. Throughout the district, 24-sheet billboards on the principal streets proclaim:

Syphilis is dangerous if untreated.

We saw one on Grand Boulevard, where once dwelt the rich, a few feet from a stately church building.

When the Black Belt was safe and homey, when white strangers were met with warm welcome instead of hot hatred, the South Side abounded with late spots where revelers usually showed up in evening dress to enjoy the cooking, the merriment and the extraordinary talents of the Negroes.

Here the late Bill Robinson, "Satchmo" Armstrong, Shelton Brooks and many other entertainers became known and progressed. Here Lena Horne, Billy Eckstine and Billy Holiday made their start. Bob Motts' Pekin began the fashion and it spread until lavish revues with dozens of light-skinned chorines were standard in the city's nightlife.

The heavy migration and the agitation for Negroes to demand equality, together with the danger of robbery and assault, drove the moneyed whites elsewhere. Now there is no lit-up nightlife in Bronzeville, not even for its own people. Flat-parties, guests usually bringing their own gin, or gatherings on street corners or in alleys and hallways, as well as in the tawdry taverns, now encompass the evening and night activity. Of the famed and favored spots only one remains with a floor-show, Club De Lisa, owned by a white pal of the late Capone. It is not heavily patronized. The Hotel Pershing is the place to go, but white folks are stopped at the doors.

A hot spot is the Du Sable Hotel grill, at 39th Street and Drexel Avenue, in an oval basement room with an endless bar. It runs all night and caters to the sporting element, but the only whites are an occasional fairy or lesbian. A malodorous dive, across the street from the nostalgic White City, which was a world-famous amusement park, plays a colored chorus, but the principals are Negro homosexuals, who not only entertain on the stage but act as hostesses and B girls, so feminine in dress, mannerisms and makeup that a stranger would accept them as female.

There are ballrooms which draw the wrong people and picture theatres which show the wrong kind of movies and taverns that cater to the wrong types of trade. Records show 268 taverns in the small area comprising the Fifth Police District, several to a block in some sections, and many drugstores that sell by the drink, a raw violation. Many of the liquor joints are owned by white outsiders who pay Negro managers to front and represent themselves as owners. In that way, when a license is revoked, the ostensible Negro owner can have it restored where a white man wouldn't have a chance. This sets up again the phenomenon of the Negro in the political position of the "master race."

There are many instances, not surreptitious, which prove

this. Chicago's taxi ordinances, like New York's, forbid more than one party riding in a cab. This is enforced except as to cabs owned by Negroes and driven by Negroes, who may carry as many riders as they wish and pick them up when their cabs are not filled. Many act as jitneys, cruising the boulevards and taking fares at 15 cents, also forbidden by law. Cops have learned not to bother Negro cab drivers on these or other traffic violations. They don't want to tangle with Dawson.

Chicago's vehicle license commissioner is boss of the city's taxicabs. It is his duty to put them out of business if they violate the ordinances. Edward J. Gorman was the commissioner until he resigned under fire in January, 1950.

Gorman's friend, James B. Veitch, is the Chicago agent for the insurance company that writes most of the policies for independent cabs. Mr. Veitch, in turn, has a friend. He is Congressman Dawson.

There are 350 cabs, owned by others, but rented by the day by Negro drivers. They run a sort of unlicensed bus business along South Park Way and Indiana Ave.

The Illinois Commerce Commission ordered the practice stopped. Gorman did not break up the racket and at this writing it is still operating. Applicants for new licenses were sent from Gorman's office to Veitch's for insurance, and there, one veteran was told it would cost $2,000 as "ice" to get a license.

Four of the other major Negro islands are also on the South Side, one near 63rd and Ashland, a second at 95th and State, and the largest centered around 111th and Ashland. The fourth is at 135th and Cottage Grove.

Each of these is a Bronzeville in miniature.

But most surprising about the movement of Negro population was its invasion of the West Side, large parts of which have been taken over completely, and the North Side, about which more later.

5. GO WEST, TAN MAN

THERE ARE two principal Negro sections on the West Side. One is new, from the south border of Roosevelt Road—12th Street—extending from the River to Western Avenue. The other is north of Madison Street and runs from Racine Avenue to Kedzie Avenue. This is an old habitat which formerly ended at about Ashland Avenue centering on Lake Street, which was undesirable real estate because there the elevated ran through the street instead of, as is usual in Chicago, through alleys. A certain degree of Negro stability was established there, the children were peacefully accepted in schools and there was little conflict. As far west as Paulina Street, it formerly ran through the borders of one of the cheapest and foulest licensed prostitution areas, which was not the fault of the Negroes, though they did sneak a little on their own. But no such extremes as those found in Bronzeville developed there then or now.

This section is known as West Town. Many of its people are railroad workers on a higher economic and social scale than those in Bronzeville, though by no means as handsomely housed except in the mansions of once social Warren Avenue. West Town is known for its mulattoes and every year a "Miss West Town" is chosen amid high to-do and the winner gets $1,000 in cash and a free trip to Mexico. There are several all-Negro nightclubs along Lake Street and white people find it reasonably safe to patronize them. They imitate all the ways of such places elsewhere, some have excellent floorshows and all have B girls with a side door to closer relations. We were solicited by a handsome quadroon, the head hostess, who offered to help us get acquainted, not only with the hustlers, but in person if we'd come back later.

But this is not as picturesque as the other west side settlement mentioned above, which has engulfed one of the most colorful cosmopolitan melting-pots of America. Around Halsted and Maxwell Streets swarmed the Chicago ghetto, with many thousands of Jews from Russia and eastern Europe, who spoke no English, who arrived with tickets pinned to their clothes and placards hung around their necks. Streets and tenements teemed with bearded patriarchs and their families. Stores sprang up with pullers-in on the walks and everywhere were pushcarts which sold everything from garlands of garlic to women's drawers. The Jewish wave followed closely on the Irish, and with Blue Island Avenue the accepted dividing line, there were wonderful ruckusses which kept the Maxwell Street Station house humming.

Lait covered this beat, which was a key police center with a big lock-up and courtrooms. To the north were Polish, Bohemian and Italian newcomers who populated the district of Congressman A. J. Sabath, at this writing the dean of the House, and his brother, who was the police judge.

This conglomerate mass bred fierce gangsters, indescribable vice, but also some of the outstanding characters, including James C. Petrillo, who tooted a horn for a few weeks but soon began taking over the national Musicians Union. Hull House, founded by Miss Jane Addams, was planted there because nowhere was it needed more.

In time, paralleling the virtual evacuation of the downtown ghetto on Manhattan Island, the older people died, the younger ones grew and many prospered, honestly or notoriously, and moved to more happy abodes. As the Europeans left, the new Negroes came. The sector, while regarded as in another part of the city, is only about a mile across the river from the original South Side Black Belt, stretching toward Bronzeville. On the fringes of the Maxwell Street circle came a deluge of Mexicans, Greeks and Sicilians. Some Jewish merchants who moved out retained their shops and beggars and millionaires still come there for bargains, from job-lot work-shoes to minks and grand pianos. But the luxury trade is evaporating and many stores are shuttered.

Living conditions here are as low and lousy as could be found anywhere in the world. Negroes live in hovels without roofs, caved in on the sides, steps missing, tilted like miniature towers of Pisa. As many as a hundred live in a shack meant for two families. They sleep in hallways, some even standing, leaning against stairs. Whole families exist under stair-cases. Filth overflows to the walks and weedy lots and everywhere junk is piled. At night, Halsted Street thereabouts is a fantastic riot of smells and colors, a jammed jamboree of Negroes, Mexicans, skull-capped Jews, Filipinos and Levantines. From the reeking cafes come rancid odors of cheap cooking. You can buy anything on the street from a girl, price $5, to a stiletto, price $2.50. Street-hawkers sell guns openly at $20, knives, Spanish fly, contraceptives and obscene pictures and other crude pornography. Guns are sold to children and recently a 15-year-old boy shot his 14-year-old playmate to death with one he had bought on the street from a man who first offered him dope.

This is also the home and hunting-ground of Chicago's gypsies. Few are permanent residents, but this is the clearing house for itinerant caravans that work the plains of the Middle West. They are complete parasites, thieves and terrific drunks. They prey on the ignorant and superstitious whom they swindle by offering to lift curses or bring good luck. The "workers" are the women. The men never even steal. They sleep all day and their principal non-alcoholic pastime is beating their wives. A gypsy woman who is not thoroughly thrashed sets up a wail that her man no longer loves her. There is virtually no inter-racial immorality with gypsy females, though they use all the teasing wiles to trap men. The police boot them around, as they have no votes, pay no taxes and can drum up no influence.

Some of the most bizarre crimes of Chicago's long panoply transpired hereabouts. One of them was the kidnaping of the Furlong baby, the child of an Irish laborer, a girl who disappeared from a heap of slag on which she was playing, unwatched. Amid a furor and theories of sex maniacs—the child was only four years old—a long and tremendous hunt went on, because the incident had caught the imagination of the community. Lait was sitting in the Maxwell Street Station when a drunken man pussyfooted in, called him aside and swore that while he was having an affair with a street-walker in a frowsy hotel at Halsted and Washington Streets he had heard a baby cry. The search was so intense that nothing was being overlooked.

With Captain John Hanes, Lait hurried to the woman's room. There was nothing suspicious in sight, nor had any of the hotel employes seen a baby where a baby would be highly conspicuous. Against the wall stood a wobbly wooden trunk. Hanes pushed it aside, as a thorough policeman would. There, on the floor, asleep, lay the Furlong baby, safe and well. The sides of the trunk had been perforated with air-holes. The woman, with a frustrated instinct of mother love, had seen the child, snatched it, carried it off under her shawl and kept it in her room to fondle between tricks.

During Prohibition, millions of barrels of wine were made in the cellars hereabouts, to supply a large part of the country. The ace gangsters were gentlemen compared with the social swill here that fought with machine-guns, bombs and butcher-knives for the profits of this trade. By common usage that ward, the Sabaths', was known as "the Bloody 19th."

6. HONKY TONK ROW

WEST MADISON STREET, once the dirt road over which the farmers brought their produce downtown and to the Haymarket, is wide and solidly paved, but still thrives on dirt, every kind conceivable.

Beginning at the river and west for more than a mile is the Skid Row which surpasses the Bowery in everything that is unspeakable.

("Skid Row" is a common misnomer for "Skid Road." The derivation is not from men who skidded, though the good Lord knows they have, but is a term of the Northwest, where log roads were greased for dragging timber. As parts of the forests were felled, other lanes were set up and along the abandoned ones transitory huts where lumbermen and hoboes got drunk were set up. But the error is so common that we will use the term Skid Row, in order not to appear didactic and too damned educated.)

Chicago's Skid Row is classic. For generations panhandlers, bums, seasonal workers, ex-convicts and other ragtag have gravitated to Chicago. They came riding the rods, in boxcars or on foot, to the great freight-yard terminals. West Madison Street, a short walk from all roads, became the rough labor employment mart. Here agencies specialized in mass shipments of ice- and wheat-cutters, railroad construction crews, cooks and dishwashers and other unskilled migrant manpower. This turned the section into a succession of fleabag flophouses, bulk five-cent whisky saloons and all the corollary accommodations for the dregs of humanity. Here were the first nickel lodgings, on pineboards worn in grooves where lay the heads, the feet and the middles. Under every neck was a hinge. At seven o'clock in the morning the bartender in the barrel-house below pulled a lever and all heads dropped into space. That was the only way to bring back to life the sodden, shaky boozers. As they came down, they were each given one on the house—out of the slops of any beer, liquor, tobacco, everything, which had been poured into a keg the moment a drinker took his hand off his glass or turned his back. Each got a tin-cup of this. It was called "a rub of the brush," because that was how it felt going down. This gave the bozos enough of a lift to get them past the door.

This was in the Eighteenth Ward (old) which rivaled the First, with its dominance by "Hinky Dink" Kenna and "Bathhouse John" Coughlin, made absolute by repeaters recruited from the floaters. Here Alderman John J. Brennan was the boss.

Lait, only a few weeks after he became a reporter, was assigned to expose vote-buying in the Eighteenth. He dressed in faded overalls, scuffed shoes, a torn shirt and a beat-up cap, streaked printer's ink across his face and checked in at the Salvation Army lodging-house, in the heart of Skid Row, as a tramp who had just beat it in from Kansas City. He was so slender then that the other 'bos labeled him Kansas City Slim.

This was four days before June 1, Judicial Election Day. He was soon approached, given a drink of terrible hooch and told he would get 50 cents for each vote and would be expected to vote eight times in as many polling places. Together with others, he was briefed and given eight names, which were either of dead men or entirely fictitious registrants, and was told to vote under those names in the order of the slips. He voted three times and each time got a half-dollar. He telephoned his paper, and at the fourth place, on Halsted Street south of Madison Street, a photographer and an officer of the Election Board were posted in the window across the street. Here Lait was paid by Brennan, in person, and a photograph showed the transaction. Brennan and eight of his henchmen were arrested and Brennan and four were convicted.

That system of voting was old then and is still new today.

If anything, West Madison Street has sunk even deeper. There are virtually none left there who seek work or ever expect to find work or to have work find them. In those days there was a sprinkling of seasonal workers, who got high pay for severe labor and saved up enough to loaf until they were ready to earn some more. These were hoboes, but not bums.

The tramp as an American institution has about disappeared. In his category were yeggs, who roved in packs, lived in roadside jungles, cased small-town banks and robbed them. The famous James Brothers and Younger Brothers were exaggerated yeggs. There were also skillful beggars and men with trades who worked at them in the city when they went broke. Now there is no one left on Skid Row with enough gumption, manhood or physical vitality even to steal beyond rolling a lush or swiping shoes from another derelict. Even the panhandlers are furtive and clumsy as against the old pros who had the decency to lie and wheedle and set up on the good corners. These human cockroaches beg only when they want to be pinched and sent to a nice warm cell where food is brought to them.

Time was when Skid Row was worth reporting, when Howard Chandler Christy made his reputation drawing humorous cartoons of a cheerful mendicant whom he called "Nervy Nat." There isn't even a caricature left in them any more. Now and then the Chicago newspapers solemnly "expose" Skid Row, describe the composition of "smoke," go into detail about the "winos," and reveal with gasping surprise that some of these lost souls once were men, even gentlemen. We will spare you their miserable lives and their unmourned deaths.

A few feet to the north stood the storied Desplaines Street police station, near the Haymarket. This was the focal point of a section of two-bit whores, every conceivable manner of violence, and the general leavings of the higher grades of low life. The lords of the surrounding territory of cottage hookshops were "Mike the Pike" Heidler, "Monkeyface Charlie" Genker, and "Mike the Plumber," who seemed to have no last name. Mike the Pike, in addition to running four cathouses and taking the earnings of two or three women in each, operated the hangout where all the pimps drank coffee and played stuss all night long, waiting for their broads until four o'clock, which was the closing hour, except for "all-night stayers," usually men too plastered to get on their feet.

It was Mike who gave to the world in one line a deathless summation of love as it was bought and sold west of Halsted. He ran a two-story four-bit brothel on Peoria Street. There was no "parlor," but the reception room, which had no paving on the floor, was for standees, and on busy nights they filled it and lined up in an overflow on the sidewalk. Toward the back was a flight of stairs to the girls' rooms. As each girl came down, the man she had just entertained went out the rear door and the first customer in line got her. There was no picking and choosing; it was an endless-belt operation. As he was paired, he handed Mike fifty cents, which, with his usual poetic promptings, Mike rang up on a cash register. He tossed the girl a brass check which she would cash in later for a quarter, and she and the man went upstairs. Mike had a push-button to every room, the fee bought fifteen minutes, and at the end of that time he rang a bell in the room. If the teamster or coal-heaver wasn't out by that time, Mike sent up and charged another quarter.

The Republican State's Attorney raided Mike's joint, and he was pinched. But his trial came up before a Democratic judge and Mike knew he would be discharged. The assistant prosecutor on the job was a good Christian and a Sunday School teacher. He presented in evidence a little red notebook found in possession of the defendant. There was no objection and Mike, knowing the outcome, was strutting his stuff. He sat in the witness chair in the regular pimp's uniform of the day, a white silk shirt open at the throat, no necktie, but a three-carat diamond screwed into the front. The representative of the state thumbed the book, and the following colloquy ensued:

"On page under date September 4, would ask defendant the meaning of the following item: 'Mabel, 22'!"

"That means," said Mike, "that Mabel went upstairs that day twenty-two times."

"On page under date September 18, what does this mean: 'Flossie, 28'?"

"That means Flossie went upstairs that day twenty-eight times."

"In view of the extraordinary testimony already adduced from this amazing defendant, I ask the significance of this incredible entry: 'Gladys, 35'!"

"That means Gladys went upstairs that day thirty-five times. I guess it was a Saturday night."

"My God! I should think it would have killed her!"

"Well," observed Mike, "running up and down them stairs ain't no fun."

This was in the zone of the Desplaines Street Station, which was torn down last year after a historic existence since 1882, when the neighborhood included mostly semi-rural homes of the well-to-do. With the Haymarket Riot of 1886, in which eight policemen were killed and others were wounded in an outbreak of anarchists, the locality retrograded. But during its decline it produced perhaps a million crimes and some famous cops.

Among the best known was Inspector Ed McCann, who took the Joliet rap for the Democratic grafters to whom he delivered $35,000 a week in collection from prostitution, gambling and protected crime.

His official collectors were two detectives. They were about the toughest team that ever worked the force. They both died violent deaths, years later.

They called regularly at the West Side gambling joints, the red light dives, the all-night saloons, the hangouts for known thieves. The allotted amounts always awaited them in manila envelopes, the bills not folded.

Then for dessert, they usually gave the proprietor a beating, busted up a few chairs and a window or two, and departed smiling.

The cops would kick in as follows:

The inspector, whoever he was, sat at a roll-top desk. In the center of it, below, was a drawer. When they or other collectors entered, the inspector would get up and walk toward the rear of the room where stood a water-cooler. While his back was turned and he was taking a drink, the envelopes would be slipped into the drawer, which was closed by the time he started forward again.

The inspector could thus swear in good faith that no one had handed the money to him, that he had not seen anyone put it anywhere.

The envelopes were delicately referred to as "the documents." The inspector always managed to get to his desk and see that the "documents" were in the drawer before the collectors got beyond the reach of his voice. Like all dirty dough it had a habit of shrinking as it passed through hot hands.

The policemen assigned to pick up and pass on the money felt that was part of their assigned work, as they still do. None ever rose up in the wrath of high conscience and refused.

One night, downtown in detective headquarters, where a lieutenant was in charge, the drawer was hastily opened and it was found empty.

Ensued a verbal passage between the lieutenant and a West Side captain, a giant in the old-fashioned, frog-fronted, long uniform coat and tan Pawnee Bill hat:

"Captain," called the lieutenant. "I fail to see the doc'-ments."

"Well, lieutenant, I certainly put them in the drawer."

"I am holding the drawer open. It contains no doc'ments, captain."

"Do you mean to say I didn't deposit them there, lieutenant?"

"I mean to say there is nothing in the drawer, captain."

"I have been on the force as long as you have, lieutenant, and you have never heard my honesty questioned."

"I not only never heard your honesty questioned, captain. I never even heard it mentioned!"

A more picturesque inspector there than McCann, who went to jail broke, was John Shea. He was a handsome, hard man, not overly tall, but built of steel. He was known as "Black Jack" because no razor could remove the shadow from his cheeks. Despite the political situation, Shea had a constitutional hatred for law-breakers. When he was a dick, still comparatively young, the mighty man suffered a stroke and emerged paralyzed from the waist down. The scourge of malefactors was assigned to desk work and was so efficient that he was given charge of this rough bailiwick. He developed uncanny skill in handling his ball-bearing wheel-chair, in which he lived during working hours. His office was about 40 feet square and he spun around it with more agility than those able to walk could match by running.

Along the muddy alley at the side of the station was a

block of grog-shops above which slatterns lived, hustled through the open windows, and enticed the Skid Row habitués for pleasure at a quarter a throw. Sprawled on the floor of her crib they found the remains of a trollop named "Hunchbacked Kitty." She was face down and in her distorted spine a knife had been sunk. Shea blazed. He sent for Egan and Norton, a famous, tough team.

Shea couldn't stomach a murder in a room into which he could look from his own window. Shea examined the knife, which was of peculiar design. His men scouted cutlery manufacturers and found it was a broom-cutter's tool. Shea ordered a canvass of all broom factories and a round-up of all hands who hadn't worked that afternoon. The search soon came down to an immigrant from the Budapest waterfront and investigation showed he had been taking money from Kitty. He was brought in. He shook his head and mumbled that he spoke no English. He was husky and heavy. But Shea wheeled himself out, shoved his huge hand down into the man's collar, dug his knuckles into the suspect's Adam's apple until his face turned blue, and then, with the most amazing feat of physical strength Jack Lait had ever witnessed, he lifted the 180-pound prisoner off his feet and threw him half the length of the room, against both walls of a corner, cold and limp.

"When he comes to, he'll speak English and plenty of it," said Shea. And he did. As the man's eyes began to open, Shea whirled himself at him and sat over him. He started to reach that right arm out. The man on the floor cowered, covered himself with his arms and started his monologue, a full confession.

"Take him away before I strangle him," Shea ordered. "It's a good thing for him I haven't got the use of my legs!"

On cold nights, 500 to 600 wrecks, who couldn't even summon a coin for a flop (called "kip dough") slept in the old station house on the floor. But in the new lockup which has replaced it, at Monroe Street and Racine Avenue, there are 14 cells with seats for 140 and a bullpen which seats 20. It is a stylish place and will not accept more scum than it can receive with comfortable hospitality. It has such luxuries as a refrigerator, a stove, a sink and a $60 table. Prisoners' fare is no longer black bread and coffee, a slice of bologna has been added. There is modern plumbing instead of the old running troughs. In this $250,000 haven a watch is set, so the guests won't unscrew and steal the faucets. It is already infested with vermin. A suggestion for delousing equipment was turned down by the Corporation Counsel, who feared some of the thin-skinned clientele might sue if subjected to it.

As one wanders west on Madison, he finds Skid Row giving way to Strip Row. This is the mecca for the sucker trade and there are dozens of the places peculiar to Chicago, the long converted stores with a low stage set up to give a view, from all locations, of a succession of strip-teasers accompanied by three loud musicians. Beer is 50 cents a bottle, bad whisky is 75 cents. Madison Street's joints of this character are as lewd as any in a city which is plastered with them, and which will be further described. The infamous L and L Club, an ant-hill of homos, is near the Flamingo, where, immediately after each coarse coocher has given her exhibition, your waitress solicits you for her. These joints, like all others which violate law and decency, are politically taken care of through the usual pipelines, which lead to the big Syndicate.

John Touhy, the Democratic district leader, a business partner of Alderman Sain, representing it, writes some 90 per cent of all the insurance policies issued on all these and collateral dives. That is the side-money system originally founded by Bathhouse John in his First Ward. Dope is sold everywhere, as are denatured alcohol, bay rum, canned heat, fermented cider and anything else that will produce a jag. Many of the hookers on the streets are runaway bobby-soxers. Black Bronzeville need not take any back talk from white West Madison Street.

7. THE NEW TENDERLOIN

THE NORTH SIDE of Chicago is its newest and nicest. The broad expanse of its beautiful parks and its lake-front boulevards still bespeak the dreams of those who loved Chicago and planned it. Near the Lake and the extension of Michigan Boulevard are fine hotels and elegant shops. Lake Shore Drive's glorious mile was once lined along its single building-fronts with stately mansions, and there are still homes, there and nearby, of the rich who choose to cling to the city. Here was the gray stone mansion of Mrs. Potter Palmer, who was not only the first society woman of the Middle West, but perhaps of the continent. When she went abroad, her trunks were labeled "Mrs. Potter Palmer, Deliver To Buckingham Palace."

In time the bourgeoisie went north as commerce extended along the Lake front and honkytonks and assignation houses ruined the back streets, with the waves that washed up from near North Clark Street, which was always a hellhole, but was confined in its open degradation to below Chicago Avenue. At the turn of the century it was a compound for yeggmen whose national headquarters was the Revere House, kept by Steve Crowe, brother of Pat Crowe, who attained national notoriety as the kidnaper of the Cudahy baby. All around it were saloons where life wasn't worth a nickel. The saloon-keepers were thugs. Along the west side of the street were hundreds of street-walkers' hovels which were robbers' roosts. Over the region reigned "Hot Stove Jimmy" Quinn, one of the "Gray Wolves" of the days when Chicago streets were being sold to Charles E. Yerkes, an ex-convict himself, and spittoons for City Hall were being bought for $400 each.

It was the custom of Mayor Carter H. Harrison II to walk home to his house on Goethe Street. He usually would go up LaSalle, but one day he took Clark Street. He had no sooner crossed the bridge than a drunken hustler grabbed the silk lapel of his Prince Albert and said: "Come on upstairs, baby. I'll show you a good time." Lait was dangling his feet on the sergeant's desk in East Chicago Avenue Station when the effete mayor came in, fighting. For two or three days the women were kept off North Clark Street—the only time in its history.

But it has changed. It seemed inconceivable that a further blight could descend on North Clark Street. Yet it came—with another Strip Row, which added Woolworth perfume to all the familiar stenches and for a solid half-mile the wiggle-and-leer joints have displaced some of the oldest drinking-dives of the murderers and safe-blowers.

McGovern Brothers' Bar ran for a generation. Everything went there—except women. They wouldn't even let one scrub the floor. They bragged that they wouldn't let a female cat in. Today it is one of the biggest and most brazen strip-teaseries, and advertises itself as "Chicago's Biggest Girl Show." It even plays matinees and employs probably twenty-five peelers, and those are not its only distaff drawing cards.

Chicago lives through one unbroken round of conventions. It is overrun with stop-overs, tourists, buyers and sellers and smalltowners in for a fling. North Clark Street is two minutes' walk from some of the busiest hotels, and the guests mill along Clark gawking at the framed photos outside the stripperies, and then rush in with their eyeballs bulging. Prices here are higher than on the West Side, but furtive gentlemen will approach you and offer you anything you can name. Everything they sell is illegal in a black market for any kind of drug or weapon or unspeakable circus, bi-sexual or homo-sexual, human or beastly. For $500 you can buy a virgin, and name your own choice of color; for $3 you can have a hag, with the same selective discrimination. You can buy untaxed champagne and rotgut right out of the washtub. Nowhere this side of Port Said or Marseilles are there such bargains!

East of Clark Street is Rush Street. Clark gets the dregs, Rush gets the cream. The richest gangsters, the best-kept mistresses and the more prosperous of the show people drink and play there, in hotels and the converted residences where uniformed butlers once swung open the portals to the best people. All around them in apartment and transient hotels are gamblers and their women and all the other colorful folk of the new world, the half-world and the underworld.

This sector, as of the Chicago Crime Commission records, contains hundreds of premises which violate one or more, or all, of the laws concerning:

> B girls soliciting at bars, clip joints, catering to homosexuals, bars and cocktail lounges operated after hours (many run around the clock and never close), gambling, assignation houses, permitting soliciting for immoral purposes in lobbies, and allowing bartenders, etc., to sell narcotics.

Similar conditions exist in many sections, but nowhere are there as many infractions in so small an area. This is not essentially a tourist location, though steerers do bring suckers. Your reporters entered a cab stationed outside a West Madison Street dive and asked to be taken to the Loop. The driver asked us whether we had had fun. We said not too much, and pretty cheesy. He agreed, saying: "Them dives is for the rube trade. You gents look like you want the real thing and would pay for it. There's a place on Rush Street where pretty young girls take off everything and do tricks."

We went. It was rather like the run of such establishments, except that the girls were juveniles, two no more than fifteen years old. There were other men there, but the talent seemed to attract many lesbians. The stripping was complete and the "tricks" were obscene, but circumscribed by lack of imagination. The prices were high and the cabby told us he got $5 for every party he delivered. We had to be okayed by him, as it is in a remodeled private house. There is no sign and the doors are not open to strays. The inevitable B girl was at the bar and she, too, was a juvenile who should have been asleep after doing her homework. Instead, she was surrounded by obvious lady-lovers who were pawing her and buying her drinks.

This drink-buying has never been developed anywhere else to such rapacious acquisitiveness. The B girls are not necessarily for sale, but they are harpies who slip in and sit beside men and plead, "Please buy me a drink, mister." If you nod, a waitress brings a round, duplicating any earlier orders in addition to serving the girl a whisky glass of what is supposed to be absinthe and vermouth. It is colored water with a drop of non-alcoholic flavoring to simulate the ingredients, which the girl will ask you to smell to convince you that she isn't stalling and that her swill is worth a dollar-and-a-half. She has barely swallowed it before another round appears on the table from nowhere. Should a man protest, she begins to cry, says she understood it had been ordered and if it is not accepted the entire cost will be charged to her. In one place we told her that was a lot of malarky and, instead of letting her run up bills for drinks we didn't want, we gave her some money under the table and told her to talk. She said she was not a whore and that she was not allowed to leave before 4:30 A.M., at which time she could make any arrangements she chose, and that sometimes she did date a man. But not for nickels. She was a young Puerto Rican from New York, where she had to give in to tramps and Chinamen and then was badgered and robbed, often stuck up with a knife or gun. She couldn't make a living and if she hustled openly a pimp would take her over by brute force. Here she was making about $200 a week, knocking down 50 per cent of the gross on her own drinks, 75 cents on each served her at our table. She also got an occasional tip from some man trying to make her. She said the waitresses earned at least $100 a week. But the strippers, the attractions, earned from $40 up to $75, and had to pay 10 per cent to a booking agent.

Burlesque bars are few on the near North Side beyond the mile of Clark Street dumps. There is only one open stripper on Rush Street, the Spa. Most establishments are restaurants or cocktail lounges with only a singing pianist, male or female, for entertainment, plus the inevitable B girl. The initiates hang around to drink, talk, meet old friends or pick up new ones. But the bartenders will get you anything you want—tell you where there is a crap game, contact call girls or take a bet on the horses. Throughout Chicago, bartenders function to a much wider extent than they do in any other known place. It is the fashion to advertise their names in connection with saloons and restaurants, as though they are stars. And some of them are, with individual followings because of their wide usefulness. Their local appellation is "the mixo," and they are heavily tipped.

If Chicago has anything resembling a bohemian section, it is the near North Side. Bughouse (Washington) Square attracts the nuts and the exhibitionists. The made-over flats and the remodeled mansions harbor all that is left of Chicago's artistic and literary colony. What was once on the way to being the center of a new school of civilized culture has dwindled to a pocket edition of the remains of atmosphere in New York's Greenwich Village, with candlelighted teashops, a few sawdust-strewn saloons where the avante garde reads effusions of its confusions to other would-bes, and the pet drinks are grappo and vino rouge. Such habituals always draw the distorted and the perverted and that melange of middle-sexed jobs which nature started but never finished. As a blind for allowing more serious toleration, the police swoop down now and then on the pathological misfits, but they soon return.

The out-and-out parlor-houses are in business again further north, around Division and LaSalle Streets, a mile-and-a-half north of the Loop. During the war, the Army cracked down on them. The housing shortage made it impossible to move and open surreptitiously until caught. Now there seem to be no difficulties except occasional squawks from respectable neighbors who own their houses and cling to them, and as the squawkers don't pay off, they get little action. Some of the madames are in business after years of retirement or money-making in less flagrant fields. Strangers are steered by taxi-drivers, bellboys, bartenders and full-time commission salesmen who work hotel lobbies and bars. The minimum in the traffic is $20. Most of the places sell liquor and champagne at inflated rates. Beer, the old hookshop standard, is out above the ground floor.

Lake Shore Drive, Lincoln Parkway and Sheridan Road, fine avenues facing the Lake, are still Chicago's glamor boulevards. Most of the sprawling homes of the mighty are gone, as unsuited to the mood and the economy of the times, or have been converted into schools and institutions—or, in one case, the U. S. Court of Appeals. But in the modern apartment houses and on adjoining cross streets live most of what is left of the wealthy. But these super-flats keep roofs over the heads also of kept dames, big-time gamblers, thriving saloon-keepers and the richest and most powerful of America's new and rising nobility—the top racketeers of the Syndicate. If anybody is old-fashioned enough to attempt to bar them, they buy the joints, either through respected real estate dealers or openly at auction, if necessary.

These northward drives, really continuations of each other, run into the swank suburbs. A few blocks inland is the extension of North Clark Street and its branching arm, Broadway. These are the North Side business thoroughfares. Their entire length is dotted with saloons, taverns, dingy nightclubs and the full range of restaurants. Many have gambling setups in the rear or are blinds for bookmakers. Broadway and Clark meet at Diversey, another neighborhood Tenderloin with all the fixings.

Five miles north of the Loop the Bismarck Gardens flourished, a huge restaurant and al fresco acres where played famed European bands and 75-piece orchestras. This was in the fashion of Continental Europe. There were sylvan spots, walks, rural bridges, trees, grass and even a miniature zoo. With war against Germany, the name was changed to Marigold Gardens. Came Prohibition and it was all switched into an attempt at a modern nightclub with floorshows and all the accessories. Chicago couldn't see it. Now the old Marigold is dingy, depressing and often dark. When it runs it is a fight arena and dance-hall.

Farther north is the Wilson Avenue area. That was the trading point for respectable residential developments which flourished especially with the continuation of the elevated railroad through to Evanston. A few undesirables seeped in, but it remained largely a business and small-time theatrical district, close to Wilson Beach, a beautiful public playland of fun, with fond memories for many comparatively young Chicagoans. Now the beach is filled in and the land is extended out into the Lake. That is in tune with many changes there, mostly for the worse.

Wilson Avenue is an express stop on the North Shore

Electric railway, which runs past Fort Sheridan and the Great Lakes Naval Training Station. During the war period hundreds of thousands of young strangers were processed and stationed in these posts. They still maintain large complements. Men on leave find they save a half-hour on their way to the fleshpots by getting off at Wilson Avenue. So a conglomeration of cheap assignation houses, dope-peddlers and the ubiquitous burlesque bars, with their hustlers and all the accoutrements for clipping sailors and soldiers, sprang up there and have never left. They drove out the old-fashioned bars by outbidding them in rentals and poisoned the entire locality.

On Wilson Avenue near Broadway is the Silver Palm. Here the notorious Satira got her start. She was doing a chorus strip-act on the raised platform behind the bar. She had a sinuous figure and her "work" brought her prominence. She attracted many men, including the married lover she was to kill on his boat in Havana Harbor. One of the owners of the Silver Palm financed her defense. The grateful Satira, later a Page 1 sensation, did her time, got out of the can, and promptly booked herself into his opposition saloon. Satira returned from her Cuban murder stretch a heroine. Women as well as men flocked to see her. She was quoted and lionized by columnists, wooed and pursued by well-heeled wolves. It was predicted she would be a star. Soon she was—in a honkytonk in Calumet City, patronized by steel-puddlers and slummers out for hell-raising.

We went to the Silver Palm where she had originated. We also traveled to Calumet City to see her. The woman has no quality, even in the disgusting specialty which is her calling. Since these words were put in type, Satira got herself a male partner and put on a "modern" Hindu dance specialty. And as for the Silver Palm—we have covered nightlife and seen everything in San Francisco, New Orleans, Tiajuana, Paris and Panama City. But we bow to the Silver Palm.

Here, on the raised stage behind a long bar, is a continuous and interminable parade of peelers, wigglers and muscle-dancers, most of them moronic even for their trade, unsightly caricatures on the undraped female body which, in repose, has been the inspiration for masterpieces. Minsky's women, a byword for the whole burlesque institution, were glorified Ziegfeld duchesses alongside the troupe from which sprang Satira. And the patrons befit the entertainers.

The audience, almost entirely stag, consists largely of old lechers with peeping-Tom expressions and young delinquents who drink their beer from a bottle and sit mesmerized at the sight of moving female flesh. Circulating to cadge drinks are unsavory B girls, joined now and then by cast members between their turns. Running the proceedings is a bleached woman weighing a good 200 pounds, who offers unsubtle commentaries on the performers and whips up the good clean fun of the whole business in a ground-floor loft thick with smoke and crowded with seats to furnish views from all angles.

It is difficult to get indignant at Chicago. So much is so open, and law-breaking is so obvious that it comes to appear normal. There are thousands of dives running so flagrantly that they would mean jail for everybody connected with them if they operated an hour in New York, which is no Sunday school settlement. One gets used to it.

The Silver Palm is as corny and blatant and low as any. But there are hundreds as low as the Silver Palm, where Satira minced forth overdressed and pranced out almost nude. The wife of the man she killed got some publicity and she, too, wanted to cash in. She did it the way of least resistance, in another burlesque cafe, the French Casino, on North Clark Street. An enterprising Chicago agent we met there confided to us that he had a colossal idea, a project that would stand Chicago sideways: he was trying to book them both on one bill—the murderer and the widow of her murder. How can you get sore at a town like that? And he was probably right. If he put it over, Chicago would most likely cheer.

A few blocks farther north, the wayfarer sees a sign proclaiming the Paladium Dance Hall. Years ago this was the colorful Green Mill Gardens, fronted by Tom Chamales, a well-known nightlife impresario of his day, a First Ward politician who ran the Queen Hotel, which was one of many that flourished in the gala days of Bathhouse John. Joe E. Lewis, now one of our most famous and most expensive cabaret stars, worked at the Green Mill during Prohibition days. He was unknown but was soon discovered and developed a strong following among the sports who patronized expensive speakeasies. There was no actors' union, and in places like these actors worked until they got the heave. But one night Lewis turned in his notice. He was going to work in a new place, the Rendezvous, started by rival mobsters. This was strictly not according to Emily Post.

The gangsters who owned the Green Mill didn't care for it and they told Lewis so. That night, as he was about to retire in his room in a North Side hotel, Machine-gun Jack McGurn, who was Al Capone's bodyguard, and who didn't get his nickname accidentally, pushed his way in. He slashed Lewis' cheeks, cut his tongue almost off and left him in his room for dead. The surgical touches were unusual, but they were meant as a warning to other performers who might get ideas. With the exception of Lucky Luciano, Lewis is the only known person who ever remained alive after such attentions. After months he pulled through. He had to learn how to talk all over again. To this day he carries the criss-cross scars on his face. The payoff is that after he recovered Joe went back to work for the same outfit that cut him up. He is now on the friendliest terms with the surviving members thereof.

Rogers Park reaches to the northernmost border. It harbored upper middle-class householders. Under the Illinois local option system it was bone-dry, completely closed and clean during Chicago's most flaunted wickedness. The influence of the churches was strong. But the onrush of predatory profits overcame it. It is still beautiful, with wide streets, trees and detached homes with spacious lawns. Such apartment houses as were built also conform to its general plan of room and air. But now the saloons are in, perhaps more per capita than in the crowded tenement territories. For every tavern there are two gambling houses.

Howard Street, running west from the Lake, is the city limit line, dividing Rogers Park from the stately seat of Northwestern University and the cradle and home of the W.C.T.U., Evanston. Prohibition was invented there. Evanston has always been arid and its municipal government sternly means business. For some blocks, one side of Howard Street is in Chicago and the other in Evanston. Lined solidly along the south walk are taverns, stripperies and liquor shops; across the road there are none. To the oases, first open stop from all the dry North Shore suburbs, flock the students and the bibulous suburbanites. That has made Howard a honky-tonk lane and every night is Saturday night. Some of the busiest prostitutes in town practice around Howard and Paulina Streets. At Howard and Clark is a joint that runs all-night gambling.

Thursday night is Howard Street's biggest, even surpassing Saturday. On "Maid's Night Off," domestics from all the swank North Side and suburban homes come there to get drunk and picked up, and the boys are there waiting to help them.

Others not intent on romance or good times are there also. These are finger men for the hold-up gangs, who scrape up acquaintances with the girls, then lift their house-keys from their purses. When the slavey is ready to return to her employer's home, her "escort" insists on accompanying her. At the servants' door, he slugs her, and he and his accomplices gain admittance with her key.

Howard Street is gradually growing worse than Wilson Avenue, which is a thieves' and pimps' paradise. Late in 1949 hoodlums there beat up five cops sent to arrest them.

Negroes have settled on the North Side, too, the largest colony running a mile north of Chicago Avenue on the west side of Clark Street. They have a smaller contingent north of Wilson Avenue, almost to the Lake. And many are crossing into Rogers Park, interspersed in blocks predominantly white.

8. AROUND THE WORLD IN CHICAGO

CHICAGOANS boast they can eat, make love, or get killed in any language. Almost one-quarter of Chicago's residents are foreign-born. They come from every land. Yet the city is not cosmopolitan—well, anyway not as much as San Francisco, New Orleans or Boston, which, though smaller, have better-defined and more atmospheric foreign sections.

The outlanders who came here landed elsewhere first. When they finally reached Chicago they were absorbed by the town—not contrariwise, as happened in New York. Chicago is still Midwestern.

You can go through miles of streets where every name on every shop is unpronounceably Polish, Bohemian or other Slavic. These streets aren't physically different from any others. There are no quaint foreign sections which resemble some Old World city. Yet these émigrés did bring some inborn idiosyncrasies of their homelands in cooking, entertainment and customs, which they and their children follow. For mutual protection and to insure against loneliness in an alien land, greenhorns usually gather together.

This chapter is not meant to be inclusive. Nor is it a guidebook to tourist haunts. You can buy one of those on the newsstand.

A. Sons of the Prophet

You won't find any camels at 18th and Michigan. Chicago's small Arabic quarter is surrounded by Automobile Row.

If you can digest such, there are several native restaurants serving Near Eastern delicacies which you are supposed to eat with your hands. Arabs sell tapestry and rugs, wholesale and retail. Many merchants who say they are Arabs (because business is business) are not.

You will find no orgies out of the *Arabian Nights* here. Chicago's Arabs don't keep harems and if they did you wouldn't care to look twice at their women. They wouldn't be to your taste. The chief pastime is drinking thick, black coffee and playing cards.

B. Pilsner und Pretzels

Those who saw the *Prince of Pilsen* in their youth, and who now think of all Bohemians as gay and dashing Mittel-Europeans who drop everything on a cue to go into a rousing drinking song had better keep away from Chicago's Little Prague. These Czechs are solid, stolid people, the utter antithesis of the colorful folk of operetta lore.

There are more of them in Chicago than in any city in the world except Prague. Twenty per cent of all Czechs in the United States are in Chicago. They were among the earliest residents and have been prominent in the Windy City for a hundred years.

Little Prague is between 18th and 26th and Halsted and Pulaski Road, covering about six square miles. Generally, Czechs, or "Bohunks," as they once were called, are law-abiding people, though one is advised not to tangle with a Bohemian who has been drinking too freely. Because of their numbers, Czechs soon became powerful in politics as well as in the underworld and for many years they controlled the Cook County Democratic machine. Anton Cermak, last of the great Bohemian bosses and mayor of the city, was assassinated in Florida by a bullet allegedly intended for President-elect Franklin D. Roosevelt. He was a millionaire—from dubious sources of income.

Many Czech immigrants were farmers or unskilled laborers. Their early years in Chicago were sustained in adversity. They fought and conquered their handicaps and were acclimatized, Americanized and assimilated into Chicago's warp and woof.

Little Prague is noted for restaurants which specialize in sauerkraut and dumplings and fine draught beer. Czechs love to drink and dance and make love. Bohemian girls are fair, well-built and, it is said, not puritanical. The people are athletically inclined, go in for mass drills and exercises in their numerous Sokol halls.

All is not peaceful in Little Bohemia. The Kremlin is at

work and many local Czechs changed their politics when their Fatherland did. You may expect dissension here.

C. Our Little Brown Cousins

If you see a smallish guy with slanty eyes, who might be Chinese or Japanese, with a big blonde, he's neither. He's a Filipino. His compatriots compose Chicago's second largest Oriental colony, outnumbering the Chinese. Filipinos are not concentrated in any section, but many live on N. LaSalle near Little Tokyo.

An estimated 10,000 of the little brown brothers are in Chicago, but again it must be pointed out that these figures are clouded. For many years, entrance of Filipinos into the country was illegal, and many are afraid of being deported.

Why the blondes? There are less than 30 Filipino women in the entire city. The babes never left the home islands, and that is a pity, because the average Filipino girl is cute and cuddlesome, a sort of Oriental doll with Latin characteristics.

The absence of women is not particularly regretted, because most Filipinos seem to prefer buxom, beefy blondes. They keep them on the community plan. It is a practice among less affluent Filipino boys to chip in for one flashy automobile, one smart suit of clothes—which they can all wear, because they are all the same size—and one flat in which they all live and keep or send for one blonde. Each uses the car, the suit and the girl on his day off.

Chicago's Filipinos are probably the most prosperous in the country. There was never the same prejudice against them that made them pariahs in California, nor were they all reduced to menial jobs, as they are in New York.

Though numerous Chicago Filipinos work in restaurants as busboys and dishwashers, you'd be astonished at how many are doctors, lawyers, barbers, merchants, and even practitioners of the arts and sciences. All Filipinos read English, which they speak badly, but they prefer to talk Spanish or their national Tagalog.

Filipinos are members of the Oriental Council, composed of Japanese, Chinese, Koreans and themselves.

They are industrious workers and seldom are on rolls of

unemployment or other relief. They are not intemperate drinkers, but they show a disproportionate incidence of reefer addiction. Filipinos seldom use guns but prefer knives, with which they are experts.

There are no Filipino restaurants in Chicago, so most of the colony does its wining and dining in Chinese, Japanese or Spanish eating places or private homes and clubs.

Due in part to the lack of female companionship, Filipinos are inveterate gamblers and spend most of their hours at card-playing.

D. Die Wacht am Lake Michigan

During World War I, some Chicago Germans expected the Kaiser to win, and they prepared for his triumphal entry into the Loop.

But most of them had learned their lesson by the time of World War II, and Hitler did not have anywhere near as many boosters in Chicago as he did, say, in New York's Yorkville, or on Long Island, or in northern New Jersey. Chicago's Germanic population was by then almost completely native-born, many of the fourth and fifth generations. Immigrants no longer were coming inland, but remaining in the coastal towns.

The first German arrived in Chicago in 1837, and by 1848 and 1849, when they flowed out of the old country in shiploads, the German colony was one of the largest in town.

Before World War I, Chicago was said to have had more Germans than any other city in the world except Berlin. Anti-British Mayor "Big Bill" Thompson justified his attitude toward the British by saying, "After all, there are more Germans here than in Hamburg." He threatened to punch King George V on his snoot if he showed it in Chicago.

Germans were the most important of all second-table elements in town. Their influence was felt in industry, education, politics, the arts, society, and with comparative infrequency, in crime. Public school teachers took sabbatical leaves to study in German colleges. Deutsch was taught in grade schools. The Prussian system of education was imitated in the setup of the public school system.

Germans influenced the meat-packing industry and brewing. Chicago was full of breweries and beer gardens. There was an atmosphere of good living. These were wholesome people. The influence of the Germans began to wane during World War I, when so many had intermarried and bred patriots. In the meantime the wave of Slavic peoples made the Germanic star wane.

There are many German colonies. Though there are more Germans in Chicago than in New York, the city does not have one large German section like Yorkville.

If you are looking for Germanic atmosphere you will find it in the vicinity of North and Ogden Avenues. Here are night clubs and restaurants featuring Viennese waltzes and Bavarian sauerbraten. One of the most famous German restaurants in the country, and among the oldest, is the Red Star Inn on North Clark. Near it is the famed old Germania Club.

During the war most of these German restaurants took on a coloration of red, white and blue, and today you find little pro-German sentiment among their patrons.

Maybe a few are Nazis, but they still "ain't saying nothing."

E. Lunch, She Served

You will be as surprised as we were to find 75,000 Greeks in Chicago. These people are usually thought of as living in seaport towns. But, according to Chicago historians, here is the oldest Hellenic section in the United States. It is a block north of the Mexican settlement, on the near West Side, forming a delta at the intersection of Halsted, Blue Island and Harrison Streets.

Generally, Chicago's Greeks are law-abiding. They are hard workers, frugal with their savings, and usually end up owning their businesses—fruit-stands, candy-factories, lunchrooms and shoe-shine parlors. There are many extremely rich Greeks in Chicago. These are the importers of olive oil and wine and the wholesale provision merchants.

Like Filipinos, Greeks originally brought few women over here. There has been a heavy migration of them in recent years. The shortage of women accounts for the gambling-clubs and coffee-shops where most of the men spend all of their spare time. Greeks, like other people of Near East origin, are habitual gamblers for high stakes. Gin-rummy and poker have become their games.

Gambling is controlled by a local Greek syndicate, which is closely allied with the Italian mob. Many of the important figures in Chicago's underworld are of Greek descent.

Tourists and locals visit the Greek section in search of delicacies, such as baklava and sampali. Americans who think of Greek food as the tasteless stuff served in lunch-wagons will be amazed at the exotic and highly seasoned courses in bona fide Greek restaurants. Most of these are too strong for American tastes. A specialty is lamb and rice.

F. Everything's Pizza

Most Italians are peaceful people who would rather eat spaghetti, drink red wine and sing *O Sole Mio* than throw their weight around.

But among them is a core of cruel, quick-tempered men, bitter and defiant of law and authority. These trouble-makers prey on the good and deeply religious people of their own nationality as much as they do on others.

Italian-Americans now make up the dominant racial group in Chicago, having taken over the city in much the same fashion as they annexed New York and many other large American cities. This phenomenon will be considered in a later chapter.

This is the place for a few words about Little Italy. Though Italians are found all over the city, and in large numbers, Chicago's largest Little Italy is around Taylor Street, from Halsted to Western Avenue.

The poorest Italians live around 23rd and Wentworth, near Chinatown, in a section of evil-smelling huts with living conditions as bad as the worst in Bronzeville. The indigent, ignorant Italians who live here are gripped by the Black Hand, forced to pay tribute from the pennies of their penury. From this neighborhood comes an outpouring of criminals, gunmen and juvenile delinquents.

Boss of the local Sicilian Union is Bruno Roti, who runs a tavern which is patronized frequently by underworld figures.

One of the worst points of friction is the borderline between Italian and Jewish neighborhoods, at 3600 Roosevelt Road. Jews, too, like Italians, have a long record of pacifism, but here gangs of young Jewish and Italian boys engage in bloody battle. Conditions are so bad, the authorities are forced to call in leaders of both colonies in an effort to force the young hoodlum gangs to lay off each other. All the fine talk about the melting-pot and the rights of minorities is forgotten in the stress of stern reality.

After the last such war, the elders agreed to keep all Jews on one side of the line and all Italians on the other.

A second Little Italy is in the vicinity of Grand and Milwaukee Avenues. Wherever Italians live in large numbers, you will always find they are victims of Black Hand extortionists.

There are many fine pizza palaces in these sections, where tasty Italian food and wonderful chianti wine is sold at low prices.

G. Children of the Book

What was once Chicago's Jewish ghetto has been taken over by Negroes and Mexicans.

But the Jewish businesses and the kosher restaurants still remain in the neighborhood of 12th and Halsted. To them are drawn Jews from all parts of the city.

As the Hebrews prospered, they spread all over town. As they do everywhere in freedom, they became assimilated, and now there is no such thing, practically speaking, as a Jewish colony.

Many middle-class people of Jewish origin live on the far West Side and in the better sections of the North Side. Many localities are almost entirely Jewish, but up to date and Yankeefied. The wealthiest Jews moved into the swank North Shore suburbs.

Jews are leaders in every business and profession and are in the forefront of the arts and sciences.

Until recently, they were in the top echelons of the organized underworld, too, but are being supplanted by Italians, as will be explained hereinafter.

H. On the Shores of the Midwest Baltic

Chicago has 100,000 Liths, most of them around 31st and Halsted Streets. They are hard workers and good citizens who seldom get into trouble except on Saturday nights after too many boilermakers—whiskey and beer.

Chicago is the Lithuanian center of the U. S., and has been since the 1880's, when the earliest settlers moved in from the Pennsylvania coal-mines. These are gay, homeloving people, who go for community singing and community athletics.

The average time spent in the United States by the typical Lith is now 50 years, but they still love the ways of the old country and teach their children the language in parochial schools.

Few tourists visit the Lithuanian section, which offers no color of its own. Those who like strange foreign foods are recommended to kugeli, a sort of potato pudding.

I. Jumping Beans

Chicago escaped the tragedy of New York, where hundreds of thousands of Puerto Ricans were brought from their sunny, tropical home into Harlem tenements, to face rigorous northern winters.

There are few Puerto Ricans in Chicago. Its sole Latin-American colony of any size is Mexican.

These people, all peons at home, came to Chicago working on the railroads. Many live near and work in South Chicago steel mills. Others settled in the Maxwell Street district, previously described. On one side are Italians and Negroes and on the other are Greeks. The part of the slums reserved for them is the dingiest, dirtiest and stinkingest. They are painfully poor people. When they get a few dollars they spend them on tequilla, their national drink, or on marijuana, their national smoke, or whoring, their national pastime.

The portion of Blue Island Avenue which runs through the Mexican section is not only one of the toughest in all

Chicago, but probably has more streetwalkers per square foot than any other save 35th and State in Bronzeville, and Quincy Street, downtown.

Though many Mexicans are employed as reefer peddlers or make their livings pimping or picking pockets, they do not go in for as much violence as their Puerto Rican cousins do in New York. Neither are they organized from up on top, nor are their crimes protected, because their numbers are negligible and they are not citizens with votes.

In their native land these were farmers and laborers. Many tried to earn their livings in the Middle West as seasonal workers on the large farms and in the orchards of Michigan, Wisconsin and Minnesota, but the bright lights of the city spoiled them for such husbandry and humdrum.

They are ill-equipped to face the biting winds off the Lake. The neighborhood abounds in reeking restaurants, selling enchaladas, tortillas and chile con carne in foul, rat-ridden places catering to customers as dirty as they are.

Young Mexican girls, because of their Indian blood, bloom extremely beautiful, but as they approach maturity they begin to fade and get sloppy. Many are professional prostitutes. The non-professionals don't play hard to get either.

J. Warsaw Rhapsody

As befits a city of magnificent distances and great proportions, most things in Chicago run to the superlative. And so it is no wonder that Chicago's Polish population is one of the largest urban ones in the world.

Poles began coming in trainloads exactly 100 years ago, and by the turn of the century were already a dominant force. Their power has continued to increase and the Polish vote is of preponderant importance to any political party.

To some extent Poles are the Irishmen of Chicago. Instead of names like Murphy and Clancy on the police force and in the civil service, you find long, unpronounceable cognomens ending with many z's and x's and y's. The Polish Chicagoans are spread throughout all residential districts, but the chief section, known as Little Poland, where the people of that nationality come to trade and have fun, is on Milwaukee

Avenue, near Division Street and Ashland Avenue. Here are stores selling handicraft from the old country, restaurants serving pierogi, a Polish variation of ravioli, and Polish theatres, dance-halls, social clubs and gambling joints.

Most Poles are hefty, with a tremendous capacity for food and liquor. They eat rich, heavy viands and guzzle unbelievable quantities of such liquid poisons as slivovitz.

During the week, Poles are hard workers. They are mechanics, expert craftsmen and small shopkeepers. You will find the girls working in offices, stores and factories throughout the city. But on Saturdays, 100,000 of them get dressed in their best to congregate in Little Poland and get roaring drunk. All Saturday night, the cops are busy locking them up and the ambulance surgeons get weary patching up broken heads.

The girls get dressed up and go to an early movie; then to a tavern, where they sit at the bar and drink until they get picked up. After that there's dancing and more drinking and fighting and romancing.

Polish girls are handsome, if you like the type, big with wide foreheads, cheekbones, waists and hips.

Though most Poles are well-behaved, and the group compares favorably with any other race or nationality, those Poles who break the bounds are ferocious and capable. In addition to personal crimes of violence there are many Polish pickpockets and neighborhood hoodlums. Many stick-up men are Polish.

Though Poland is now a Soviet satellite, Poles in Chicago are bitterly anti-Communist. They remain devout Roman Catholics. In this, the Polish colony differs from the Czechs.

K. Catherine Was Great

Chicago's Volga boatmen live on Ashland Avenue between Division Street and Chicago Avenue. These are old-time White Russians, who got out of the land of the czars when Lenin rolled in. They are religious orthodox Greek Catholics.

Many of Chicago's Russians claim to have been nobles or high army officers under the Romanoffs. Now they work as short-order men in lunchrooms or as doormen in front of nightclubs, though a handful are artists and professional men.

The group is negligible in size and importance. There has been no large-scale immigration from Russia in more than 30 years and these few are refugees who got out by way of China or Turkey.

What the colony lacks in size it makes up in the interesting backgrounds of its members, who will tell you all about it—as long as you buy the vodka.

L. Svenska Poyka

Numerically, Swedes and other Scandinavians make up one of the largest segments of Chicago's population. They are important in every field of endeavor, have added immeasurably to the city's wealth and well-being. Their girls are entrancing.

But they do not belong in a book of this nature, because they have provided little local color. The sections in which they live are indistinguishable from other neighborhoods. They are remarkably minor in crime, vice and gambling, and not important in politics.

The chief Swedish trading area is in the vicinity of Belmont Avenue and Halsted and Clark Streets. Here are some native grocery stores, delicatessens and restaurants. The Julian Theatre presents Swedish movies and the Viking Temple is where they have their dances, lodge meetings and social events.

There are many good Swedish restaurants in Chicago, specializing in smorgasbord, the native hors d'oeuvres. Swedes are either teetotalers or wonderful stews. Their favorite drink is aquavit, a colorless liquid with a concealed kick.

9. LITTLE TOKYO

WANT a little Geisha girl? You can find one. Like saki? You can get a binge on it.

America's second largest Japanese colony is now located on the shores of Lake Michigan. Until two years ago, there were more people of Japanese descent there than anywhere outside the Orient.

Since then some of these displaced people returned to Los Angeles. Chicago's Little Tokyo is slightly smaller than that in the City of the Angels. These new faces were added to Chicago's cosmopolitan population by war and intolerance. It is a disgraceful chapter in our national diary.

After Pearl Harbor, General DeWitt, commanding the Pacific Coast Area, ordered all persons of Japanese blood, native-born American citizens or not, transported from their homes and confined in concentration camps. There was then, it is true, considerable anti-Japanese hysteria in California and in the Northwest states. The anti-Jap campaign was no new war-born phenomenon.

Encouraged by local jingoes, DeWitt, for the first time in American history, imprisoned citizens without trial, by military fiat. With full approval of President Roosevelt and the entire Washington government, huge concentration camps were set up in the mountain states of Montana, Idaho, Wyoming and Colorado. More than 100,000 Americans were sent to them, after being driven out of their homes and businesses on the West Coast. Their crime was that their parents or grandparents had been born in Japan. Though we were fighting an equally bitter war with Germany and Italy, none of German or Italian descent were molested. Not even foreign-born aliens were hindered unless proved subversive.

While these pages were being written, the U. S. Court of Appeals, in a blistering decision, denounced General DeWitt for his action, which had the tacit, if not written, approval of Roosevelt. The court stated that conditions in some of the relocation centers were "in major respects as degrading as those of a penitentiary and in important respects worse than in any Federal penitentiary." Also it mentioned the "Nazi-like doctrine of inherited racial enmity stated by the commanding general." Another paragraph read:

"The German mob cry 'der Jude' and the general's statement, 'the Jap is a Jap' to be 'wiped off the map,' have not a remote relationship in the minds of thousands of Nisei whose constant loyalty has at last been recognized."

The Department of Justice is not appealing this decision. It is now the law of the land.

The Japanese who were committed to the so-called relocation centers were law-abiding people who for years had produced fine truck garden products and flowers, served as doctors, lawyers, teachers, merchants and farmers. A special center was set up for those suspected of sympathy with the enemy or who wanted to be repatriated. The loyal Japs were sent to other camps. DeWitt said the removal was for "their own protection."

Before the war, there were few of Japanese ancestry in Chicago. The influx began as soon as DeWitt issued his infamous order. Many Japanese packed and left the West Coast before it went into effect, and came to Chicago. After they had been imprisoned about a year, extreme pressures were put on the government to allow individual members to leave if they came East. At first they had to show means of support and to get sponsors. From the end of 1942 on there was a small trickling of young Japanese eastward bound. They were Nisei, meaning, second-generation Japanese, U. S. citizens born and educated in this country. These among the relocated followed to Chicago, where they had friends who told them they were being treated well.

During Chicago's labor shortage all help was welcome. Chicagoans were not bitter. These young Japanese found jobs. Half the hotel help in Chicago was of Japanese descent. Nisei boys and girls caught on in hospitals, institutions, department stores and restaurants.

By the end of 1943, plans were made to empty the relocation centers. But the victims were still forbidden to return to California, though it had been proved there were no spies or subversives among them. In Hawaii, where the largest single group is Japanese—one-third of the Territory's population—it was not found necessary to put any controls on those of

Japanese birth or ancestry, though Hawaii was in the center of the war zone, the most vital military spot in the whole war plan. As the Japs were released, the largest group came to Chicago. Many intended to make their stay temporary. They were from Southern California, used to fresh air and sunshine. The cold winds, sleet, snow, dirt and the noise frightened them.

At one time there were probably 40,000 Japanese in Chicago, settled or in transit. When the war ended they were free to return to California. A few did and were surprised to find the anti-Japanese attitude there had softened. The heroism of the 442nd Battalion and the 100th Combat Team, both all-Japanese, had done much to popularize the Nisei. They were the most highly decorated outfits in history, from George Washington's day on. And Nisei were not subject to the draft, could only enlist in special outfits set up for them.

Most younger Japs stayed on, found in Chicago opportunities denied them on the Coast. They became integral members of the community, set up to practice their professions and businesses.

There are now about 20,000 Japanese in Chicago, most of them Nisei or Sansei. The latter are third-generation American-born. Their average age is around seven. The average of the Nisei is about thirty. Many Issei remained, too. These are Japanese born in the old country. By our citizenship laws they are still aliens, but enjoy permanent legal residence. The average Issei is about sixty-seven.

Those who remained are moderately well-to-do. In California aliens may not own property. There are no such laws in Illinois, so wealthy Japanese found they could transact business there without the subterfuge of having deeds recorded in names of relatives or friends who are citizens.

The Japanese had difficulty finding housing. Chicago's permanents had troubles of their own. The largest Jap settlement finally evolved in North Clark Street, a neighborhood of inferior rooming houses and flat buildings. As more arrived and their financial positions improved, they broke into better homes in the East 40's, near the Lake, sandwiched between Bronzeville and exclusive Hyde Park, and uptown in the Lake View district.

The seeker of the exotic will find much that is unusual and foreign in the Japanese sections. In the North Side Little Tokyo are candy stores where you can buy yo-okan and kaki-mochi. There is a Japanese movie on West Huron, and a Japanese barber shop on North Clark. There are scores of Nipponese tearooms and grocery stores and other shops that sell Jap phonograph records and musical instruments. Others specialize in small-size dresses, the 7's and 9's, which fit dainty Oriental girls.

Though Japan and China were traditional enemies, Chicago's Chinese colony welcomed their fellow Orientals. Many young Japanese went to work in chop suey restaurants. Now many Chinese are working in Jap establishments.

Chicago showed tolerance, but there were many early problems. In Congress it was feared there would be riots if Japanese were allowed to come to the Midwest. But Chicago's civic groups made warm plans for the evacuees. Jobs were offered, efforts were made to find housing, despite prejudice against Orientals in some sections. There was some race discrimination. Some colleges and schools refused to admit young Japs, a Chicago crematorium declined to accept the body of a deceased resettler, some cemeteries turned up their noses at Japanese corpses. There were isolated efforts to refuse votes to Niseis. Some dance-halls would not admit them. Most hospitals also discriminated against them as patients, though happy to have them as employes.

This new group was patient, turned the other cheek, became the most peaceful and law-abiding of citizens. Soon Chicagoans found they were an asset.

In many cases, families had been broken up. Parents were still in relocation centers and children were in Chicago. The old conservative ways of the Japanese home were gone. Even when the parents were in Chicago, they had lost their authority. The war made young Japanese realize they were Americans. They refused to be ruled by the iron-handed father as in the old days. And young Japanese women began to demand their rights as Americans.

In Japanese families the men were served first and the women were not permitted to sit at the table until the fathers and sons had finished eating. Customs like this, carried on in

California, could not be maintained in Chicago. A few Japanese youngsters, too young for the Army, went wild with the new freedoms after years in concentration camps. Juvenile delinquency was on the upgrade for all Americans. The Japs had their zoot-suiters, too. During the first four years, fourteen illegitimate children were born to Japanese girls in Chicago.

After 1947, when problems of permanent residence were solved by return of the transients to California, leaving those who would live in Chicago, there has been no more juvenile delinquency in the Japanese colony. Since 1947 there have been no bastards born to Jap girls. Perhaps their white friends taught them birth control. But gambling among Japs is on the increase. Like all Orientals, they are born gamblers. Chicago makes no effort to restrain them in what is one of the city's main industries. But they usually patronize places where their own kind of games are played, usually in back of Japanese restaurants and tearooms. There is also card-playing in apartments. The principal game is Hana-fuda, or Gimmi 88, played with special cards. In Japan it is known as Hana-Awase, the flower matching game.

The overlord of all Oriental gambling in Chicago outside of Chinatown is a Korean, Jason Lee. He pays tribute, of course, to the Big Mob. He runs a casino at 1358 North Clark near Division, open to all.

Chicago is the soil that nurtures gangsters, so it is natural that the Japanese should contribute their share. Even before they left the West Coast there was a Nipponese underworld, controlling gambling, dope and prostitution for the colony. Some leaders of these gangs migrated to Chicago, to continue where they left off. To operate in Chicago they had to make terms with the Syndicate, which controls all sin in the United States. The Jap gangsters also deal in dope and in furnishing white women for their compatriots. There is little prostitution among Japanese women in the colony. When a Nisei girl decides to go into that, she usually angles for white men. No Japanese girl needs to search long for a husband among her nationals. This is true of most minority groups, where boys and girls marry young and there are few old maids. The number of Japanese women in the country is somewhat less than the number of men. The average Nisei girl can pick and choose. Because of this, it was profitable to supply white and Negro women for Japanese men. Prostitution is an old Jap custom, legalized from ancient days.

On the West Coast, the Japanese seldom went out socially with whites, but limited contacts to their own and occasionally Chinese and Filipinos. In those days, California law forbade interracial marriages, so if an Oriental girl went with a white man it was assumed they were out for no good, which is very good with Japanese girls. But they found Chicago tolerant and without a law against miscegenation.

Many Japanese girls are cute, though not built to American standards. When they went to work in offices beside white men, they found many anxious to take them out. This was a novelty for the little Madame Butterflies who had never seen the inside of a white man's house except as servants.

Frequently Japanese girls are daintier, gayer, more feminine than their Chinese cousins, and for that reason most "Chinese" girls in show business are Japanese with adopted Chinese names. The layman cannot tell the difference and except by dialect, most Orientals can't, either.

Chicago's Jap colony has numerous girls of the peasant type, seldom seen in big cities before. Many of the relocated came there off California farms, descendants of farmers from the old country. A large number are Okinawans. Peasant gals have shorter, sturdier limbs, bow legs and stocky figures. They're hairier, too.

The seeker of the unusual will find more than fifty Japanese restaurants all over Chi. The chief item of food is sukiyaki. It is prepared at your table, comes raw in a frying pan, a sort of chop suey without gravy. The waitress cooks it before your eyes in a gas or charcoal brazier. It is flavored to taste, with soy sauce, which Japs call soyu, pronounced shoy-u. At the Wisteria, 739 North Wabash, you take off your shoes and sit cross-legged on the floor.

The favorite drink is saki, a rice wine with the kick of raw corn whisky. It is usually served warm and tastes like hot champagne. Japs are intemperate drinkers, but there is no moral obloquy connected with getting drunk in Japan, so topers have no inferiority complexes, nor do they suffer hangovers or lost weekends. Their word for "bottoms up" is *Banzai,* meaning, "may you live 10,000 years." Since the war, during which that term took on implications of unpatriotism, some Japs have been toasting with *Kun Pai*.

It is uncommon for a Chinese woman to drink, but many Japanese girls lush. That is one way to tell if one is Chinese or Japanese. If she refuses a drink, saying "it makes my face red," she's Chinese.

After the relocation abuses, many young Japs proved push-overs for Communists. Lefties in the Association for the Advancement of Colored People seemed to be making headway recruiting Japs to join against whites. But most Japs, except the hotheads, resisted that. Young Nisei servicemen, back from overseas, added their anti-Communist voices. But there is still a Red nucleus among some from Southern California, which abounds also with white Communists and other unorthodox groups.

Remnants of the insidious Black Dragon Society also exist in Chicago, among the older folk, born in the old country. This is the fascist, militarist group that was blamed for the war.

Chicago Japs refer to those from the old country and Hawaii as "Buddha heads" or "Boochies." Mainlanders are, in turn, called "Katonks" by those from across the seas.

Though their skin is yellow and their eyes slant, Japanese-Americans are pretty much like other Americans. Among them are the good and the bad, conservatives, liberals and radicals, rich and poor, Catholics, Protestants and "heathen." Many, though not most, are Buddhists or Shintoists, who brought their churches and their worship with them.

If you're curious to see a Buddhist service, visit any of the following temples:

Chicago, 5487 S. Dorchester
Midwest, 1441 N. Cleveland
Rengo, 4457 S. Ellis
Zen, 30 W. Washington

We forgot to tell you, there are more denominations of Buddhists than of Christians. And that's the last time we'll mention religion. It isn't confidential.

10. ON LEONG, HIP SING

"They wanted Hop Sing
But winged Willy Wong,
A slight but regrettable
Slip of the Tong."

—By Keith Preston

TONG WARS have practically disappeared in the United States—except in Chicago. Here they are looked at with no more curiosity than any battle between rival gangs, regardless of race or color. But the Chinese invented them. For that is what the old-time tong wars were—contests to determine which mob was to control what territory. Like everything else, the manner of fighting tong wars has changed. The old hatchetmen are gone. The new ones, who were so inaccurate with pistols that they usually killed the wrong victims, are being replaced by killers hired from the detested whites.

Chicago's original Chinatown was on South Clark Street, directly below the Loop. The importers, merchants and wholesale grocers who supplied the chop suey restaurants in other parts of the city and in the Middle West were gathered there. Chicago's Chinatown was and is unique in this country. Geography makes it the clearing house for everything, legal and illegal. The early headquarters for the Chinese opium ring was in Chicago, which became also the main stop on the underground railway for smuggling and transporting Chinese girls from China to America. The traffic in picture-brides from the old country was also directed from Chicago. All these businesses were lucrative, but even more so was the Chinese gambling concession.

The Chinese population in Chicago was never large, but it was one of the most important and wealthiest.

There were Chinese in Chicago from almost its earliest days. A few drifted in from California, where they had been imported in great numbers to work on the Western railroads. Chicago's resident Chinese are of Cantonese extraction. There are said to be between 5,000 and 10,000, but there is no way of checking these figures because so many are in the country illegally and evade the census-taker.

Encroaching big business, overflowing the Loop, made the property in Chinatown too valuable for Chinese. While they were seeking a new neighborhood, much of the old Levee was being vacated and 22nd Street, now known as Cermak Road, and Wentworth Avenue were becoming ghost towns. Chinatown began to move into this void. A few found it possible to continue on Clark Street, and now there are two Chinatowns—a small old one and a big, more modern new one.

The transition took place as Chinatowns all over the country were being rocked by a series of major tong wars. After the smoke died away, only two tongs were left in the East, though many more were to continue active on the West Coast. Chicago is in the Eastern jurisdiction. The result was that only the On Leongs and the Hip Sings remained there, as in New York. The On Leongs were top men but permitted the Hip Sings to go along in a secondary position. When the territories were divided, the Hip Sings, the conquered, were allowed to operate only in the small, old Chinatown on Clark. The On Leongers, the winners, took the big, new one, on Wentworth, and with it the cream of the trade.

The treaty provided for everything in specific detail. Chop suey restaurants and laundries in certain sections were set aside for On Leongers, with less desirable locations reserved for the Hip Singers, who found their fantan games limited as the big, profitable fantan and mahjong play everywhere else in town except a bit of the North Side went to On Leongers.

Based on arrests of Chinese dope peddlers, the indication is that only members of the On Leong sell opium and Hip Singers sell white stuff—cocaine and heroin. Most Chinamen prefer the hop pipe. Few use the needle.

At this writing, the boss of the On Leong Tong is Moy Yu Chuck, now living in China with a movie actress wife. Harry Lee acts in his stead. The leader of the Hip Sing Tong is Chin Fung, alias Chin Song.

Federal authorities are fearful that Chicago will have a new tong war, which could spread all over the country.

The Hip Sings are sore over the division of spoils, and are eyeing On Leong territory. There have been unexplained

Chinese killings recently and some shootings in San Francisco are traced back to them. The Hip Sings are said to be enlisting the aid of allied tongs on the West Coast with a view to war.

Meanwhile a few Chinese Communists are trying to take over the tongs, in approved Soviet gangster fashion. But most American Chinese are not Red.

Though Chicago's Chinatown is the third largest, exceeded only by San Francisco and New York, it does not have the exotic or colorful atmosphere of either, or of smaller ones elsewhere. The gridiron pattern of Chicago streets makes its Chinatown look like any business district—no narrow, winding lanes, like New York's. Another factor in the non-Oriental surface appearance of this Chinatown is that most of the business there is wholesale and little effort is made to attract tourists. Not all of Chicago's Chinese live there; they have their offices in it, but their homes spread throughout the city.

The most foreign-looking structure in Chinatown is the headquarters of the On Leong Tong, at 2216 Wentworth. Because of its dominant position in the Chinese way of things, this is called the Chinatown City Hall. The titular head of the tong is known as the "Mayor of Chinatown." He is Frank Moy, Jr., son of the On Leong boss.

Chicago's Chinese are pacifists as to the white man's courts and the white man's law. Disputes between Chinese are almost always cleared up by local arbitration. If both parties belong to the same tong, it is settled within its walls. If they belong to different tongs, the Chinese Protective Association, made up of all Chinese in Chicago, takes over. If no decision can be reached, the matter is referred to the Chinese Consul, and in rare, important cases, even to the Chinese Ambassador in Washington. What will happen in the event of American recognition of the Chinese Communist regime is problematical. In a dispute between a Chinese and a white, the Orientals try to agree without going to court, even by paying more than a court could award.

When the district was still confined to Clark Street (usually described as "between Van Buren Street and Carrie Watson's whore-house") realty values were high and the whole colony employed a common attorney, who by consent became high commissioner, arbitrator of last resort, advisor of the leaders and big brother to them all. This guide and mentor of Chinatown was named Patrick Henry O'Donnell. He stood six-feet-four. When he wasn't steering Chinamen he was fomenting Clan Na Gael movements, conspiring to free Ireland. O'Donnell learned to talk Chinese as the head men of Chinatown learned English with a brogue. He blazed over injustices to his client friends, but could never shake them from their firm resolve to never engage in white men's litigation.

One chop suey establishment, making lots of money, was stuck up. Because of tax complications, it employed an American girl cashier. She was forced to turn over about $1,000. She knew the man, who was Duffy the Goat, mentioned elsewhere in this compendium of confidences. Her own father was a detective. She told him about the outrage and he hauled Duffy in. A dozen waiters and the manager, who had seen him commit the robbery at gunpoint, were subpoenaed. O'Donnell appeared as an *amicus curiae.* But neither the prosecutor, O'Donnell nor the judge could get one of the Chinese to identify the prisoner. They all shook their heads. So, despite the cashier's eye-witness evidence, the Goat was freed. The girl threw up her job. Having seen how safe was any white person who took advantage of Chinese, she came in two nights later, drew a gun and held up the place herself. She wasn't even arrested. Pat O'Donnell could do nothing.

Chicago's Chinese seldom mix socially with whites—the sight of a Chinese boy or girl with a Caucasian is rare, almost unique. Like all colonies cut off from the motherland, Chinatown is conservative, provincial, old-fashioned. All children are required by their parents to attend Chinese school after they finish their classes in American schools. There they are taught one of their ancient Cantonese dialects, similar to that spoken by New York's Chinese, known as "Fourth Village," but different from the Frisco tongue, which is "Third."

Except for commercialized gambling, dope and vice, which is not a localized problem at all, Chinatown gives no trouble to police. Their desire not to tangle with the white man's rules makes Chinese considerably above the average on the blotters. Juvenile delinquency is practically unknown, as respect for parents is the basis of all Chinese law and religion.

There are no panhandlers or relief clients among the Chinese. They take care of their own. Should a Chinaman be hard up, his family clan, by custom, must support him or get him a job. Every Chinese chips in monthly to this society, according to his means, and supports an age-old old-age social security which, like many other modern innovations, was thought of in China first. If the clan can't find work for an indigent, it must send him on to another city where there is also a chapter of the family society.

All Chinese with the same family name are by custom blood cousins. There are only 100 basic Chinese family names in the world, so this should give you an idea of how many relatives they all have. Those with the same family names cannot marry. In cases of smaller families, where there are not enough of the name to make a clan society in the location, several will band together into a protective association for all their groups.

Chinese love the good things of life, especially food, and spend a large part of their income eating, drinking and entertaining. The average Chinese meal consists of about twenty courses and takes half a day to eat.

At the least provocation, Chinese find an excuse for a feast, to which they invite all their friends and relatives. Most of the restaurants in Chinatown have special rooms for these banquets. The authentic cuisine in them is quite unlike the chop suey and chow mein of commerce. Only connoisseurs among Americans can appreciate the strange, esoteric courses of raw fish and eels, sharks' fins, bird's-nest soup and that rare delicacy, lambs' eyes.

It has been mentioned that Chinese women seldom drink. But the men guzzle plenty of potent liquors. Among these are whiskies made from the marrow of tigers' teeth and wines from rose petals and other flora. The most popular Chinese potables are mui kwai lu and ng ka py. But they also like Scotch and rye, which they down straight, and in large doses.

It is the custom at a Chinese dinner to toast each course, with a few specials for good measure. The host says "Yum sing," which means "bottoms up," and you've got to drain your glass in one gulp.

Chinese women are dainty and petite, especially in their native costume—the straight-lined Shanghai dress with the split on the side. Unfortunately, few American-born Chinese girls will wear them, preferring to look American. But our clothes are not made for their figures, which are usually flat, front and rear. Occasionally one sees an ancient woman from China in the old-fashioned blue pajamas. Sometimes one will see a young woman, obviously a visitor from China, in a Shanghai dress.

But don't ask the age-old cliché question. They'll laugh, but won't tell you.

When Dr. Hu Shi, the foremost living Chinese scholar, came through Chicago, after being appointed ambassador to Washington, reporters who interviewed him knew his was regarded as the greatest mind since that of Confucius. They wanted to know what this great man thought of America.

"Tell us, Dr. Hu," asked one. "What is the first thing you want to see here?"

Dr. Hu replied in impeccable Oxford accents:

"I want to find out if it's true—what they say about American women."

11. ACROSS THE LINE

"ANYTHING doing out in the County?" That's what an American asks when he finds himself in a closed-up city. Where do you find motels that will get you a dame or let you bring one, with no questions asked? Where's the fast roadhouse with the crap game in the basement? How does a stranger get a snifter after hours?

In any big town, except New York, which has no county territory, the answer will be: "Outside the city limits." But what happens when you get to Chicago, where everything goes? That's a problem for the suburban dice and wheel workers, caterers to all the hideaway hoopla. With Chicago offering so much so near, the County is hard put to get a play and must give more, more open, and usually cheaper.

Cook County, which is the most populous in the United States, is dominated by Chicago, its seat. The same combination that controls crime in the city runs it outside the city, generally through figureheads who are held forth as competitors. This camouflage prevails also in politics. By tradition, Chicago was Democratic and Cook County was Republican, with a close working agreement on jobs and influence. That is subject to change if the Republicans begin to take themselves seriously. The underworld runs both machines and sometimes the outside territory is useful and available when the heat is on at City Hall. The Caponesters bought whole villages, named the local authorities, and were immune.

An overwhelming majority of County residents are fine family folk. The people are as respectable as any anywhere. But some towns right beyond the Chicago confines are carnivals of crime and lewdness, outdoing the worst in Chicago at its worst. There is, on first thought, Cicero.

This village was at one time a settlement of cheap clapboard cottages inhabited by railroad workers, with a few blocks of shabby Main Street stores. Then Capone took it over and made it his headquarters. Here violence and robbery and hijacking and wholesale bootlegging were hatched as all the flagrant forms of immorality and depravity roared night and day. When Capone departed, in handcuffs, Cicero dropped out of the headlines. But by no means has it gone good. It is only less blaring and less brazen than it was. Chicago opened its arms to the Capone survivors and their successors; they no longer need to transact their nefarious businesses outside. But the Ciceros still have one source of revenue which somehow Chicago bans—the slot machines.

Here you find the one-armed bandits everywhere except in the churches. Gambling clubs run as openly as they do in Las Vegas, with no prudish prissiness about the coin boxes, which, with many other types of mechanical money-snatchers, are manufactured by an arm of the Syndicate, which holds an annual convention in Chicago where advice is given on how to thwart and bribe obstreperous sheriffs, but where all the power of the mobs have long failed to put over this one style of thievery. And it is grand larceny. Frank Costello and Phil Kastel spent a round $1,000,000 with the Huey Long gang to legalize slot machines in Louisiana. Their first year's take was $2,000,000, and they are still taking. That item alone makes men in Cook County rich. Besides, there are the usual dens of whore-mongering and narcotics, horse-race poolrooms and bawdy burlesque.

Now and then the state's attorney, the county prosecutor in Chicago, writes (for publication) nasty letters to the sheriff of Cook County, a Chicago office neighbor, or to the chief of police of Cicero, decrying conditions and setting forth addresses (also for publication) of the objectionable dens of iniquity and a bill of particulars detailing said iniquities. Immediately, their business booms. Nothing is ever done about closing them up. That is the usual procedure when indignant Chicagoans protest against the evil conditions in their city—the County is shown to be worse.

Possession of a slot machine—even in a private home—is a crime under Illinois law. The U. S. Collector of Internal Revenue has released lists of saloons and roadhouses in nearby suburbs which had to buy tax stamps, as required by Federal law for slot machines. Nothing happened, though the presence of such a machine in a building makes it by statute a disorderly house and is cause for revocation of liquor licenses.

The slot-machine king of the County area is one Eddie Vogel. He is way up in the Big Mob.

Your reporters found gambling houses as open as grocery stores in Evergreen Park, Stickney, Forest Park, Berwyn, Cicero, Morton Grove, Melrose Park, and Calumet City. In the last-named town the Owl Club had 400 playing poker, blackjack, craps and slot machines. Calumet City, to "Confidential" reporters, was a wow. There the burlesque bar has been developed to its ultimate and it seems everything with a roof on it is a saloon that sells an endless chain of strip-teasers. There are 500 such places in Chicago. All peelers look and act pretty much alike. After they have taken off everything, that's all they can take off. Yet Chicagoans drive a dozen miles to pack these hives of hussies and hustlers in Calumet City. It seems that once you get an appetite for indecent exposure you become a glutton. Business is so hot that the dens here can outbid North Clark Street and West Madison Street for top-price attractions. After Satira had become a shooting star, she worked there for $750 a week. That's a lot of beer.

If a customer is thrilled with the physical potentialities of one of these performers, he can usually make a deal—yes, with the bartender. You give him the money. It is a romantic custom in those parts to pay in advance for such services—as the madames used to say in the old Levee—"in case of fire." The bartender will ask $100, but he'll take $50. He will then escort you to a waiting cab, the driver will take you to a house a couple of blocks away and your selected stripper will be waiting. With strange modesty, she will be fully dressed. The thrifty can get run-of-commerce dames there for $20—and sometimes $10.

All illegal joints in Calumet City are wired together for mutual protection. If such a phenomenon as a sheriff's raid is on the way, or if spotters see characters who might be revenue or narcotics officers, or tattletales like Lait and Mortimer, one switch pulls a yellow light in every dive and the green-topped tables and the "actresses" are covered up.

We had this experience numerous times in the suburbs and the city. Most of the mobsters know us, but here and there we were unrecognized until some manager or barkeep made us out through the smoke and the dim lights. There was immediate panic. In the 606 Club on Wabash Avenue in Chicago there was a poor chump who introduced the nudies. The yellow light flashed and for an hour and fifteen minutes we kept him sweating, doing imitations of Harry Richman and George M. Cohan, reciting nursery rhymes and finally—you wouldn't believe it—attempting to lead the drunks who had come to see female skin in community singing! Our hearts finally softened and we beat it for a colored deadfall on Lake Street, where nobody knew us, and as a further disguise, we actually bought champagne. They had a bottle but we had to open it ourselves! Nobody else there knew how.

Back to the woods. Conditions similar to those in Cook County are found in other outlying territories of which Chicago is the immediate trading center, including Lake, Kane, Will and DuPage Counties in Illinois and Lake County in Indiana. This constitutes the Chicago metropolitan area, which is officially estimated as having a population of 5,400,000. Cicero is predominantly Polish, with a large Italian section. The Negroes have spread to East Chicago Heights and across the city-state line and into Indiana. East Chicago Heights has a Negro police force. A recent investigation of a speed trap there brought out some remarkable facts:

1. The policemen received a $2 bonus for each traffic arrest.

2. If the Negro police magistrate, William C. Scott, was absent, his wife took over the court and levied the fines.

3. State officials reported that the police, eager to earn their bonuses, arrested motorists no matter what their speed, and had them fined.

But Lake Forest, a suburb to the north, is rated as having the highest per capita wealth of any American town except Beverly Hills, California, and one or two in Westchester County, New York. Here live the descendants and heirs of the men of might and mind who made Chicago. North Shore suburbs are dry by local option and by stiff policing. Bootlegging and gambling are unknown. A streetwalker wouldn't get 40 feet. Any violence there is social, not for greed. Juvenile delinquency presents a problem in reverse, not because of underprivilege, but because youth has too much money, too high-powered cars and temptation too easily within means.

Oak Park, on the West Side, is modest and moral, temperate and well-off. It has been described as "The Middle Class Capital of America."

But the police chief of a nearby suburb sells "courtesy cards" for a modest fee, which makes motorists and truck drivers immune from arrest.

Chicago's suburbanites are almost all ex-Chicagoans and their children. Chicago's suburbs run from the vilest to the finest. They are miniature Chicagos. The satellites reflect the sun.

PART TWO

THE PEOPLE
(*Confidential!*)

12. WOLF-BAIT

SOMEWHAT as impressionable, restless, ambitious girls flock to New York from the entire nation, so in lesser degree but with parallel motivation do they stream into Chicago. Some may regard it as a stepping stone to New York or Hollywood.

Year after year, day in and day out, countless young buxom babes of Swedish, German, Polish, Hungarian and just plain Anglo-Saxon blood forsake the cow-tenders and the cowpokes for the glitter and promise of the Windy City. They come with anything up to $18 in their dime-store imitation-leather bags, their belongings in cardboard suitcases, facets in their eyes and dreams in their grass-root hearts. So much has been written about Chicago, it must be gay and luxurious and surely exciting. Compared to the crossroads in Nebraska and the whistle stops in the Michigan fruit-belt, it can be all that.

Not too long ago it was a logical market-place for the stage-struck and those who aspired to other careers. Chicago was the second stage center of the nation; in vaudeville it not only was a showplace, but an act could work fifty-two weeks there with never a journey that required more than a street car. There was much legitimate producing—at times, believe it or not, as much as New York—and road-shows booked from there for long and prosperous seasons. The early movie studios had such contract stars as Francis X. Bushman, Bronco Billy Anderson, Gloria Swanson, Wallace Beery, Beverly Bayne and Charlie Chaplin. A dozen years ago many radio network programs originated in Chicago.

Now all this is gone.

The billion-dollar model industry is said to have been born in Chicago, when a photographer named Beatrice Townsend first posed pretty girls to animate advertising. Chicago became an outstanding creative point for national ad copy and many models were used. Now most of such art work is done in New York.

We don't want to make you cry, little girl. But if you want to sell glamor or talent and don't want to sell it in a burlesque bar, keep heading all the way West or all the way East. You won't get far in Chicago. There are models there, of course, hundreds of them. They pose for local advertisers, and there is a solid field for their services in fashion and mail order houses, as well as convention demonstrators, ushers and hostesses. As this is the only form of capitalizing on youth and beauty without debauchery, thousands of attractive girls strive to crash it, which makes an already limited field a dumping ground for surplus charm. A survey indicated that only 10 per cent of the 4,000 youngsters, mostly from out of town, who annually try to become models, make it.

The foremost agents for models are Patricia Stevens, Sabie, and Connie Seaman. Stevens girls are the pick of the Midwest crop. They make from $5 to $10 an hour, but only a handful can count on $200 a week. In New York, $25 an hour is common. But when a girl gets in the upper brackets anywhere else, she begins looking up time-tables to New York or Hollywood.

Chicagoans brag of the beauty of their women. There is probably no place where the average, as you watch the passing pedestrians, is any higher. There is a preponderance of Nordic blondes and there are exotic girls of foreign extraction, many fascinating. But your New York or Paris boulevardier would shake his head and groan: they look too healthy. A Chicago paper bragged they run one less to the ton than elsewhere.

American beauties should be just as you see them by the thousands on the busy Chicago streets—wholesome stock, clear-eyed, daughters of virile men, with an intermingling of European strains punctuating the melting-pot heritage of our new world. But, of late, influenced largely by typecasting for the movies, the supersophisticate has regarded it as vulgar to admire any but scrawny, exotic and neurotic females, who spend their lives between rouging and reducing. Chicago's girls use plenty of makeup, but they do not run toward the dainty, petite and mysterious. Many wear flat heels, and too many encase themselves in slacks with a fur wrap, no less!

Their disregard of style dictates may be refreshing, but to some visitors it is astounding. The better Chicago stores have resident fashion experts in New York and Paris. But Chicago girls stand largely by their own styles, and on them, to Chicago men, they look good.

Even there, however, the contingent of hicks is conspicuous. Most of the infiltrators from Kankakee and Kokomo come in lightly financed and stay that way. Once they have throbbed and thrilled to the noise and the neon lights, they think no more of returning to the old homestead, though they have to take work as drudges and live in dingy hall-rooms. Unless a girl can qualify as a model, there are few other occupations open. To be a model a girl must have poise, must know how to dress and wear her clothes. A prime requisite is, again, a slender figure, and few girls who were raised on mothers' pancakes grow such shapes. The camera is also unkind to girls with wide cheeks or round faces.

There is no longer much demand for art models. They answered to different requirements. Facial contours were not as decisive as torsos which resembled the measurements of the Venus de Milo, still the standard of painters and sculptors, whether they believe it or not. The nudes cut a considerable figure in the bohemian life when Chicago was a center of artists and art schools. Many an illustrator and portrait man now famous studied and worked in Chicago. These were generally happy-go-lucky girls, not embarrassed as they stood disrobed before men or classes of men. They usually bedded up with artists or students, couldn't afford public nightlife, and when they lost their lines they became waitresses. Henrici's, on Randolph Street, was a snug harbor for the broken-down inspirations and some are still there, gray-haired and in the chips.

In truth, it was once very stylish to have a sweetheart who served it "off the arm" (without using a tray, which is a Henrici rule) there, and the young bloods would be at the exit after dinner, waiting for their girls, who had tramped miles to and from the kitchen and carried tons of crockery and food. The playboy who had a head waitress was considered big stuff.

Another glamor occupation that has evaporated in Chicago

is the cafe chorus-girl. Once the hottest after-dark town on the map, it is now a one-floor-show burg, with a regular line of eight girls usually playing only the Chez Paree. And once one gets in there she sticks for years, which nullifies opportunities for newcomers. Occasionally hotels like the Sherman and the Palmer put on productions with a six-girl chorus, and these must be trained dancers, usually with ballet upbringing, therefore often brought on from New York. The Chez girls are no longer courted and pampered because the taste of Chicago men has deteriorated to B girls and whores. The Chez babes are all pretty, and they symbolize the last echo of the gaiety and romance that their profession has always spelled all over the world. Their salaries are low compared to their distant cousins in New York. Most of them are natives, some of them are married, and those who are single are usually attached to musicians in the orchestra, as is orthodox everywhere in show business, for they are brought together by common interests and atmosphere, the same unconventional hours, and that greatest of all cupids, propinquity.

So, sooner or later, many of the babes who came in with stardust in their eyes finish with sawdust on the floor, working in restaurants. Even sales girls these days require references and some training, must be accepted by unions and meet the competition of college graduates. But if they still hanker for "the stage," they land on one—back of a burlesque bar. As will be described in detail later, Chicago keeps at least 5,000 busy in that line and is the focal center for booking teasers throughout the country. They start at $50 a week and many of them soon descend into extra-curricular activities. Others, and there is a wide field for them, become 26 girls, whose unique positions and institutional status will be discussed further on.

The functions of the B girls have been mentioned and they will rate added dissertation.

Smart, presentable young women, if they can make the right contacts can, even more so than in most big cities, become "party girls." These can be tarts just as far as they want to be, but they are not prostitutes *per se*. They are on call (though not "call girls") for businessmen who have to entertain customers and buyers from out of town, and, as they are regular habitues of the cafes, they make other alliances, often with married men who want to get out and be entertained, dance and flash well-dressed, good-looking dames before their friends and associates, but not their wives. There is no obligation even implied for immoral behavior, but they must be gay, witty and wise. The commercial houses, of which there are myriad, pay up to $50 an evening by prearranged agreement. Individuals do not pay, but they tip, and are expected to meet the scale.

The call girl works on a system and is a prostitute, but not always a full-timer. We know of one who has a Government job, who is highly efficient and intelligent, has advanced herself, lives sedately, but is on call every weekend, at which time she is an out-and-out whore with no shame and no strings. Others are not so bound by the calendar and their intake is subject to summons from central agencies of a complex nature which will be described hereinafter.

Prostitution is a major Chicago industry. Some of its practitioners do not even come entirely of their own volition, but are scouted and hunted in small towns and induced to take up the life. Many of the females in the borderline occupations eventually sit at their telephones waiting calls or walk the streets or become inmates of the houses or out-and-out hustlers in the taverns.

13. CONFESSIONS OF A CHICAGO CUTIE

Advice to Young Girls: do not come to Chicago in search of a career unless you have enough to support you for six months, return fare home, and strong will power.

* * *

Under no circumstances should you come in answer to a blind ad or a solicitation from a so-called talent scout. If you do, you will probably find he is a scout for the sort of talent that shouldn't be for sale.

* * *

Chicago is a friendly place for lonely people. There is considerably less formality than in most other northern cities. It is considered proper for a single woman to start a conversation with a man in the lobby of the hotel where she lives, or at a soda fountain. Our advice is, don't do it!

* * *

If you must come to Chicago, we suggest you come with another woman. That way, before you get acquainted properly you will still be able to see the city. There are few limitations on unescorted women visiting nightclubs or places of amusement, and it is not unusual to see women sans men dining in smart restaurants. But never one woman, solo, unless she's a B girl.

* * *

Here is a tip: don't enter any of the parks after dark. It is downright dangerous even for a couple to be in a park after 11:00 P.M., and it is not safe for a woman to go beyond sight of the streets at any time.

* * *

If a good-looking girl finds she is doing okay in Chicago and seeks loftier levels, she will find it necessary to get out of town, probably to New York. But before she goes she can make important contacts in Chicago which will help her along the way. Though Chicago is no longer in the glamor business itself, it is a stop along the road. Most big stars of vaudeville and radio, and many from the legit stage, play in Chicago now and then. If they are single men, or without their wives, they will be looking for companionship in Chicago and will be steered by friends to call girls or to models or show girls, depending on whether they want it the easy or the hard way.

Many Hollywood producers, directors and other executives stay overnight or longer while passing through from Coast to Coast, to visit their Chicago offices. Many a model—there—has found herself on the way to Hollywood after a one-night stand arranged by friends. Though Chicago is no longer of basic importance in the theatrical booking setup, all major offices maintain small staffs in the city, and a forward-looking girl soon gets to know all booking agents who can refer her to associates in New York when she's ready for the big leap.

The truth must be told here—many middle-aged and elderly Chicago businessmen stray from the fireside. Sooner or later, every glamor girl meets these local wolves, and can date them. Most of the captains of industry must visit New York several times a year. We don't want to encourage such philandering, but it has happened on occasion that a Chicago businessman has invited a local girl along to New York for a weekend or so.

But even if that isn't how she got her first view of Manhattan, almost any Chicago model or showgirl knows men who will write friends in New York to look out for the young thing and help her get started and settled on Broadway. Kindhearted New Yorkers are only too glad to help, especially if the babe is cute. Often the opposite number is waiting for the girl at Grand Central or LaGuardia Field and takes up where her boy friend in Chicago left off.

If you don't think so, you didn't know Marian McKenzie, a brown-haired charmer who took the 20th Century east about 15 years ago, when she was 18. Marian had come to Chicago from Kankakee, where she was born in the shadow of the State Insane Asylum, but that has nothing to do with this story. She was lithe, with long limbs, a doll-like face and a ready laugh. A few weeks after she arrived in Chicago she was already a top model, and it wasn't long before she lived in a penthouse on Lake Shore Drive. Marian figured that if Chicago was a cinch, New York would fall, too. She had a wealthy Chicago friend. He didn't want to see her go, but who was he to stand in the way of destiny?

He told her he would write to his pal in New York, who would get her a hotel room, take her around and see that she got going as a model there. The Chicago boy friend saw her off and the New York boy friend was waiting. They identified each other easily. The New Yorker had a place for her to live and took her there. It turned out he was living there, too. But Marian was still 18 and calculated this was how things were done in New York.

A short time later, according to papers which her lawyer filed in New York County Supreme Court, Marian was *enceinte*. According to her complaint, she wanted to have the baby even after her New York boy friend told her he couldn't marry her, because he was already married. Marian said she loved children. But, apparently, the prospective father didn't. Again according to Marian's complaint, he had kidnaped her and forced her to undergo an abortion. That, she thought, was ungallant. Her Chicago boy friend hadn't told her it would be like this. So she went to the Travelers' Aid Society, which took charge of the case because Marian was a traveler, having come from Chicago, and got her a lawyer. The lawyer brought suit for $250,000 for "a lost love and a torn body." The case was settled out of court when the New York boy friend said he didn't know anything about it. All he knew was that Marian was consigned to him from Chicago by his friend there.

The moral is that when a Chicago girl sets her sights for Broadway she should buy her own ticket.

Occasionally, a road-show comes through Chicago with real chorus girls from the Big Burg. The local heavy lovers can't wait to meet the genuine article. But, in truth, chorus girls in road-shows are not of the same class or quality as the originals in the Broadway edition. These rarely leave New York. The ones who troupe are known in the trade as "road-lice." They may be as desirable as girls who work on Broadway, but because of some psychic urge they accept inferiority as itinerants.

Anyway, these road-lice, who are booked out of New York and stay there mostly between traveling engagements, usually take over when the big musical leaves the Stem to tour the sticks. Most of the girls in the New York company will not sign up to leave Gotham. They have roots in New York, sweeties, husbands, families, or they're studying dancing or singing or drama. Many make extra money as models.

The road-lice may be as cute, pretty and talented as the girls they replace, but they aren't as distinguished. They can't wear clothes like New York regulars, aren't too interested in them, because they're seldom in one place long enough to get to know anyone who may be interested in how they look or dress. Usually, they keep to themselves. When they have dates, they are with other members of the company. Occasionally, in a town like Chicago, where a touring company may run for six months, they meet some locals.

Chicago men think they are meeting the real Broadway product in the second company of the big New York hit. They do research into their lives, and we will help them with some pointers on where this species lives, what it does and how it acts, in Chicago.

The average road-show chorus girl shares quarters with one or two roommates in one of the near North Side hotels like the Croydon or the St. Clair. The Croydon is preferred because here they know they will find others of their own kind. About all the average road-louse ever sees of Chicago is from the railroad station to the hotel, to the theatre, and back to the hotel. Having no contacts, she has no reason to get up in the daytime. She has no place to go. She needs to do no shopping, because she never goes any place, and usually comes to the theatre in slacks.

She gets up at about 5 in the afternoon and either makes breakfast in the room or has it downstairs in the coffee shop.

This is the best time to pick her up, because her evening schedule is probably unfilled. However, at 5 she looks like a mess, sans makeup and with her hair in curlers. After breakfast she and her roommates attend to personal duties, like writing letters or doing their laundry. At about 7:30, five or six will pile into a cab, cutting up the fare, and arrive at the theatre in time to put their makeup on before the show.

They go to work in slacks unless, rarely, they've made a date beforehand to go stepping with a Chicagoan. The show breaks shortly after 11. Then with a gang from the company —other boys and girls of the ensemble—they go to a coffee pot near the theatre or near the hotel and have dinner and sit around and gossip over innumerable cigarettes and cokes. Then they may play cards or just talk until sunrise.

Usually there is little love in these girls' lives. Too many males in the show will probably be as interested in men as they are. The principals will probably be masculine enough, but will be traveling with their wives or "doubling up" with girl friends—or, how much good can a half-dozen men do in a show with 40 or 50 girls?

Most of the road-lice are young, still in their teens or early twenties. Few care to drink, anyway not enough to make a night of it.

Those in search of alcoholic companionship always find it at their theatrical hotels, where sooner or later during the night most of the minor entertainers in the city's hundreds of honkytonk nightclubs and cocktail bars end up.

If, however, the road-louse is induced to make a date with a Chicagoan, she changes her procedure and wears a dress to the theatre. The palpitating gent who picks her up at the stage door and expects her to be stunning in the latest and smartest of New York fashions so he can show her off at the Chez Paree is in for a jolt. The road-louse has brought her dress from Oklahoma City, whence she sprang, or bought it in some chain-store along the route. She may be as well dressed as the run of Chicago girls, but she won't be that symbol of smartness that spells New York. Neither will she be suave and sophisticated. Her mind will be wandering to others in the company. The company has become to her one big family and she is unhappy when away from the other boys and girls.

Our advice to Chicago wolves is: You can do better with home honeys.

Where to Find the Prettiest

Models and theatrical students live at the Frost Club at 1046 N. Lake Shore Drive. Phone WHitehall 4-7727. If a man answers, you've got the wrong number. (It's for babes, only!)

Show gals stop at the Croydon, Eastgate and St. Clair Hotels. The Churchill Apartments is for those with more than a chorus salary.

Cocktail time hang-outs for models are the bars of the St. Clair and the Croydon, and the Cloverbar, where they dish the dirt. Also the Mich-Boul, escorted by advertising executives.

Chorines buy their cosmetics and sip their cokes in the Croydon pharmacy or the Ford Hopkins' drug store, Rush and Ohio. Models do ditto in the drug store at Michigan Boulevard and Chicago Avenue.

Nightime hang-out for the cover gals is Rickett's Restaurant, also on Chicago Avenue.

Show girls sans dates end up for early snacks at the Corner House, Rush and Ohio.

14. THE SCARLET SISTERHOOD

IN *OUR BOOK, New York Confidential,* we annoyed Bill O'Dwyer's police department by hinting that one might contrive to pick up a willing girl on certain blocks of certain Gotham streets. In Chicago there are few streets where you can't grab yourself a wench, and on some they will grab you.

But don't get us wrong. We are not insinuating that Chicago girls and women have lower standards of morality than those anywhere else, including New York. We are talking of a numerous minority of street-walkers, semi-amateur and all-professional, such as will be found in any contingent of almost 4,000,000 people—if the cops let them get away with it. In Chicago they do; in New York hardly ever.

It is no secret that one girl in so many will turn bad. Temptation and seduction and desire vary little under the big lights or under the elms. From then on it becomes a matter of opportunity. Girls who for money or for fun are seeking men will find them unless every time they wink they wind up in jail. In Chicago they don't. In New York and Los Angeles flirting is disorderly conduct. Money is not the salient factor. This goes for men or women. In Chicago it is a foremost pastime and often a guy who gets a come-on doesn't know immediately whether the bimbo is after an ice-cream soda or a twenty-dollar bill.

In the summer, Riverview Park is an open exchange where men go to find girls and girls go to be found. The public parks and beaches are alive with amiable females and amorous males. In winter the best hunting is in the dance-halls or in almost any tavern or cocktail lounge. Sailors who get past Wilson Avenue make a beeline for the northeast corner of State and Randolph, which teems with bobby-soxers and older unattached girls whose principal nightly recreation is hooking up with strange men. These are not pros, though if you stick something in their stocking they won't blow the whistle. There are so many of that type, it seems a wonder that those who make a living at it can live. But they do, and plenty of them.

When Chicago recorded such things in restricted red light districts, Chicago officially at one time had 81,000 prostitutes and 52,000 pimps, an average of one and three-fifths girls to keep each fancy man. Mike the Plumber, whom we eulogized further up, was super—he had twelve! Under the present setup, rambunctious as it is, there is no documentary evidence on how many follow this calling, but observation leads to a reasonable assumption that the merchants of bodies have not grown less. There are those who see to it that there is no decline, for their take is the millions of dollars which filter through into the clutches of the international crime and vice Syndicate of which Lucky Luciano, though exiled in Sicily at this writing, is still the active head and probably has more money than the Italian government. His share reaches him regularly and was banked for him during all the years he served in Sing Sing and Dannemora.

His Chicago links, the bosses of the setup there, are the three Fischetti Brothers, cousins of the late Al Capone. Vice-President in Charge of Prostitution is Jack "Greasy Thumb" Guzik, who was the cashier for the Capone mob and who got his sobriquet when he was a waiter in his brother Harry's whorehouse in the old Levee. Harry, who died in 1949 in Florida, was the cause of the Mann Act, introduced by a Chicago congressman to wipe out a hotel run by Harry, called McCarthy & DuVal's, where women were brought from all over the world and from farms and coal-mine towns, and sold and shipped to houses throughout the nation on quotations along the lines of stock exchanges and wheat pits.

Under him Jack Guzik got his education, academic and practical, and he has risen high. He owns vast real estate and has bragged, "I have more cash than Rockefeller." He has more influence, too. Any cop who raises a hand at him—and this is not hypothetical—is not only broken, but he is arrested and indicted for violating the civil rights of Greasy Thumb Guzik and he is hounded forever after by open and unseen forces. Therefore, nobody bothers Guzik any more.

Bagnios are easy copy. Their activities are concentrated and there is still a lurid interest in places where you can walk in, have assorted women line up, take your pick and go to bed. But this method is by no means the chief segment of the system. Most of the infamous trade is worked through call girls, who have been organized as efficiently as the central bureau for extras in Hollywood, which within an hour can get you any number and any number of types—for entirely decent purposes, of course. The Chicago call girl setup, however, imitates in some features its regulations: being available by telephone at stated hours, so situated that there is quick and constant transportation to central points, being registered and card-indexed and cross-filed for age, complexion, size, weight and range of accomplishments.

An illustration of how it works is highlighted by "Stingy" Dorothy Reisner, Queen of the Madames, whose payoff goes directly to Guzik. At this writing Dorothy's executive headquarters are at 4417 South Ellis Avenue. She has 2500 girls on her lists. Every girl must phone in every hour or after she has finished a call, and if she is out she may be assigned to another impatient patron before she gets home again. The telephone system is much like that of services that handle doctors' calls when they are out of their offices. In December, 1949, Dorothy's switchboard number was Atlantic 5-0442.

The girls collect $20 to $50 per call, depending on the length of time they're expected to spend and the liberality and delighted appreciation of the clients, whom they meet in hotel rooms, assignation houses, autos, on boats, in apartments or wherever they are sent. The madame gets half of the gross. This is cut all the way up the line. For 50 per cent of the take, the girl is protected against arrest, or if, in the event of an unexpected cleanup drive or a rumpus, she is pinched, she is bailed out, gets a lawyer and a fix. Moreover, the service, which is costly to operate with the graft and the auditing and the overhead, keeps her supplied with a steady flow of men such as she could never depend on hooking on the streets. Some girls with followings are said to make as much as $1,000 a week.

Another busy madame on the South Side is Marie Griffin, who occupies a three-story flat building on 42nd Street near Cottage Grove Avenue as a double-duty public utility, with a dozen or so girls for on-premise services and hundreds at the tip of a plug for call purposes. On the near North Side is another call-board, covering that area, operated by Ollie Arnstein. Some of the coin that passes through there keeps on going to a police officer in the East Chicago Avenue Station and eventually flows out to designated officials.

Ollie, a bleached blonde of indeterminate age, and her husband, Pete, also sell flesh in person at the Devonshire cocktail lounge, 19 East Ohio Street. The night we were there Ollie offered to take care of a man in our party on the following basis:

Ten dollars for a hotel room key, which she carried in her copious bosom, $2 for the room clerk, plus the girl's charge—$20 to $50—to be arranged after the couple went upstairs.

They secure replacements for their nefarious business by advertising "Lots of Tables for Ladies" in the amusement throw-away guides. Actually there are only two small tables in the lounge.

Those who prefer an advance look and a chase—or being chased—will find pavement-pounders on North Clark Street near Bughouse Square; on the south walk of the Public Library, at Washington Street and Michigan Boulevard; at the southeast and southwest corners of Clark and Van Buren, and at the old stand, which has been free territory for wielders of the big hand-bag, trademark of the street-walker, even during years when pedestrian prostitution was frowned on—on Quincy Street, between State Street and the old Post Office.

Here, in the days when the prosecutor's office lived on fees and fines, two picked cops, usually Ike Rosenthal and Monte Cannon, would pass along that block and hold up two fingers. That meant that all the girls had to report to them on the Post Office steps at 2 A.M. There would wait several old-fashioned police pie-wagons, the girls would enter and be backed up with a flourish to the Harrison Street station and lock-up. There Ike Roderick, who had the concession and the monopoly, would bond them all out at $5 a head. On Monday morning an equal number of women, often not the prisoners but their maids or others who could be up and out by 9 A.M., would line up to the august bench of Judge Prindiville or Judge Caverly, plead innocent and be fined $10 each.

The defendants gave palpably phony names, such as Sadie Smith and Annie Jones, and when asked in routine their occupations, they were waitresses, seamstresses, salesgirls, telephone girls, servant girls, chambermaids and anything but what they were. At one session, after a score or more had claimed such clean methods of livelihood, one little redhead with a bun on, when asked: "Occupation?" answered, "I'm just a whore." "Discharged," ruled Prindiville. "I sympathize with you—you have so much amateur competition!"

The frails on the flaggings take you to cheap assignation hotels—there's one on Quincy—which charge all they can get, and the women get a kickback on the rooms. Their direct charges are lower than those of the call girls and house girls, and a deal can be made for about $5 per "trick," though they will haggle for more. They, like all body-sellers, expect tips after giving their all. In professional patois that is known as "luck money."

Some hotels on South Michigan and South Wabash, in the heart of the old Levee, cater to interstate truckmen, who unload nearby on South State. These inns have a plentiful supply of cheap talent on hand for the visiting drivers.

As in other cities, some so-called private dance studios, especially on the near North Side, are blinds for other things. These are not organized and have to observe reasonable caution, though they pay off to patrolmen as a rule. If a stranger looks suspicious, all he gets is a dance lesson. But most men who want to educate their feet choose the well-known legitimate academies, usually in national chains. Private masseurs also often use more than their hands. Some have "parlors" and others are outgoing visitors. This is an old Chicago plague, also not blessed by the racket-boys and precarious to operate or patronize. The police raid the "parlors," some of them luxurious, and often confiscate equipment for sadism, masochism, fetishism and other distorted desires.

Some of the most notorious, according to a confidential report released in December, 1949, by the U. S. Army, are located at 100 East Chicago Avenue, 1029 North Clark, 2258 West Madison and 1419 North Clark.

Despite the Mann Act, which is as religiously enforced as the FBI men can enforce it, and they act usually on nothing except traffic for purposes of professional prostitution, girls are shipped out of Chicago to Florida in the winter, to lake and ocean resorts in summer, and wherever the seasonable demand dwells. They are also recruited here for houses in smaller prairie towns and for Latin America, blondes preferred. The interstate trade is strictly controlled by the Syndicate and the residue is counted with Guzik's greasy thumb.

It is well to warn the unwary that more and more each year it has become the practice of prostitutes to rob and steal, often with use of chloral hydrate tablets (knockout drops) which they carry in their purses. These are tasteless and colorless, dissolve instantly in a drink and will immobilize a man in ten minutes. This pernicious perversion of the true purposes of a pickup was described in full detail in *New York Confidential,* in the chapter headed, "No Pain, No Fun." Let it be said, however, for Chicago, more so than in other major cities, chances are that the pilgrim on the primrose promenade will find an honest tart with an honest heart.

15. JACKS AND JILLS

IN *OUR BOOK, New York Confidential,* we called attention to the sad state of young love in Gotham, where cramped living quarters and multiple occupancy dwellings play havoc with romance.

Erotically speaking, Chicago can laugh at the so-called wise burg on the Hudson. Here—in Chicago—young boys own flivvers or can borrow the family car, and there are places outside the city limits to drive to, and plenty within it as well.

And many hundreds of thousands live in private homes, or two- or three-family flats, where the kids can neck on the front stairs or in the sun parlor, or on the back porch or in the yard.

Chi is divinely gifted with parks, miles and miles of inviting greenery, where friendly bushes hide those who have something to hide.

The long Lake front, with its magnificent beach, provides the opportunity for contact by day, during which the wares are shopped for, and a soft sandy bed by night, for frolicking under the moon.

(*Note:* Stick-up men and sex degenerates often hide out in parks, on beaches and "Lovers' Lanes," and attack neckers.)

All private homes have back porches and rear entrances, but most flat-buildings also have *individual* porches and exits in the rear.

This is the greatest boon to Romeos ever thought of by the mind of man. It is impossible to estimate the number of lives thus saved, which would have been sacrificed in other cities when husbands came home earlier than expected, and boy friends had no way of getting out.

Alleys bisect almost every block throughout the city, and though they are a great inducement for crime, Chicago's citizens could not do without them, because they provide an ideal means whereby the surprised lover, who has to leave unceremoniously by the back entrance, can be swallowed up into the night.

Chicago is a man's town. It is booby-trapped against the babes. The excess of female population is estimated at 100,000, with much in the nubile brackets.

Daily, the six railroad terminals disgorge more young things into the Loop, all as green as the alfalfa fields they left behind.

Where everything has a price, love is similarly ticketed. The Chicago wolf is in the convenient position of being able to buy whatever he wants, whenever he wants it. The very existence of such a system works as a depressing lever on non-prostitutes, who find they have to be amiable if they want male companionship at all.

In most other American constituencies, save Hollywood, the man is the seeker, and pays heavily for the privilege. But in Chicago, only chumps give and spend, a possible explanation for the verified fact that fewer Windy City damsels, per capita, possess minks and other costly furs than do their opposite numbers in far less wealthy towns. Even the best-kept wear flashy platinas instead of the rich minks and martens.

A phenomenon that will be observed immediately in the Loop, and the surrounding down-town bright light belt, is that fewer couples go night clubbing. When you see a man and woman in a cafe or supper club, you can almost always put them down as visitors or suburbanites.

Your Chicagoan does his hunting solo or in packs at a considerable saving in energy and loot. Not for him is the necessity imposed on men of other towns to contact the frail earlier in the week, set up a date, buy a corsage, then wine and dine her on a gamble. When the urge for dalliance strikes Chicago's lords and masters they set out unencumbered, then secure their romantic companionship on the fly.

If they wish it to be purely commercial there are hookers at every hand, as told about elsewhere in this tome, but if they don't go in for crassness, they find little difficulty in meeting girls who are merely out for a good time, too, and who can be picked up at any cocktail lounge downtown, including those in the best hotels, or at drug store soda fountains, in elevators and elevateds, and wherever the million who daily come to the Loop congregate.

Lore of a Loop Lupo

Midwest dining hours are considerably earlier than on the two coasts. If you're making your dinner date at the last minute, call before six, otherwise the frill may have already found a provider, or eaten at home. (What a break!)

* * *

If she lives in a residential area, and you're downtown, don't offer to pick her up, as it may consume two hours of your time, and a sawbuck of your currency. Even the flossiest are used to traveling by "El." She won't be sore if you tell her to meet you.

* * *

Always remember, there are thousands of lonesome young things staring at the four bare walls of their dinky furnished rooms, who'd give anything for a night on the town.

* * *

Late-daters are the best. Let the other chump spend to take her dancing and get her loaded, after which she kisses him off and meets you elsewhere.

* * *

The ratio of eligible males to susceptible femmes is so much in your favor, you don't have to spend to keep them happy. A gag is worth a gem.

* * *

Never give a babe a break, or her folks your right name.

* * *

Some secretaries and salesgirls are awfully pretty, and most models are beautiful, but *don't date them.* There's no profit in having the sweet pastry chirp "good night" at 12:00 because she's got to get up at 7:00.

* * *

Chorus dames are O.K. for dates, but make sure that when she tells you she's got to go home to ma, it's not an oboe player instead. *Note:* Cross the chorines off your list during rehearsals. A hardboiled dance director can ruin your love life.

* * *

There's a phone booth in most ladies' rooms, and when the pigeon takes longer than usual she's probably calling another.

* * *

When you call for the babe at her hotel, if you notice she leaves her room open on the way out, don't believe she lost her key. It's so her real lover can get in before she gets home.

* * *

Don't pull the old one about "Say, didn't I meet you some place before?" That's corny and you'll only get the brush. Instead, up to her with "Honey, you're lovely. Are you in show business?" She'll be so flattered, she'll talk to you instead of yelling for a cop.

* * *

Don't get romantic in public. The doll knows what you're after, but if you're so obvious as to throw it in her lap before she's had a chance to digest the dinner, she'll brush you off —even in Chicago.

* * *

Only dopes dance. The frills are practically inexhaustible, but why tire yourself out that way? Furthermore it gives them a chance to sober up.

* * *

The smart lupo aids his girl friend's career, helping her to stardom if possible. The selfish dope who holds her back is anchored with her in the end.

16. OLDER THAN THE "OLDEST PROFESSION"

THE BONES don't rattle and the wheels don't whirr as openly as they used to.

But, though most of it is sub rosa, there is plenty of action. Ask any bartender or bellboy or try a friendly bull. Bookmakers, policy-slip pushers, lottery-peddlers, bottom-dealers, dice-clickers and wheel-riggers are still as thick as the thieves they are. Within walking distance of City Hall, he who seeks may find horse-rooms, crap-games, stud, roulette, blackjack and many other forms generally standard in the realm of hazard. Some games and tools are honest. Most are not.

This is not a diatribe against gambling, which is too old and too well-known to call for an editorial on its wickedness and crookedness. The Roman soldiers diced for the garments of the Saviour. It was an ancient practice then. Through all the ages and in every climate, in mansions and cowpatches, there has been and there is now gambling. This is merely a report on how it operates in Chicago.

There it is the handmaiden of gang warfare, assassination on the public highways, intricate racketeering and political pollution. Except in countries where gaming is an open public monopoly, it is always controlled by the underworld. It brought Chicago its first contact with that underworld.

In 1840, Chicago was the most important gambling point north of New Orleans and already tied together by bosses who had closed their contacts, though there was then no local law against it. The first offense ever prosecuted in the fledgling community at the junction of the Chicago River and Lake Michigan was running a swindling cardstore, using "seconds"—pasteboards with certain edges shaved and infinitesimal, irregular space along the edges so a dealer with a deck in his hand could produce high cards or low cards, etc., at will.

Gamblers were in the city even before women came to make eyes at the pioneers. The first headquarters of the gamblers-grafters-gunmen was then, as it is today, located directly north of what is now the Loop, in a shanty on what was called the Sands. Crime and vice also fanned out from this point.

After the great fire of 1871, Michael Cassius McDonald, a huge, tough, shrewd and ferocious man, started to tie in direct with City Hall, commanded so much revenue and dispensed so much residue that he became the purveyor of privileges in and to the underworld and the political patronage in the city and county. Chicago Crime Commission records show that, 65 years ago, McDonald's bookmaking cartel alone, with control of Chicago and Indiana racetracks, took in $800,000 profit in one season, then a fabulous figure.

His own gaming house, at Clark and Monroe Streets, housed the municipal government, to all intents and purposes. McDonald was so powerful that when Joseph Medill, founder of the *Chicago Tribune,* partially suppressed gambling for a while during his term as mayor, McDonald entered a candidate who defeated him at the next election. A scratch on a leaf from a pad by McDonald's hand named chiefs of police and ruled the aldermen and county commissioners. Mike and his family and friends were immune to arrest, even for murder, which McDonald committed freely. There is still wide immunity for big underworld murderers in Chicago.

The McDonalds got away with murder until he was old, and even then beat the final rap.

Mike could control anything except his wives. Every one went sour on him. In his dotage he fell for the grass widow of Sam Barclay, a ball-player. She had been well known around the Loop when she was Dora Feldman.

Dora, who had played with Mike's children, was Jewish. McDonald adopted her religion, was circumcised, and married her with a skull-cap on, before a rabbi.

One afternoon, veiled and befurred, she appeared at the door of a cheap little studio where crayon portraits were enlarged from fading photographs. The door was locked against her, but she took out a gun, dashed in the glass panel, and riddled a handsome young man named Webster Guerin. Guerin had taken unto himself a bride, a beautiful auburn-haired ex-schoolmate named Avis Dragan. He had been carrying on an affair with Dora McDonald, who had taken an oath to Mike that she would not betray him during the short span of life left to him.

Dora was arrested, lodged in the County jail and indicted for murder in the first degree. Mike, the man of violence and power, now in his deep seventies, the laughing-stock of the town he had owned, proved a mighty good loser. He engaged James Hamilton Lewis, later U. S. Senator, the most eloquent of pleaders in criminal defense, and gave him a $50,000 retainer. Mike died before Dora was tried and he provided generously for her in his will. J. Ham turned on the tears.

"Will the grass grow greener," he asked, "on the grave of that luckless youth, if beside it is buried this unfortunate woman who sinned and who already has paid the bitter penalty in agony and shame?"

The jury thought it would not. She was acquitted on a plea of temporary insanity, but she didn't live long to enjoy her freedom and inheritance.

His first wife, an Irish girl, beat a murder rap, too. She shot a cop to death in a joint. She ran away with an actor and Mike chased her to San Francisco and brought her back.

After 1900, the grip on gambling was divided between three syndicates. The North Side belonged to Mont Teness, who started with a saloon at Centre Street and Sheffield Avenue and who first thought up and refined the national racetrack news-gathering, dissemination and distribution. This has since become one of the major money-makers in American gambling, and innumerable murders followed in the involved attempts to monopolize it, the most recent of which at this writing was that of James M. Ragen, which will be again discussed in the dissertation about the two red-blooded cops who had the good courage and bad judgment to arrest Jake Guzik, the high commissioner of vice, after they had arrested the murderers of Ragen.

The South Side was run by Jim O'Leary, a typical old-time Chicago character. When a reform mayor and a sheriff raided him, he moved across into Indiana, where there was no specific law against poolrooms (horse-playing enclosures where bets were openly made and reported and paid off on the spot), which was O'Leary's principal business. When the Indiana authorities attempted to move in on him, he insisted he was within his rights, built a stockade of huge logs 18 feet high, chained together around his big barn, and stationed riflemen above on the ramparts, with orders to shoot anyone who attempted forcible entry.

The Loop and the Levee, by far the most prolific and profitable, were the undisputed property of the two First Ward Aldermen, Hinky Dink and Bathhouse John. Their machine later fell into the hands of the Sicilian mob and became the nucleus of the international crime combination, which has since closed a stranglehold on Chicago and is growing more powerful by the day, in scopes never visualized even by the bold brawlers and raw fixers who early became integrated into Chicago's history.

In his highest ascendency, the Chicago Crime Commission reported, Al Capone drew an annual net income of $25,000,000 from local gambling alone. The men who succeeded him went far beyond him. America's annual gaming bill is now placed at 25 billion, more than one-half the national budget.

Gambling, according to those who have made scientific studies of it, is not a sin unless it becomes a disease, causing the afflicted to sacrifice family, business, everything else. The chief and the most dangerous problem is that, as long as millions want to bet and gambling is illegal in every state except Nevada, the result is corruption, which grows until the illicit traffic sets up a super-government. When the head of a police department or a district attorney can get more a day than his post pays him a year, authority meets tremendous temptation. Once an official takes big bribes he is hooked and becomes blind to other crimes, which offer further fortune.

The report is fairly well authenticated that a politician whose nod or no was the last word in Chicago, and who eventually became mayor (not Kelly or Kennelly) received $1,000,000 a year in advance, over seven successive years, and he did not even undertake to protect gamblers or their interests; all he promised and carried out was that the police would not originate raids, smash property, or bother suckers who flocked in to be trimmed.

Any administration can eradicate 90 per cent of all gambling and at least as much of other organized racketeering overnight. We are not howling for this to be done. We don't care much. We are only telling you what is, and what is not being done and why. New York has long kept gambling fairly within bounds and there is comparatively little Syndicate prostitution. There is no city in the United States where you can't lay a bet with a bookmaker or where you can't find someone who knows where there's a game going. But this is kept surreptitious. You usually have to know someone to get in and as a result youngsters at least are kept away.

Mayor Kennelly, the incumbent at this writing, has shown how easily this business can be controlled. He has ordered crackdowns on the casinos which operated shamelessly in the flossier nightclubs, many of which since closed because that was what they were open for. He has by no means chosen to get tough with gambling in other places, perhaps because he is naive or perhaps because his underlings sell him a bill of phony information. You can't find horse-rooms, wired in and shooting the works, in every block, and there is a certain degree of thin secrecy, so you must be known or recommended after you first find out where such spots are alive.

There is more diversified betting in Chicago than in any other environment we have found. The boys work openly in both of the city's major league ball parks. They will quote you instant odds on a final result on any inning, on any batter, how long a pitcher will stay in, or on balls and strikes. Football, softball, basketball, hockey, fights, engender a big and wide turnover. Bookmakers are no novelty to us. There are four in the building in which we work in New York. But they are still not as thick as the Chicago layers, who are legion.

Between 9,000 and 10,000 taverns, cigar-stores, newsstands and candy-shops take bets. They have special telephones under bars, desks or counters, connected by direct wire to central Syndicate headquarters. A half-dozen king-sized gambling joints, also wired in, are within a few yards of City Hall.

At this writing, there is a place going full blast at 217 North Clark St. The owners were Mel Clark and Tony Accardo, alias Joe Batters. But Clark was told to "take a walk" and Bernie Korshak, brother of Sid Korshak, attorney for underworlders, went in instead. He is fronting for Charlie Joey, alias Gioe. Tony is now the "Enforcer" for the Sicilian Syndicate, succeeding in that exalted position Al Capone and, later, Frank Nitti.

This enterprise has wires direct to all the nation's race-tracks. Its net profit, after payment of all expenses, overhead and "ice," is in excess of $25,000 a day, which comes to a neat $7,500,000 a year, clear.

Another major wire-room, operating at this writing, is at 10 North Clark Street, a block from City Hall. It is owned by Joe Epstein. At the time these words were being written, Epstein's place had 200 telephones. Chicago's wire-rooms never had difficulty getting phones, even during the war, when private citizens and legitimate industry couldn't wangle a number or an instrument. Epstein's place is a hangout for dope peddlers. Addicts know they can find someone there with the stuff. His partners are Joe Grabiner and Eddie Stern.

Mayor Kennelly lives on the North Side, at the Edgewater Beach Apartments. Twice a day—in the morning and evening—his car passes the premises at 215 North LaSalle Street. There, in back of the "Gym Club," at this writing, is the biggest betting club in the Midwest. This is no low dive, but a handsome hangout where society gamblers rub elbows with stage stars and the elite of Mobocracy. Its owners are associated with Babe Baron, a friend of Democratic leader Jake Arvey. Baron, a former athlete, and wartime lieutenant-colonel, killed Jimmy Walsh in front of Henrici's restaurant on Dec. 3, 1929. In 1934, when arrested as a suspect in the Gus Winkler murder, he was carrying a loaded gun. He owns an auto agency and has a contract to repair Chicago's police cars.

These are important gambling dives. But there are hundreds peppered all over the city. Many political clubs are only fronts for gambling. We saw no attempt made at all to hide the fact that several card-games were going full blast in West Side Democratic leader Touhy's political club, which is directly across the street from the Chicago Stadium, where Franklin D. Roosevelt was first nominated for the presidency, with Touhy's fervent and fervid support.

Bingo games are another lucrative cornucopia for the underworld and its political allies. These games are staked out to all neighborhood leaders. Though the take from each customer is moderate, the gross is tremendous. This is a poor man's game, but many can play at once. Like Woolworth, the gangsters are getting rich on nickels and dimes. Even the multi-millionaire mobster Jake Guzik, doesn't think it beneath his dignity to operate a bingo game. He has one, which runs weekly in a hotel operated by a nationwide hotel chain.

Many bingo games are run under the guise of charity, or for the benefit of political clubs.

The raid on one that took place while these words were being written indicates better than any way we can tell you, how the take-over of Chicago's crime and politics was accomplished by the Sicilian Syndicate and its allies. Police smashed a big bingo bazaar in the 35th ward, on the Polish Northwest side. The Chicago Crime Commission charged that Alderman Walter J. Orlikoski was tied up with the games. A few days after the raid, Alderman Orlikoski shouted that the Polish political leaders and their "people" were being pushed around in selection of candidates for important public offices.

In a letter to Democratic County Chairman Jake Arvey, the local district of the Polish National Alliance, which Orlikoski controls, charged, "It has become increasingly clear that certain groups are trying to eliminate Americans of Polish descent from getting top places." Recalling the bingo raid, and suggestions that Orlikoski should be ousted as the party's ward committeeman, the letter went on: "We need not state that similar games of chance take place nightly in all sections of our city. We cannot help but wonder why the powers that be have suddenly chosen to raid establishments only in wards where a Polish-American happens to be alderman."

All defendants were found not guilty.

The Chicago area has an unusually large number of cases of defalcation by trusted bank employees. It is generally found that the absconding official stole the money to play horses in the crime Syndicate's gambling dens. That happens more frequently here than elsewhere, because gambling is easier to find.

From time to time Chicago newspapers publish lists of

premises where gambling games are openly operated or where bets are being accepted. Rarely does any police action follow. On the contrary, business for the resorts immediately improves, as customers have a choice catalogue of addresses.

The demand for bookmaking facilities is so great that, with the approval of City Hall, no premise is legally considered a "horse-room" unless it is larger than 20 feet by 20, or caters to more than 12 bettors at one time.

On the rare occasions when police step in on a gambling enterprise, you can be sure that the raid has been ordered because the handbook operator was not paying off or was out of favor with the Syndicate.

From time to time it is regarded as good strategy, a sop to public opinion, to make token raids. A given number of fall guys are selected. They are pinched, immediately bailed out, and then usually acquitted when they come before the court. The easiest way to do this is for the police to make sure there is a technical fault in the case. Many Chicago judges are ever eager to protect the constitutional rights of defendants, especially when they are tied up with the gambling Syndicate.

A typical case was the discharge by Judge John Gutknecht of eleven men arrested on a charge of playing dice in an apartment on South Kedzie Avenue. The arresting officer said he saw the men through a window. He had no warrant, but raided the apartment. The judge upheld the defense motion to rule out the evidence. Then the court sternly stated from the bench: "This whole thing is a farce—a big farce. But the city is willing to go through with this farce, so I will play my part in it." He thereupon discharged the defendants.

In most places policemen do not need warrants to make arrests when they see a crime committed. Apparently Chicago has a special magna charta—for gamblers.

The foregoing explains the mechanics. The visitor to Chicago who merely wants to bet on a horse in the Third at Hialeah is not interested in how it's done, he wants to know where to do it. Just call your bellboy or ask the bartender or the girl at the cigar-stand. They won't hold out for fear you're a dick, they know all the dicks know all the places.

17. QUEEN OF THE DICE GALS

ON FEBRUARY 2, 1943, Estelle Carey, Chicago's richest 26 girl, rolled snake-eyes.

The voluptuous ex-model was the victim of one of Chicago's de luxe murders, still unsolved. She was scalped, her throat was slit, she was beaten, and her legs were burned off. After torturing her, her killer set fire to the apartment. The murder focused wide attention for the first time on Chicago's unique dice girls.

At the coroner's inquest it was testified that Estelle was Nick Dean's girl friend. She worked for him as a 26 girl in the cabaret he operated. Nick was a big shot in the Syndicate. His sweetie didn't work for a measly $50 a week, like the others. Blonde Estelle Carey made $500 a week.

She lived with a friend, Maxine Buturff, in a five-room apartment at 512 Addison Street, a pleasant upper-middle-class location near the Lake on the North Side. The girls paid $75 a month rent, unfurnished.

Estelle was 34 when she was found dead by firemen who were called at 3 o'clock in the afternoon by neighbors who smelled smoke. When they found her body, they notified Town Hall Police Station, where Acting Captain William Drury was in command.

Leads were slim, but it was ascertained death was caused by the flash fire which, apparently, had been started by contact with the contents of a broken bottle which lay near the body.

This was one of those perfect mysteries you come across rarely except in detective fiction. Firemen said both the front and rear doors had been locked from the inside; they had had to break in. The killer could not have escaped from the windows, because the apartment was on the third floor and there was no fire escape.

Estelle's address book contained a number of men's names. On investigation, many were found to be reputable businessmen. There were also letters from a good-looking young soldier. Though the murderer apparently walked off with two fur coats, no other valuables were taken and the place was not ransacked. The police thought the fur coats were a blind to make it look like a robbery.

Estelle's father had died when she was two. She was put into an orphanage, where she remained until she was seven, when her mother remarried. After quitting school she worked in a factory and then as a telephone operator, until she decided to try to live by her wits. She was a striking blonde, 21 or 22 years old then.

Her climb up began as a waitress. While she was working at Rickett's, a sort of Lindy's on the near North Side, where actors and gangsters hang out, Nick Dean saw her. Dean, whose real name was Nick Circella, was way up near the top of the Italian underworld hierarchy. His was a name to be feared. People bowed and stuttered when he spoke to them. Because Chicago is the last place in the country where gangsters are still glamorous and where chorus girls point them out and consider it an honor to be dated by one, it was big stuff for Estelle to be noticed by the great man.

Al Capone had been sent to Alcatraz. The top leadership of the mob was in the hands, temporarily, of a committee of regents. Nick's influence was strong. He was a powerful catch soon to become even more powerful.

Dean and another Italian mobster, Lawrence "Dago" Mangano, were said to be the owners or backers of the Yacht Club, a swank café on Rush Street, since then closed. There was a gambling room in it, which proved its operators were with the big shots, or they couldn't be running.

With Dean as her sponsor, Estelle quit the restaurant to be the house-girl back of the 26 board at the Yacht Club. She soon became one of the North Side Tenderloin's most looked-up-to characters.

Later the ultra-ritzy Colony Club opened on Rush Street. It, too, was reputed to be owned by Nick Dean. Dean, however, claimed that it was owned by his brother, August, and Henry "Sonny" Goldstone, a professional nightclub manager. The Colony compared favorably with any café in the country outside New York. There were few that excelled it. The main floor had a battery of 26 games. Upstairs there was a complete gambling layout with roulette and all the fancier games. Estelle was promoted to its 26 department.

But if Estelle got her place in the sun through the influence of her lover, she held it because she was an efficient worker. They say she once took $10,000 from a gambler at dice in two hours.

By the time Estelle's tortured body was found in her apartment, she was in charge of the battery of 26 girls at the Colony and had a piece of the profits in the gambling concessions.

When Willie Bioff was brought to trial as a result of racket exposures by Westbrook Pegler in the Hearst papers and Arthur Ungar, fearless editor of a trade paper, Hollywood's *Daily Variety,* things began to happen in Estelle's little world. At about the same time, Constance Bennett and Anita Louise were robbed by jewel thieves and it was charged they had been fingered at the Colony. These were important names and newspapers went to it, with the result that, regardless of the Colony's protection, the city had to close it up. It has been shuttered ever since.

When Nick Dean went into hiding after he was wanted as a material witness against Bioff and Browne, Estelle dyed her hair black and went with him.

Dean was indicted in New York for conspiring with the pair. Two months later, in December, 1941, he was arrested in Cicero and flown to New York. He pleaded guilty and was sentenced to eight years and fined $10,000.

For this the underworld gave him a vote of thanks. Had he elected to stand trial, embarrassing disclosures about his pals might have been made. Then they found out that he had dickered for a short sentence—copped a plea after he had sung!

Estelle was banking the extortion take in his absence and had $2,000,000 salted away.

During a trip to Florida for her "sinus," Estelle met one of the boys from the New York mob, Eddie McGrath, who was an associate of Frank Costello and Joe Adonis. McGrath was in Florida at the request of the cops, who were prosecuting him for a labor racket murder in Key West.

When he was acquitted, shortly after New Year's Day, in

1943, Estelle thought he might be good insurance for her, so she helped him celebrate the victory—McGrath promised her the boys wouldn't harm her. In fact, she had phoned from Chicago to McGrath in New York at 11 A.M. on the day of her murder.

Though Estelle had numerous lovers during this period, police were unable to find any clues that linked her sex life to her demise. After she was slain, Estelle's safe deposit boxes were found to contain only a couple of thousand dollars and two small insurance policies. If she had a fortune hidden somewhere, the police never found it. But maybe the mob did. Maybe that accounts for the torture. Either it was that or to punish Dean for double-crossing the fraternity.

The story goes that Dean spilled because Estelle had told him the Syndicate had taken the nest-egg which she had kept in hiding, awaiting his release from jail. Those who tell that story say Estelle might have swiped the dough herself. They say that's why she was murdered, because her lie led Dean to inform against the mob.

(*Note:* Dean was "singing" the day she was slain, but clammed up when shown the headlines by his wife.)

To this day the murder remains unsolved. Was she killed by a burglar, or a jealous lover, or a wife whose home she had ruined?

Or was she rubbed out because she held out on Dean, or double-crossed his partners, or because, as it later developed, she had been picked up and held for questioning by the F.B.I.?

Contemplate the Carey case, all ye who want to find all the elements of a Chicago story wrapped together:

Illicit gambling; gangster-lover; millions of dirty dollars; tie-up with racket extortions; double-cross; killing, with torture; vanishing millions of crooked dough; no solution, no witnesses, no punishment, no aftermath.

Sex, blood, fire, money, murder, mystery, fade-out. Motive still confidential.

The Estelle Carey murder will probably go on being a mystery forever. But, palpably, the death of Chicago's most famous 26 girl had to do with her underworld connections. Police, when not hampered by pressure from above and allowed to work unhindered, usually solve private crimes. But gang murders almost always go unpunished. In the last 638 gang murders in Chicago there were only thirteen convictions. And not all the thirteen, by a long way, went to the electric chair. The sentences of some were reduced. Others were pardoned. Some were just forgotten.

Who is the 26 girl and what does she do?

You see these pretty pigeons on high stools in almost every saloon and nightclub.

She is something unique to Chicago.

For several years, Chicago has been on its best behavior—for Chicago—as to open gambling on public premises. If you want to play a game of chance you have to go to a layout in a private house or in a back room behind a garage or a store, or hunt out a protected favorite who can "run" over a saloon.

For some reason inexplicable to your authors, the 26 game is not considered gambling, though on its face it is that and illegal.

It is so much a part of Chicago life that natives don't think twice about it. The game is found as generally in the finest North Side restaurants as in the dissolute dives.

The excuse for this particular dice device is that it is played only to help induce better business at the bar.

For the record, winners are given slugs or chits, good only for merchandise. In actual practice, 99 per cent of the 26 games pay off in cash.

For the enlightenment of those who have never seen it, this is how the 26 game is played:

The player is given 10 dice. He can choose any number from 1 to 6. He is then entitled to 13 throws in which to make 26 points. For example, if he should choose No. 5, it would be necessary for him to throw 26 fives in his 13 throws, a total of 130 chances to get them.

If he throws 26 or more, he wins $1 for his 25¢ investment. If he throws 33 or more, he gets $2. If the player throws 11 or less, he also gets $1. For 12 he gets nothing. For 13 the pay off is 50¢. For from 14 to 25 he gets nothing.

There is a variation in this, known as Hooligan, played with five dice. The player is entitled to 21 throws. On the first he selects his number. For example, if there are two 6's, he might select the number 6. The girl would then set aside the two dice which came up 6. The player then has three dice remaining. On the second throw he uses three dice. If one 6 appears, the girl pulls out the die which showed 6.

On the third try the player rolls two dice and if he throws one 6, he will have, in the three throws, made the total of four sixes, and a total of 24 points.

Then he begins all over again. In his first roll in the second series he may, for example, select 3. Suppose in that series of three throws, the 3's appear in the exact manner the 6's did in the first series. He would then have four 3's, or a total of 12 points.

This process is repeated until the player has gone through the entire series of numbers from 1 to 6. He then must also roll a Hooligan. This consists of consecutive numbers of 1, 2, 3, 4 and 5, or of 2, 3, 4, 5 and 6. The Hooligan counts 20 points. He can throw for the Hooligan at any place in the game he thinks it is to his advantage.

To win, the player needs a minimum of 86 points. On a 25¢ bet he would win $1 with that. On 98 points or more, the prize would be double.

In this game it may become obvious after the first two or three throws that it will be impossible to make the necessary points, and the game will be terminated.

When played for cash instead of tokens, the player must select his point before he makes his first throw in each series. The percentage is high against the sucker in Hooligan, far higher than in the 26 game.

It is not uncommon for the 26 game to be converted into a very fast dice game called Bing. This is played with only two dice. It requires a larger layout than the 26 game.

Frequently establishments will have two 26 games going with a removable partition between them. It is easy in this setup to remove the partition and convert it into Bing. In that game there is an operator who runs a table. He makes the initial throw. For example, if with two dice he throws a total of 6 points, the players clockwise around the table each throw once to beat the dealer. Each bets against the dealer and the payoff is made as each bet is won or lost.

If the point is 6, each one making 6 or under loses; 7 or more wins. If on the first throw the operator throws two 6's he collects all around the table without further play. If he throws two aces he pays all around the table.

If the operator throws 7, the players can double their bets if they wish. This is a "come-on." In the Bing game, the player is never permitted to handle the dice. They are placed in a cup. Obviously, the operator is in a position to switch dice and to inject crooked ones at will.

If the point is 6 and the player throws two 6's he is paid double his bet. Bing is an extremely fast game and strictly for cash.

Each spot now owns its game and hires its own personnel. A few years ago, the 26 game was centrally controlled by a syndicate and it was necessary to hire the 26 girls directly from that syndicate. That no longer prevails. But police captains receive a specified stipend to permit the game to operate.

Earnings of the 26 girls vary. In the smaller taverns, in neighborhoods where the take is low, the girls usually work on a straight salary of $50 a week. In busier locations, some start with a guarantee of $50 a week and a commission on profits. Some operate on a straight commission. Frequently the girls double as hat-checkers, waitresses and B girls. Sometimes singers, dancers or strippers pick up extra loot by doubling behind the 26 table.

The game is supposed to be used primarily as a trade stimulant, but it is a source of income for the house. A man may spend a long time at the bar over one or two drinks. The 26 game, on the other hand, can take in a sizable amount in a few minutes.

We were told by experts that, if the dice are not crooked, the player can average a $1 win once in about five games. In other words, for $1.25, to play the five games, he would average back $1. That's 5 to 4 against him—and investigators have found all kinds of crooked devices in various 26 games throughout the city, raising the odds to any proportions whatsoever.

As previously indicated, all these games are illegal and the police are paid off to permit them to operate. They are tolerated as "ticklers" for bar business. But sound liquor wholesalers decry such gimmicks as injuring the industry, opening it to assaults and jeopardizing it.

While these pages were being written, a 17-year-old boy played 26 in a tavern and won a couple of dollars, which he thereupon spent for drinks and got good and plastered. He was arrested. The probabilities are he would not have gotten drunk had he not won in 26. He was paid off in chits good only for liquor and only in that place.

The girls who operate these games are, as explained in another chapter, up near the top of the local glamor-girl professions. While good looks and a pleasing personality are essential to the job, the girls must also be alert and acquire considerable skill in fast, accurate addition. A smart girl soon learns not only how to cheat the customers, but how to trim the house.

The 26 game operates around the clock, throughout all hours that bars and taverns are open, legally or illegally. The girls work in shifts. One who is on the make quickly finds plenty of opportunity to make contacts with gents who have money in their pockets. In addition to the customers, they meet the regulars and the owners and the backers of the cocktail bars and resorts in which they work. Many become girl friends of the bosses and sometimes of important gangsters, as did Estelle Carey.

That 26 games are stimulators of something is proved by the sad story of the young expressman who had a strong suspicion of banks. He even distrusted the steel box in which he and his wife kept their savings. He told police he carried the $2,700 with him, for security. The bankroll gave him a sporty sensation. So he visited a tavern on West Madison Street, and had a couple of beers. Meanwhile he played the 26 game. His luck was bad, but Mary, the dice girl, kept coming to his table to console him.

He flashed his roll when he paid for her drink. She told him he'd better be careful, he was on West Madison. So the young expressman took her advice and tucked the money away in a safe place, while she watched. When he asked her to go with him to another dive she said she would, when she was through, at four; that he should wait for her on the corner of Albany Avenue. He was right on time.

But, instead of Mary, two thugs were waiting for him. After a short chase they collared him and went directly to the pocket where the moolah was stashed. Then they swung on him and left him in the gutter.

When police questioned Mary, she said she remembered him. She even recalled making a date with him.

"I make dates with a lot of my customers," she cooed. "But, of course, I never keep them."

18. ALCO HALL

FEW CHICAGOANS realize it, many have no knowledge of it at all, but there are dry places in Chicago and they are growing.

Illinois is a local option state. Under its peculiar laws elections can be called not only for cities, counties and townships, but for precincts. About one-eighth of the population of the state now lives in dry areas. That's about 1,000,000 people. Most of these hug the Kentucky border and the Mississippi, across from Iowa. But there are Saharas deep inside Chicago.

Voters have three choices in addition to voting all-out wet:

1. Shall the sale at retail of alcoholic liquor be prohibited?
2. Shall the sale, except beer, containing not more than four per cent alcohol by weight, be prohibited?
3. Shall the sale, except by package, not for consumption on the premises, be prohibited?

Under provisions of that law, whereby political precincts within the city limits can vote to exclude intoxicating potables, the drys have made steady, if not too important, headway. There isn't much publicity about it and the campaigns are restricted to the districts, where they are intensive. In this wet, wild town which hardly had a dry square block during national Prohibition, 130 of 3,400 precincts have been closed to liquor sales of every kind.

With 3,400 precincts in all, there is as yet no trouble digging up a snort. But the implication behind the local option prohibition of any part of this metropolitan city is rather startling. The 130 victories for the arid forces mean as many plans, moves and successes by a powerful minority, working in manners and methods far more slick than the old hammer-and-tongs battles against bars and bottles which captured the nation, but which are forever passé.

Anti-Saloon Leaguers, who long ago discarded that name,

which revolted America and caused the civilized world to snicker and to wonder, have developed a foxy system. They enlist property-owner leagues to sell the voters on the proposition that they can increase real estate values in their neighborhoods. Their line is something like this:

"We are both men of the world. We both enjoy a nip. We don't want to close Chicago. All we want to do is to run the dives out of this particular little section and watch the values go up. We can always buy the stuff a few blocks away, where the people aren't smart enough to see this opportunity."

This is a powerful sales talk in districts where a large proportion of the citizens live in private or two-family houses. It is logical because many Chicago taverns are in shanties and decrepit stores, a blot anywhere. Meanwhile, these pinpoint bombings are financed, without showing the hands of such influences, by Methodists, Baptists, the W.C.T.U., the United Drys (successor to the Anti-Saloon League, a national organization) and—here comes a heavy hidden factor—other saloonkeepers.

A grog-shop owner on the edge of a precinct will have competition across the street. By putting the rival out of business he gets all the latter's trade in addition to what he already has. Knowing the neighbors, he can calculate how soft they would be for local option closing in their own precinct and free access to liquor twenty feet beyond it. This short-sighted throat-cutting maneuver has helped in most of the early elections the drys have won. But the professional reformers, once they had tasted blood, found they could get some more and began to initiate aridities on their own.

Few Chicagoans were or even now are hep to this combination which is slowly, stubbornly working at and dreaming of a dry Chicago. Enforcement would not be as simple now as it was until 1949, when the city was Democratic and the state Republican, with the state government then vengefully wielding the law. With Democrats in Springfield again, it is questionable whether the state would override the city bosses if this spread to where it threatened their outlying cohorts.

So far, most of these 130 dry precincts are on the Southwest Side, from 87th Street to 119th Street and from State Street to Western Avenue. The second largest zone is on the Northwest Side, a half mile in either direction from Cicero Avenue, near the city line.

Only one campaign raised a city-wide furor. The taverns in parts of East 63rd Street were scandalous. They aped those in other sections which we have discussed at length. There were no closing hours. Prostitution of all kinds was encouraged. Crummy burlesque shows were run behind the bars. Toughs and thieves and degenerates were attracted until it was unsafe for decent people to walk by. Parents complained that they were afraid to let their children pass those corners to and from school. The liberal-minded voters knew no other way to rid themselves of these evils except to wipe out liquor.

Illinois, and more pertinently Chicago, furnish prime examples of lame liquor laws. Whether this is due to ignorance or premeditated political design, the State Board is required—not permitted, but required—to issue a liquor license to any applicant without a criminal record who pays the fee if the local authorities approve. The State Board has no police power in practice then or thereafter. A license can be revoked only by municipal officials. And they do that only on the advice of the local police precinct captain.

Picture that cinch for graft and gravy! To run at all, a saloon is at the mercy of a police captain. You marvel how saloons at present costs can sell what they advertise, "a shot and a glass of beer for 25 cents," and live, let alone pay off. But there are many such places in almost every police district and a man who could put the shake on them at $5 or $10 each per week would do handsomely.

Bootlegging and speakeasies are out. Not because of conscience or enforcement, but because legal saloons are always too near and by Illinois law there is no restriction on possession, transportation or delivery to homes in any territories, including those closed by local option. The statutes specifically so provide, but the Syndicate has foreseen the remote possibility that in time an entire main section of Chicago could be dried up, and the downtown mob, with facilities trained and ready and in use now supplying non-liquor counties and whole states, would move in. They control a great deal of the wholesale liquor distribution now, with trained rum-runners and speak operators.

Illinois has two forms of on-premise licenses. Taverns do not furnish food and are required to close at 2 A.M. on weekdays and 3 A.M. after Saturday nights. Cabarets and restaurants, which pay a higher license fee, may stay open until 4 A.M. weekdays and 5 A.M. Sundays. Of course, with the trade run by ward authorities, there are no closing hours where the joints can afford a payoff. Many saloons have no keys. You can see drunks on the streets at all hours. Bartenders work in three shifts.

Bottle sales for off-premise consumption are licensed not only in package stores, but in drug stores and groceries, also. The result is furious competition with often a dozen retail outlets in one block and price-wars to push brands which are not price-fixed. Premiums, often vile ones, go with the bottles. There is no barring of minors from buying. In some neighborhoods a pint flask of gin, probably a refill from a loose supply, can be had for a half-dollar.

Of course, there are many fine liquor-dealers, as there are fine bars and taverns, some of which are listed in the Appendix. There are 7,000 licensed taverns, not including restaurants and nightclubs permitted to sell, making a total of about 10,000 doors through which you can enter and drink standing up or sitting down. Most of these are conducted by decent, upright citizens. Some are managed by ex-convicts. When the Chicago Crime Commission exposed the records of numerous criminals in the business, their places were temporarily shut down—until the Liquor License Appeal Commission of the City of Chicago ordered most of the permits restored. One such place was shown up as a hangout of gangsters, as bad as the owner who served them. It was proven that liquor was being sold to minors and it was shut down. After it was reopened, a bartender shot and killed a patron. Nothing has been done about the place since. But collections rose from all the other nefarious dives because some had been shut for a few days.

It is impossible to set forth all the ramifications that went into influencing the original state and city laws and the build-up of the systems whereby even these are constantly and lucratively sidetracked. The same ring which bribes police and their political superiors and gouges vast revenue from the outlets to protect them in their flagrant violations reaches down through the entire long state of Illinois to Cairo, on the Delta at the confluence of the Mississippi and the Ohio Rivers.

This little burg, which has no airport, is far below St. Louis in the inbred region scarcely ever mentioned in Chicago, known as "Egypt." It is the concentration point for bootleg booze shipments to dry territories in other states, especially Kansas, Missouri, North Carolina, Mississippi and Oklahoma, the latter two the only completely bone-dry states left in the Union. The Fischetti cohorts are said to take in $500,000 a week from supplying bonded stuff to bootleggers in those and other states. Cairo has more wholesale liquor dealers per capita than any other town in the world. In wet Illinois territory, they purchase legally from nearby Peoria for deliveries at their warehouses, the orders marked "For Export," and thus exempt from Illinois tax.

During the dead of night the cargo is loaded on rafts and barges and boats, which float down to dry Mississippi, to partly-dry Arkansas, and for trans-shipment to Oklahoma and the prohibition counties of Kansas. From river points trucks and planes and even helicopters owned by the mob deliver into dry areas of Kentucky, Tennessee and the Carolinas. The combination even owns and maintains airports and planes at strategic landing places.

19. THE BOBBY-SOXERS

HOMES BROKEN by divorce and estrangements, bad environment, crowded housing, callousness to law and order, glorification of gangsters and the example of adults who, in Chicago, apparently live by the code that there is a price for everything, are the underlying causes for the deplorable picture of juvenile delinquency.

Stories like these, taken at random from police reports, are no isolated exceptions:

Robert Munday, a student at Montefiore School for Incorrigibles, took 3½-year-old Thomas Laux into the basement headquarters of the neighborhood's "Hangmen's Noose Club" and strung him up to a beam. Munday confessed the slaying and said he was angry because the child had taken his pet kitten.

Howard Lang, 14, son of a woman who had been married and divorced five times, came from the same type of neighborhood. In October, 1947, he stabbed Lonnie Fellick, 7, and crushed his chest with a rock. Investigation disclosed that a gang of children, including girls up to 17 years, had participated in sex parties in the rundown area. Howard, acquitted due to legal technicalities, has begun a new life under a new name in a home outside the city.

There also was the killing of William Gervais, 13, by Rafael Villasenor, 15, in Fuller Park, not far from the Munday home. There authorities found children were using the park—provided to divert them from such activities—for after-dark orgies. Billy was marked for death by the neighborhood in which he had been reared. His mother had divorced and remarried. Billy's elder brother, a war veteran, had killed his stepfather when the latter attacked Mrs. Gervais in a drunken rage.

Villasenor, so tough his gang buddies called him "Rocky," strangled the boy after committing a sex act. He stuffed the body in a conduit in the park where the gang gathered with their juvenile "molls" to hold sex parties, drink cheap wine and beer and smoke marijuana. Villasenor also escaped prison on a technicality. He is now in a state home for boys.

Nine-year-old John Navickas, who disappeared a year ago, lived in the same neighborhood. Police believe he met the same fate as Billy Gervais.

Another delinquent was Roy Adams, 14, who smothered eight-year-old Nancy Schuler on May 27, 1948. Roy had quit school after the fourth grade and was known as a "problem child." His parents were divorced. He confessed that he killed Nancy because of a sexual motivation. He got fourteen years.

James Hartmann also came from a broken home. He killed Mrs. Gracelyn Bush, wife of a minister, while attempting to snatch her purse, in September 1947. He got twenty-five years in prison. Previously he had held up a young mother and forced her to submit to sexual indignities.

Here is the record of a grieving mother who told a coroner's jury her 18-year-old son, dead of drug addiction, had used narcotics with her knowledge since he was fifteen. She said she had done little about it and had even given him money to buy dope, because she feared the narcotics-peddlers might do violence to the boy if she interfered. She said she first discovered his use of drugs three years ago, when she found a doped cigarette in his pocket and noticed needle punctures in his arms.

She did not go to authorities until two months before he died, when the boy had greatly increased his use of cocaine. Because of her complaint he was sent to the Federal Narcotics Hospital at Lexington, Kentucky, but resumed the use of drugs when he was discharged a month later.

The same day the foregoing appeared, a judge in Family Court sentenced a 23-year-old colored girl to 90 days for selling heroin to a 16-year-old boy.

Soft sentences are the tipoff for the prevalence of juvenile delinquency in Chicago. First, cops look the other way. Second, if they do make a pinch, the judges discharge or give mild punishment.

As will be seen in the chapter dealing with the narcotics

racket, reefers are readily available all over the city. Children are introduced to them in high school and sometimes even in grade school.

Usually, the dope-peddler passes them out free to the kids to get them hooked. After that they are forced to turn to petty thievery to procure the money to buy the weeds, and through this means are recruited into the underworld.

It is considered smart in all high school circles to smoke marijuana. The stronger reefers sell for $1, but greatly adulterated cigarets are supplied the school trade at 25 cents. These are sufficiently strong to "send" the kids. After they become habituated to them, they are forced to seek the more expensive reefers or go to "hard stuff"—cocaine and heroin.

Reefer-peddlers wait outside high schools until after the final class. Sometimes the local candy stores handle the weed. In many cases upper-class students have been found selling them to other children.

Along with the general breakdown in morals, the school kids are always eagerly searching for newer and smarter ways of getting a bang. Already old-fashioned is aspirin in Coca Cola. Much more potent is a sleeping pill or "goofball" dissolved in a glass of beer. Under its influence the kids lose all restraint.

Benzedrine fiends are common. The latest fad is to insert an aspirin tablet into a cigaret and smoke through it, so that the nicotine becomes diluted with aspirin fumes.

Police and U. S. officials estimate that more than half of all Negro students in Chicago high schools use narcotics in some form. Whereas reefers are overwhelmingly favored by white youngsters, colored ones find they need something stronger to give them a lift. U. S. narcotics agents have told us it is not uncommon to find a 12-year-old Negro child deeply habituated to "main-liners," an extreme form of dope addiction, in which the subject gets no kick out of cocaine and heroin unless he inserts a hypodermic into a main artery in the arm or leg.

In one brief period, less than a month, two special agents found more than 150 high school students, between the ages of 13 and 17, using cocaine or heroin. One 13-year-old boy died from an overdose of adulterated heroin.

Juvenile delinquency is almost out of hand. On a recent night, sixty young hoodlums armed with clubs and brass knuckles raided a malted milk and hamburger store on the North Side and beat up ten patrons, most of them pupils at Carl Schurz High School. Some of the rioters traveled to the scene in stolen cars. Police were able to arrest eighteen. Two of the victims went to hospitals.

Authorities said their investigations convinced them the attacks were not the result of inter-school feuds, nor were they racial in origin. These young hoodlums, it seems, fight for the sheer lust of fighting. Sometimes as many as two or three hundred boys and girls gather on corners and disrupt traffic.

Police ascribed much of the present-day juvenile delinquency to leniency and oversentimentality. Just a week before, fifteen young hoodlums belonging to the same gang mentioned above were arrested, but were discharged by Judge Drucker in Boys Court.

Crime prevention authorities assert also that overprivileges showered on the youth these days are largely responsible for the gruesome conditions. All classes in Chicago have a high per capita of wealth. Negroes, especially, are better off in Chicago than they are anywhere else in the country.

The youngsters have cars to ride around in, spending money to buy dope, guns, blackjacks and contraceptives. They spurn work and study, so have the leisure in which to get into trouble. No longer are they forced to help support struggling parents. The child labor and relief laws snuffed that out.

A typical teen-age riot was thwarted while these pages were being written, when police seized twenty-two boys, a number of them high school students, who had formed a battle-line to engage a rival gang, at Milwaukee and California Avenues. The planned fight was said to have resulted from quarrels between two girls from the Logan Square district and two girls from another neighborhood. Two of the bobby-soxers returned to the grill where the argument occurred and began calling boy friends.

At the scene, police found two baseball bats, four two-foot lengths of lead pipe and five rubber hoses.

Reference has been made in earlier chapters to gang wars on racial lines between young mobs of hoodlums. However, all evidence indicates that this is a negligible factor insofar as juvenile delinquency is concerned. The youth of Chicago has been taught to jump over racial fences. A phenomenon noted in all schools and neighborhoods where whites and blacks come together is the many romantic attachments between young Negroes and young Caucasians. When that happens it's a colored boy with a white girl.

The silent corridors of the Art Institute and the Public Library play host to colored youths making love to white girls. Every concert at Orchestra Hall will find a blonde bobbed head snuggled on a manly black shoulder.

When a gang of eight teen-agers went out to commit a robbery, they rented a gun for $65 on the instalment plan, because none owned a weapon. Another young mob was broken up after police discovered they were stealing guns and selling them to grade and high school pupils.

But it must be borne in mind that not by any means are all juvenile delinquents colored, nor, as aforementioned, do they come from blighted areas.

The four teen-age girls who figure in this story live in exclusive Hyde Park, near the Lake front. They blithely admitted they had threatened the wife of a packing-house executive with a knife and attempted to steal her auto for a joyride. They told how one threatened the victim with a pocket knife while another carried a brick fragment in her purse to swing like a blackjack. The girls are all 2B students at Hyde Park High and all seemed to come from happy homes. A University of Chicago psychiatrist labeled all four "potential murderers."

But that's only childish prankishness in Chicago.

20. THE JUNKIES

THE NUMBER of narcotics addicts in Chicago grows at an alarming rate. The disease is affecting people in every age bracket, but especially teen-agers and young men and women. The unsung Narcotics Bureau of the U. S. Treasury is one of the more thorough enforcement agencies of the government, despite the handicaps of its limited personnel and niggardly government appropriations.

The Chicago police, too, make valiant attempts to keep dope out of the city. All cops hate drug-peddlers and pimps. When coppers aren't handcuffed, they go to work on such swine with right good will.

Not even the most complacent municipal government dares call the law off drug-peddlers. The cops are told to do their duty, but they can accomplish little, because the problem is far too big. Though the authorities do not spare drug-pushers, and frequently make examples of wholesalers, they do not go above local levels. The kings of the Syndicate, who bring the dope to the country and arrange for its nationwide distribution, are not molested.

The poor Negro, Italian or Mexican peddler, who may make 50¢ profit on each deal, does not name the higher-up when arrested, because he usually doesn't know who that is, and a squeal means his life. If he keeps quiet and pleads guilty he gets a high-priced lawyer, a minimum sentence of a few months, and a bonus.

Dope-dispensers are thick as flies on both North Clark and South State Streets. Another concentration point is at Wilson Avenue and Broadway. You can buy white stuff on West Madison Street and in front of the Pershing Hotel, in Bronzeville, also at Paulina and Madison and 47th and Calumet. And on almost every other busy corner in town.

Enforcement agencies are hampered by the leniency of Federal judges, who are loath to impose stiff sentences. Many hesitate before allowing any convictions at all. When possible, the agents prefer to prosecute under the state law, but there the maximum sentence for a first offense is only one year.

Illinois has no law against dope addiction, which means that the junkies can't be picked up and made to tell where they got the stuff, nor can they be sent away against their will for treatment. Governors Green and Stevenson vetoed such a bill.

Reefers are almost as common in Chicago as cigarettes. A U. S. Narcotics agent told us that 90 per cent of band musicians in Chicago not only use them, but sell them to young men and women who come to their places to dance.

The best marijuana sold in Chicago comes directly from Mexico. Much of the bum stuff is grown locally. Marijuana is a weed that grows without care and can be raised in back yards, window boxes, gardens or vacant lots. There are farms that find it profitable to raise no other crop.

Even the Sanitary District, an independent governing body created by the State of Illinois to operate Chicago's Drainage Canal system, found itself embarrassed with a bumper yield of 150 acres of marijuana, some of it 20 feet high, growing on public land. There were acres and acres. It was estimated that it would take five years to eradicate the growth. The Commissioner found a 35-acre tract at Lemont and a similar one at Tessville, villages near Chicago. Most of this marijuana was seeded on the quiet by addicts or sellers in the Chicago market. The people who plant it manage to slip out at night to harvest it.

In another case, an arrested marijuana seller admitted to police he had planted and picked a marijuana field at 91st Street and Harbor Avenue, within the city limits, in the hope he could raise $15,000 to buy a small café and retire. When arrested, he was selling the cigarettes, which he grew on the abandoned lot, at 50¢ to $1 each.

Though marijuana does not create habituals in the same way that heroin and opium do, it has been banned by law because of its psychological and physiological effects. It is closely related to hasheesh, the ancient Oriental drug which conquering emperors fed to their soldiers to make them fearless killers. We get our modern word "assassin" from it.

Marijuana is the Mexican variety of the weed. The alkaloid derived from it is not as potent as the Asiatic stuff, but it is sufficiently powerful to cause the smoker to throw off his inhibitions. Under its influence he feels he can accomplish anything; that he is a superman above laws, and that he possesses the strength of demons. It is an incentive to rape. Most sex-criminals smoke it.

That there is also a close tie-up between reefers and sex on the commercial level was demonstrated early in 1950 when Federal and police narcotics agents raided a flat at 823 Sheridan Road which they described as one of the city's major marijuana distribution points and as a call girl center.

The cops seized four small address books listing the names of persons to be dealt with at hotels, and names and addresses of customers. They believe one set of books was for reefer customers and the other for men using the call girl service.

The flat was equipped with two phones, one for calls from addicts and the other for lonesome gents. A filing system listed the customers on variously colored cards, according to their wants—sex or narcotics. Many were both.

Most professional killers dope up on marijuana before they commit their crimes. It gives them the added nerve to pull the trigger and the added strength for a getaway. The records of police departments all over the country show that 80 per cent of all crimes of violence are committed by reefer-smokers and that all such addicts are "cop-fighters" who hate the law.

Though marijuana, itself, is not much more habit-forming than tobacco or coffee, it is the inevitable case history of all who use it that they must go on to the hard "white" stuff eventually, when they no longer get a wallop out of reefers.

Heroin sold on Chicago streets comes to town from the Mediterranean through New York and from Mexico through Lower California. Opium is no longer a major article of drug addiction. Most of it bound for the Chicago market comes from New York, though recently some good stuff has been coming from the Orient through San Francisco. Cocaine comes from the West Coast of South America through the Canal and Atlantic and Gulf ports. Most morphine, which is similar to heroin, but weaker, is diverted from legitimate U. S. channels.

Chicago, because of its location, is the central depot in the wholesale dope trade for the entire Midwest. Stuff comes into the city and goes out by plane, train and car. Though couriers bring considerable stuff into the city in commercial planes, the use of private planes, bought as army surplus, usually fraudulently, is swelling. The dope racketeers have acquired numerous private airports in the Chicago vicinity and near the Mexican border.

Chicago is being flooded with dope made synthetically. It is believed the Syndicate has set up drug factories in Illinois for that purpose. Their operations are now on a limited scale, but soon will have enough capacity to supply manufactured narcotics for the entire United States.

The magnitude of the problem is indicated by the fact that in one month recently, 387 sellers were arrested in Chicago. Seven were juveniles.

A ring of dope-peddlers specializes in the sale of heroin, cocaine and morphine to teen-agers at high schools and neighborhood and parochial school playgrounds in the Second and Third Wards. All involved here are Negroes.

Two peddlers were caught in the act of injecting heroin by hypodermic needle into the arm of a 14-year-old boy. Two 15-year old girls admitted they had been taking cocaine for months. All police know sales of the narcotics are handled by teen-age and bobby-sox pushers who charge from $1.50 to $2 each for capsules.

Narcotics addicts soon become criminals, because it takes more money than even prosperous adults can afford to continue to feed the habit. The arrest of three thieves captured looting a North Side grocery led to the smashing of a dope-ring when the trio confessed taking part in purse-snatching and burglaries because they "had to get money to buy dope."

One of the dope syndicate's top sources of revenue comes from people in the upper brackets. Respectable persons are "hooked" at parties, where they are first induced to try a shot, from curiosity and "for the fun of it." Smooth adventurers set up swank apartments on the chi chi North Side Gold Coast and, plentifully supplied with money, manage to get into the best social circles.

An investment of $10,000 is considered justified to hook a stage star, banker, or wife of a big businessman. These people are not supplied with $1.50 heroin capsules. They soon find their dope bills running into hundreds of dollars a week. At present prices it costs a moderate user $15 to $30 a day for heroin or morphine, $60 to $80 a day for coke. Opium is $40 a smoking session. It is not uncommon for the ring to bleed people of as much as $1,000 a week, causing them to commit crimes and defalcations and to hock their jewelry. But even more profitable than the sale of narcotics to those in the money is the opportunity for blackmail, which employs an entire department of the Syndicate.

The society woman who has "a monkey riding on her back," which means she is hopelessly habituated, soon finds she is called on by a character who threatens to expose her to her husband or to the authorities unless she comes up with a weekly stipend.

Many Chicagoans who want to go on dope binges travel to Milwaukee, only a little more than an hour away. For some bureaucratic reason known only to the great brains in Washington, Milwaukee, at this writing, has no representative of the U. S. Bureau of Narcotics stationed there. The nearest resident agent is in Madison, the state capital. Though Milwaukee has a fine municipal police force, it is helpless to cope with the highly organized and immensely wealthy drug ring.

Thus Milwaukee has become the dope resort for Chicago. Opium parlors are running wide open there. They cater especially to well-heeled Chicagoans, who are supplied also with other forms of excitement when they come up for weekends. For the same reason the drug ring finds it advisable to use Milwaukee as a storage center for the wholesale Chicago supply. The stuff is brought down in small quantities, minimizing the hazard of losing a big haul to the Feds, who are always on the ball, but can't cover much territory.

Contrary to public belief, most opium smokers in America are not Orientals. Big shot gangsters and gamblers favor the pipe, as do their molls and some women of the theatre.

It may be news to their henchmen, but the narcotics dicks list Willie Heeney, underworld boss of Cicero, and Tony and Rocco de Grazio, Mafia rulers of Melrose Park, as hopheads.

Morphine and heroin, which are opium derivatives, are "habit forming." Cocaine, made from the South American coca leaf, officially is not. The law and the pharmacopoeia ban it, however, because its effects are similar to those of marijuana and more so. Sooner or later most professional criminals become cokies.

21. G STRINGS—B GIRLS

"*MUSCLE-DANCING*" was introduced in the United States in a big way when the late Sol Bloom, as an entrepreneur at the Chicago World's Fair, celebrating the 400th anniversary of the discovery of America, presented "Little Egypt" in a series of contortions while she stayed on her feet, known as the "hoochy koochy." It became world-famous, drew millions and was the only concession at the Fair that cleaned up.

"Strip-teasing" is a comparatively new fashion in public performance. Nudity is ancient and its possibilities are limited, because a girl can't have on less than nothing. But in about 1925, in Paris, a cookie who knew something about sex appeared in a café and, instead of showing herself nude, showed herself naked. There is a distinct difference. Nude means with nothing on. Naked means with everything taken off. She was a sensation as she gradually removed one bit of clothing after the other, keeping in motion and sustaining suspense. This became known as "teasing," and was quickly adopted in stock burlesque, which it eventually ruined in many towns because it brought the law down. It was transplanted to floor-shows, where the authorities didn't interfere for a while.

In this country the strippers adapted the kooch as an element of the strip and sounded out all the suggestive and provocative possibilities, with many variations and improvements in the nuances of disrobing, garment by garment, fluff by fluff. Gypsy Rose Lee developed it into an art and was accepted as a stage performer by the others. Margie Hart and two or three more, by skill and with physical beauty of face and form, did well and lingered on a while.

Sally Rand, who is still a star, and Faith Bacon, are fan dancers, not to be confused with stripping, though many peelers do both.

But, about ten years ago, when even the stars of this field quit it at their height because of its disrepute, the act was considered washed up in New York and it was prohibited in many other places. But in Chicago it not only never died, but went wholesale and became, as has been shown, an industry.

No one can estimate exactly how many are employed in the city, carrying with them an average of twenty others, including bartenders, 26 girls, B girls, waitresses, hostesses, masters of ceremony, musicians, managers and bouncers, directly, and supporting secondarily agents, politicians, coppers, purveyors of food and liquor, electricity, furnishings, advertising and other collateral participants, including landlords. So you see, if these women ever had to keep their clothes on it might cause a financial panic in our second largest city.

After much early experimentation in the circumscribed possibilities of supporting all this, by opening buttons, hooks and zippers, the strippers have finally divided themselves into three classes: "fan-dancers," who keep up the pretense of hiding their nakedness as they enlarge it; "grinders," also known as bumpers and belly dancers, who feature undulations and various wiggles and squirms; and "talking women," who utter sly, usually dirty, observations about themselves and the customers, on animal subjects apropos of their anatomy as it is exposed bit by bit.

The burlesque business, as it is called generically, is divided into three basic divisions: the lounges, at which the shows are presented behind big bars on raised platforms or on stages at any extremity of the room; burlesque theatres, which are no longer traveling troupes, but stationary, in which the women are changed and in which generally no beer or liquor is sold; and the burlesque bookers, stationed in Chicago, who engage and route countless peelers through the local dives and everywhere in the nation where such stuff is tolerated, especially through the Middle-West belt to the Gulf of Mexico.

Burlesque lounges are found in every part of Chicago, in the Loop, in residential sections and in the wastelands. The worst of them have been described, but some are luxurious neon-lighted resorts with modern and costly décor. The performers range from fat and scrawny heaps who are glad to take $50 a week, to advertised and publicized beauties who have been known to earn $1,000 a week.

One thing all lounges have in common is continuous shows; another is no minimum or cover charge. Some open as early as two o'clock in the afternoon and run through till four o'clock in the morning, and in the suburbs until breakfast time.

These dumps employ from five to twenty girls each. After a cute exit and a grinning grateful bow, there is usually a brief intermission, filled in with piano or instrumental music. Sometimes, in the classier dumps, there is an M.C., male or female, who kills time with nasal songs, often smutty parodies and monologues dealing with the coarser bi-sexual and homo-sexual subjects, always nauseating and giving one a sense of shame even deeper than that which is spread by the sight of a clumsy female attempting sensuality and attaining only bestiality.

When the heat is off, there is no limit to which some strippers descend. Novelty is the spice, but few of these women have any flair for it. They do know that the customers want nakedness, and that they give as far as they are permitted. Beyond this climax they are sunk, and that includes the talking women, who have more range, but stay down on a level with their audiences, which seem to want four-letter words and blunt toilet-talk.

Prices for drinks run from 50 cents for beer to 75 cents in the best saloons, and 75 to 85 cents for hard stuff, which is terrible booze, served by the thimbleful. Drinks for B girls, as has been mentioned, run to $1.50. Many of the strippers double in that capacity, but all such places employ others on the floor, who solely solicit drinks. All men without women are worked. As a rule the B girls are not thieves, but they have been known to roll a drunk or to surround a man alone, and while he is kept interested one of them picks his pockets. If a patron flashes big bills he may be fingered, followed and hit on the head.

Some burlesque bars have back rooms where good or well-known customers can retire to dimly lit booths with almost any of the women on the premises. They have back entrances through which spenders can take them out unseen. Necking and such in telephone booths, halls and passageways is not unknown.

Many B girls work as long as 15 hours a day, especially on weekends. A young, smart girl can make $150 a week at the bar and tables. These girls do not have to hustle, but many do on their own, after hours, having made dates with the chumps they met in the room.

Some of the tonier burlesque clubs like the French Casino have evening-gowned girls waiting on a long bench at the entrance, instead of circulating from table to table, to the possible annoyance of customers. Here the lonesome man can pick out the one he wants when he comes in and have her join him.

At some burlesque bars, the waitresses size up their customers. For men who look like sports, they offer to act as intermediaries between the girls in the show and the patrons. At the Flamingo, on West Madison Street, our waitress said, "Do you wants Toots to come out?" Toots was a talented red-headed grinder who had just finished her number.

The time of day means nothing to the faded girlie-shows on South State Street. According to a reporter for the *Daily News,* at 2:30 in the afternoon he found the Pink Poodle running full blast at 502 South State Street.

Eight B girls, two of them scantily clad in kimonos, stood near the door waiting for customers—the polite name for the chump who'll buy drinks.

Four tried their time-honored "Honey, buy me a drink" routine on the "customer" and professed great sorrow over the news he was "broke." A continuous strip show was in progress at the bar, while thirty other customers nursed their 50-cent beer watching the B girls take their turns as performers.

With one exception, the investigator found girls stripped to G-strings, and dancing that way for several minutes before gathering their clothes and parading past the bar to a basement dressing room.

The exception, a pudgy number with black net underthings, stopped short of nudity after a man looking suspiciously like a policeman stationed himself at the door.

"Leave it on," the bartender muttered to the girl after noticing the lounger at the door. By 3 P.M., the bar was packed and the two-piece orchestra had grown to three. Two of the girls were loudly kissing their customers and one heifer-sized miss was encouraging "daddy" to forget about the kimono.

"They usually strip all the way," a detective in a squad car outside informed the reporter. "Maybe they have a lookout upstairs and see us."

Farther down the street other girlie saloons went begging for customers, apparently scarce on a Monday afternoon. Several girls were perched on bar stools in each one and begged the reporter to come in.

"Just looking for a friend," the reporter said, backing out of one place. "You'll find one here," a male lounger declared. "Find anything you want here."

Two days after the foregoing was published in the *Daily News,* your authors visited the same addresses. Nothing was changed.

Conditions in the bars could not exist without political protection. Payoff is made to dozens of local police captains, who pass the dough to the ward committeemen. You must first be okayed by the Syndicate.

Burlesque theatres on South State and West Madison Streets do not sell liquor or refreshments. The grinds go on and on, alternating stage shows and old "for adult only" movies. The lowest degenerates patronize these houses.

The burlesque influence has spread from Chicago all through the so-called Bible Belt. Into this Strip Strip, Chicago sends thousands of peelers. Though the adjacent territories are long on prohibition, hell-fire and damnation, the leathery-skinned peasants go strong for the titillating human form, female and visible.

All the way to Texas, by way of Iowa, Kansas and Oklahoma, every stop turns up an oversupply of nudes—fat ones, homely ones, some pretty ones, but all down to the inevitable G-string. And all send their 10 per cent commission back to an agent who works out of his hat on Randolph Street. The Middle West has been called "the backbone of the nation." But its trademark is the navel.

22. GANGDOM—HOW IT BEGAN

WE HAVEN'T harassed you with much history. But the roots and the growth of mobocracy, a uniquely American manifestation which has spread over the map of the United States, cannot be portrayed without looking backward. Though it has spread everywhere, it is indigenous to Chicago, which is still its most fertile and flowering garden. The story of organized vice is so closely interrelated to its origins and spread in other cities that we will have to open and pull in the shutter as we attempt to project the picture.

Gangs go far back into our native history, and we are all familiar with the hoodlumism of roving robbers after the Civil War, of the New York Hudson Dusters and similar outfits of plain plunderers and street fighters in all our major cities. But these were not racketeers.

The origin of the word "racket" goes back into the early Tammany days, when each petty leader threw for himself an annual benefit, in a local hall. The din and the drunkenness and the loud brass band all mingled into the common appellation of these affairs as "rackets." This pure English bisyllable then became the word to express physical and political pressure whereby unearned money was gotten. The racket hall might have had a capacity of 1,000. But many times that number of tickets were sold to saloonkeepers, pushcart peddlers, tradesmen, public job-holders, as pure graft, under threats of annoyance or arrest or revocation of licenses and other privileges, or with fists and clubs swung by the toughs sent out to collect. Some of these rackets became highly profitable; and the next echelon of politicians stuck out their mitts and demanded a cut-in, on pain of running rival rackets or killing the revenue by giving protection to those who were kicking in to avoid beatings or other terrorism. Thus the word covered the entire institution as it flooded into every avenue and lane whereby oppression on the one hand and favors on the other, backed by political drag, the brass knuckles and the gun, could invade all shady businesses and many honest and orderly enterprises.

Though racketeering is, as we have said, an American manifestation, its origin is European. It was always restricted in the old country but was never entirely suppressed, from times before the Holy Roman Empire to this day. In Sicily and Italy extortion has always thrived, enforced by the stiletto. There is an entire literature around the bandits of Britain, including Robin Hood, who were racketeers, using force for profit and making deals with punitive authorities. Similar practices were and are known in Turkey, Greece, Spain, Portugal, in certain parts of France, in the wilds as well as the cities of Russia, in Poland, the Baltic States and on that entire continent, except that there was practically none in the Scandinavian regions, which grew barbarian invaders, conquerors and rapists, but not racketeers.

The early history of the Nazi movement, when Hitler and his first few followers were busted bums, is replete with racketeering in its every element.

The point of all this is that, while our native stock developed rustlers and robbers, desperados, murderers and claim-jumpers, racketeering has been the contribution of our immigrant hordes.

These came here, lived like animals in poverty and inferiority, mostly in squalid slums. Inter-racial hostility was intense in those crowded tenement and shanty sectors. And out of the oppressed, which gave us some of our finest and most useful citizens, came also bullies and crooks, ward-heelers and sluggers. For entire generations these stronger and bolder newcomers used the forces they had found in their sly brains and their cruel muscles without realizing the potentialities of power in a free country. They became the gas-house hoodlums and in time roved in packs, which gave them mass power. The native politicians saw what that meant toward throwing elections.

After toughs had broken a few heads and discovered that they had helped to make big men, they began to demand a share, or other adequate reward. The marriage of violence and politics soon became organized. But elections are far between and the gangsters began to turn to other game.

Withal, racketeering as an end in itself, as a profession which swung presidencies, which made countless millionaires and created fifty times as many murderers, came with the descent on our earth of that weird angel from heaven whose name was Prohibition.

The father of big racketeering was the same Big Jim Colosimo whose story runs like a thread of crimson and black through the tale of Chicago during the last fifty years. Colosimo, a swarthy Sicilian dock-walloper, got in a little trouble in Palermo and fled in steerage to Baltimore. He got a job on the B & O Railroad, laying ties, and was sent to Chicago. He liked it there. He became a ditch-digger, settled in the early Italian First Ward section around Harrison and Wells Streets. He was husky, handsome, cunning, literate, temperate and ambitious.

Whatever his ultimate aims, his immediate rise to comparative affluence came with his marriage to Victoria Morosco, the proprietor and madame of four wooden brothels on Armour Avenue, designated with the flattering over-all nomenclature of "Bedbug Row." There were two $1 houses and two $2 houses.

The bridegroom immediately recognized that a man willing to spend $2 wants twice as much or twice as good as one who ventures only $1, and besides, the $2 girls were not as busy as the $1 girls. Back of Bedbug Row was an unpaved alley. All the houses had rear doors. So Colosimo made the girls interchangeable, shooting the $1 girls into the $2 houses when the demand was brisk and the $2 girls into the $1 houses—a bargain—when there was a waiting line in the $1 houses.

Such a man was bound to rise in a land of opportunity.

In the four houses were usually about forty women. Each woman had a pimp, and with the servants and the Colosimos, that ran up to fifty votes. It was not then a populous precinct and fifty votes gave a man some standing and a voice in the control of the precinct. Hinky Dink and Bathhouse John, the lords of the ward, began to take notice of this upcoming American and he was soon a precinct captain. That was as high as you could go in the First for years to come. But with his new status he saw room for expansion. Saloon-keepers and gamblers and purveyors of prostitution in his fief and on his borders were urgently advised that they had better "see" Jim Colosimo. Those who didn't, woke up in alleys, if they woke up at all. While the two aldermen exercised a general sovereignty over the badlands, each satrap had some latitude in the poorer precincts. Jim did so well that he soon was collecting not only for Jim, but he was so efficient that the two bosses gave him other territory, mostly hard cases, as their official graft-gatherer.

Colosimo opened a gaudy cabaret-café on Wabash Avenue near 22nd Street, where eventually he was assassinated almost thirty years ago, and on which the sign still reads "Colosimo's." There he held court and did business and there he swaggered and was a good host. And there he brought Johnny Torrio. And there Torrio brought a hoodlum, on the hideout from Brooklyn, whose name was given as Al Brown, but who became Alfonse Capone.

By that time, though Hinky Dink and Bathhouse John were still the political heads, and were allowed a certain cut of the swag, Colosimo had taken away from them their goldmine, their underworld. This was due to his perspicacity when he, who had fattened so in Democratic life that he had even sold Bedbug Row as no longer worthy of his stewardship, switched in a tight election to a big ex-cowpuncher named William Hale Thompson, a Republican running for mayor.

That was shrewd, daring double-crossing, and it upset the old balance of the First Ward dual dictatorship. But the miracle came to Colosimo with the passing of the Eighteenth Amendment and the Volstead Act.

When that disaster struck, Colosimo was ready to turn it into a phase of our civilization which created a unique era of money, murders, ways of life and eternal history. He conceived and executed organized bootlegging of liquor and beer, with all that followed it through thirteen years of social anarchy, a hundred million people on a mad jag with a handful devouring the dividends of what was perhaps our Number One industry.

But Colosimo's major element of power has not yet been mentioned here. After years during which the Mafia (Black

Hand) flourished in Chicago in Little Italy, on the North Side, fourteen official city chiefs of it had their heads blown off with sawed-off shotguns by their own rivals. Then Big Jim moved in and it was the second men, with ideas of displacing him, who got it—and with machine-guns. The "Unione Siciliano," with its crews of killers working for Colosimo, stopped all court revolutions.

Most of the gangs were run by Irishmen, though there were Jewish, Polish, Bohemian and Hungarian outfits. For a time the Mafia gang worked as it did in Sicily for a thousand years, defying kings and Mussolini, where even today a bandit chief is holding off the entire Italian government. It levied tribute from Italians in Chicago, ranging from a fruit-stand peddler, who paid twenty cents a day, to Caruso, who was blackjacked for 10 per cent of everything he earned. Colosimo got the gunhand over his own people in Chicago. Then, a penetrating and expanding soul, he became convinced that Prohibition was in the bag and he quadrupled his force of "persuaders."

We will not here go into the oft-told tale of the gang slayings for supply and territory. But in Chicago the first shots were fired; and on the orders of Colosimo. Among three ace torpedoes he and his successors enlisted in his grandiose and gory undertaking was Frank Yale (Uale) also from Brooklyn, who was murdering for Colosimo when Capone was still opening the door of his car. It was Yale who planned the killing of Dion O'Banion, who had set himself up as the North Side boss, and who started the heavy slaughter when Capone attempted to bring under his thumb O'Banion's gang and the West Side mob, both mostly Irish.

O'Banion's execution was carried out by two Sicilian torpedoes, John Scalise and Albert Anselmi. While in jail on suspicion of the killing, they plotted to rub out Capone himself and take over the mob, but unfortunately confided in Machine Gun Jack McGurn in an attempt to win his support.

McGurn ratted to Al. Upon their release from the clink, which was foreordained in Chicago where the authorities never like to inconvenience hot-shot gangsters, Capone threw them the orthodox "coming-out party."

All guns were checked at the door. After the usual toasts, Al got up and made his speech.

"I want to show you how much I appreciate loyalty," he said, and called the two guests-of-honor to his side for their rewards. Then, while McGurn and other aides held them, Capone beat them both to death with baseball bats. Their mangled bodies were left by a lonely roadside in the country.

Colosimo did not quite make it. But Capone did, except that he allowed a little business to be done by others, after many gaudy funerals and a "peace" conclave in the Hotel Sherman, which was reported in the newspapers, and a frank statement issued on territorial divisions within the city. Yale, believed to have carried out Colosimo's demise, had found tougher men than he was and had returned to Brooklyn, where he, in due course, was murdered. Johnny Torrio, a relative of Colosimo's first wife, who had immediately succeeded Big Jim, was forced to the curb and part of his jaw was shot away. He was taken to St. Luke's Hospital, where another attempt to kill him was made in his room on a high-up floor. That was enough for Torrio for the time being, and he fled down the fire escape with bare feet and in his pajamas, and was next heard from back in Italy. That was when Capone, the most savage of them all, seized the Unione Siciliano, the whiskey industry, the underworld, and in time, all Chicago. All during the 1920's Capone battled Irish and Jewish mobs and they fought back. Like nations exhausted after warfare, they occasionally called armistices and drew up treaties. But the Italians stuck together with a racial bond, whereas Irish fought Irish and Jews fought Jews, gradually eliminating each other as the Mafia grew stronger and more solid and more re-enforced. There is no question that many gangsters of other origins were sentenced to death mainly because they were of other blood-strains.

As of today, the Mafia and the Chicago and nation-wide underworld Syndicate are one and the same.

On the surface the Unione Siciliano is a social brotherhood which brings together all those who have taken a solemn secret oath in a membership denied to those of other consanguinity. The Mafia leader is not necessarily the active king of the underworld, any more than the men who rule steel, oil, finance, etc., are presidents of their corporations. But he is the man with the last word. It is believed that Capone insisted on being the active one-man head of everything and that he ruled New York through his agent, young Charlie "Lucky" Luciano, a heartless assassin, whose prime minister was Frank Costello, a brilliant organizer, political contact man and business executive.

The story of how Capone operated has been the subject of many specialized books. President Herbert Hoover ordered his dominance destroyed. There is a story, though apocryphal, that Hoover came into a hotel and noticed that a stranger was getting more attention than he was. He turned to his secretary, Larry Ritchey (Ricci), who had been a Chicago Secret Service agent and knew the shady characters there, and asked who that man was. When he heard it was Capone, he is said to have uttered two words to Ritchey, "Get him!" He perhaps, with all his world affairs, tribulations and crises, never spoke two more momentous monosyllables.

The Intelligence Unit of the U. S. Treasury caught up with Capone when he was at his historic heights, with a personal income estimated by Government auditors at more than $2,000,000 a week. There was much prattle about the backbone of the underworld being broken when Capone was convicted and eventually sent to Alcatraz, though he had put over a deal with the prosecution for a nominal penalty. The Syndicate, without Capone's forcefulness and genius, kept going places after he was put away, because now a lot of trained brains which Capone had kept enslaved began to fulminate.

Though Capone had eliminated all important rivals in Chicago by rubbing them out or making them join with him in tributary capacities, there still remains an occasional oldster of the Irish and Jewish survivors in the now all-Italian-dominated Syndicate. Some were kept because they were specialists at handling vice and crime peculiar to their people; some were irreplaceable experts in particular lines. But the Mafia, which controls everything in Chicago and its environs, infiltrated—mostly with other Italians—into the big money in other cities.

New York was a fertile field, the world's richest, and it was there for the taking.

The three chief operators in New York at the time were Owen "Owney the Killer" Madden, boss of the Irish mobsters, who controlled the West Side; Arthur "Dutch Schultz" Flegenheimer, who controlled Harlem and the Bronx; and Irving Wexler ("Waxey Gordon") who was the boss of Brooklyn, the East Side and the New Jersey suburbs. The latter two were Jewish.

Italians, however, were becoming more and more influential in Gordon's mob. Both Gordon and Schultz used Italians as torpedoes. Madden was sickly and fighting a losing battle.

Some time around 1928, a mysterious and shadowy character began to commute regularly between Chicago and Brooklyn, where he had lived since his arrival from Italy. He carried with him instructions which were to change the entire picture of America's underworld, and eventually of the crime setup of the whole world.

This man was a 210-pound, 6-foot-3 giant, who at that time was 35 years old. His real name was Gaetano Ricci, alias "Bobo," alias Anthony Goebels. We shall call him Goebels.

It was slightly embarrassing to him just at that time to get into a brush with the Chicago police. It was the only time, before or since, that he was mugged. On April 5, 1928, Goebels appeared in the Chicago Municipal Court on a charge of carrying concealed weapons. He had been arrested along with Louis ("Little New York") Campagna on State Street by Bill Drury, a colorful cop about whom more later. When these individuals were searched it was found that Campagna was armed with a .45 and Goebels with a .38. The court, in typical Chicago fashion, held that the arrests were illegal because the policeman had no warrant to search the prisoners' persons. The defendants were discharged, though the weapons in the case were confiscated by the court. As far back as 1928, Campagna was considered one of the more important members of the Capone Syndicate.

But no one seemed to know who Tony Goebels was. Even today he is a man of mystery, without other police record.

However, the picture was developing. Tony was the go-between who arranged for the take-over of New York by the Capone Syndicate and the Mafia. You will be reading more about him in these pages.

Goebels continued to make many trips back and forth between New York and Chicago. The long-distance wires were constantly open between his residence in Brooklyn and the headquarters of the Syndicate in Chicago.

The Unione Siciliano in New York, which was loosely connected with its opposite number in Chicago, through the world-wide setup of the Mafia, continued to grow stronger, but not anything like its more vigorous brother in the Windy City.

The first Eastern boss was Ignazio ("Lupo the Wolf") Saietta, a relative by marriage to Ciro Terranova, infamous as the "Artichoke King."

The Mafia was a pretty loose organization in New York. No one had ever become as dominant as the leaders in Chicago. Sometimes there were a half-dozen local chiefs, until Boss Masseria took charge in the 1920's. As in Chicago, the Unione was the social front for the underworld and quite often not all its members were gangsters. Sometimes prominent Italians, especially politicians and others in the public eye, joined as one might join the Masons or Elks, for business reasons or votes. Sometimes even a non-Italian who did work for the mob, such as a lawyer, found himself a member of the Unione.

Before 1928, however, the Italian mob leaders were still sitting at the second table. It is true they were greatly feared because of their ruthlessness. As Craig Thompson and Allen Raymond said in their revealing book, *Gang Rule in New York,* "Even for mobsters they were bad and everybody feared them. They kill calmly today as a matter of business and they will bear watching tomorrow." This book was written in 1940.

The Unione Siciliano was closely tied up with the East Side mob of Waxey Gordon, in which Lepke and Gurrah, later to form Murder, Inc., were important characters. Waxey's boys were the most brutal of murderers in the ranks of New York's Big Three.

When Tony Goebels returned from Chicago in 1928, he

brought with him the word that the Italians were going to annex New York. It took the Italian boys a good half-dozen years to gobble up the world's richest city, and by the time they were successful Prohibition had been repealed and it became necessary to find a new source of illicit income.

During all that time, the fight to dominate New York was directed from Chicago, first by Al Capone, then by his lieutenants when he was sent to Fort Leavenworth, before transfer to The Rock. It was accomplished by brilliant generalship.

Tony Goebels, commuting constantly between New York and Chicago, was the central clearing-house, and through him all the orders were delivered. Though the boys were confident they were above the law, they often trusted neither the telephone nor the mails.

The object was attained through many media. Violence was used only when necessary. The leaders of the Big Three New York mobs were all disposed of, each by different means.

In the beginning, the Chicago chiefs went after Waxey Gordon, who was the boss of the outfit in New York in which they were strongest, and which they aimed to absorb as their nucleus. This was consummated through adroit scheming. Gordon was betrayed so the law was able to get on his trail and convict him. Young Tom Dewey, then assistant United States Attorney in New York, sent Gordon up. This was the first time a major gangster had been convicted on anything other than income tax charges. It made Dewey a local hero and was the first step toward his becoming governor and twice a presidential candidate.

When Waxey was convicted and sent to prison his boys, especially Lucky Luciano, who was his chief aide, assured him everything would be held for him until he got out. But the day he went away the Mafia walked in. When Gordon was finally released from jail, he was penniless, and he remains so till this day, thwarted by the law at every turn.

Another tack was used to eliminate Owney Madden. Madden had long been out of jail on parole from a sentence for an old murder. The boys had his parole revoked and he went back to Sing Sing.

When Owney—a little demon known to "level" with his

kind, who was well-liked by most in the underworld and many honest people with whom he mingled socially—came out of the Big House, the top mobsters called a huddle with him and advised him to retire. His health had been further impaired in the penitentiary. He sold out, moved to Hot Springs, Arkansas, where he married the postmaster's daughter, and is now a prominent citizen in that playground of hoodlums. He was hiding Luciano there until Dewey got Lucky.

The Mafia leaders were charitable. They arranged for Madden to have a steady income from New York, and he is still reputed to be half-owner of a lucrative New York luxury restaurant. He remains a respected elder statesman of the underworld and often the big shots from Chicago run down to see him in Hot Springs and ask his advice. His is a case of personality. We know him well and can't help liking him.

"Dutch" Schultz was a tougher nut to crack. He led a charmed life. It seemed he was armored against the law, as he long was to rival gangsters' bullets. But finally the Chicago boys put him on the spot, dining with two henchmen he thought were his friends in a Newark restaurant.

Though the Italians had now eliminated their three chief rivals in New York, they found other important Jewish gangsters arising to take their place. Among these were the aforementioned notorious Lepke and Gurrah, who had slanted the activities of the underworld to the profitable protection and union racketeering businesses after Prohibition. While professing undying friendship and affection for Lepke and Gurrah and other members of Murder, Inc., the Italians managed to get them out of the way again by allowing them to fall into the hands of the law. Bill O'Dwyer's prosecution of them helped make him Mayor of New York. After that there was only one mob in the United States—and that was the Syndicate, united, supreme.

After Capone was nailed in Chicago, the affairs of the Syndicate were handled by other top members of the Mafia. For a time it was believed Al would be out quickly. It was said they couldn't keep $100,000,000 in Alcatraz. But they did.

Capone's No. 2 man was Frank Nitti, whose title, "The Enforcer," struck terror into the hearts of Chicago hoods. He was the boy who executed the gang chief's orders—and the gang chief's enemies. As Capone went away, Nitti took charge of his affairs and the bank-roll.

Frank began to like the spot for himself. Through devious methods known only to the underworld, Nitti pulled the proper strings to see to it that even if Al had a chance for parole he must serve his full term. Political pressure was obvious.

After Scarface's release, when he emerged a sick and broken man, Nitti used his local drag to send Al up again to the Cook County jail for a one-year term which was still hanging over him.

During the years of the regency, while the king was away, Nitti was the No. 1 front man, though the Unione Siciliano directed his efforts. Most of the rivals had been eliminated by the early 1930's, but the Mafia boys occasionally had trouble with non-Italian gangs that operated on the far West Side or in Cook County territory. Parts of the county were still strongholds of the remnants of the Irish combination, and Bohemians, important in county political affairs, wanted some of the racket take.

Chicago's Czech Mayor, Anton Cermak, a powerful County Democratic leader, sent word to the Mafia that their power was to be curtailed. The police were ordered to get rough with Nitti and his associates.

A detective, acting under orders, shot Nitti in the neck, a wound from which he recovered. The underworld vowed vengeance against Cermak.

Tony Cermak went to his grave believing that Giuseppi Zangara had fatally wounded him by mistake on February 15, 1933, in Miami. Cermak and the nation at large thought the anarchist was firing at President Roosevelt. But to this day, underworld grapevine insists Zangara had been hired to get rid of Chicago's militant mayor, who stuck his neck out and told off the Mafia, and the assassination was planned to look like an attempt on the President's life, to camouflage the crime Syndicate's plot.

No one will ever know the full truth about it all, but we do know this: the underworld had made up its mind to get Mayor Cermak. Had he escaped Zangara's bullets, another triggerman would have gotten him. In fact, a futile attempt had been made to plant a bomb at the Chicago World's Fair, on an occasion when he was speaking there—reminiscent of the assassination of an earlier mayor, Carter H. Harrison, Sr., at the Columbian Exposition forty years before.

Nitti now gambled that the crime crusade would blow up with the death of Cermak. His theory was correct. From 1933 to 1943, when the Federal Government stepped in and smashed the Syndicate's movie extortion plot, leading to the suicide of Nitti, Chicago gangland had its greatest period of prosperity and immunity from arrest.

Even that crusade against the extortioners probably would not have been undertaken by Uncle Sam had not the gangsters overextended themselves by levying tribute against the billion-dollar movie industry.

One of the top bosses at that time was "Little New York" Campagna. Paul "The Waiter" Ricca, not to be confused with Tony Ricci, was said to have become local head of the Mafia.

Capone had four brothers—Mimi, Ralph, John, and Matt. None proved to have the leadership proclivities of the peerless Al, but Ralph and Mimi rose high in the councils of the mob. After it became obvious that Al, wasting away with a disease, would never return, there was furious jockeying for power and position. Some killings punctuated the situation, all internecine because all non-Italian opposition had been wiped out, forced to retire, or absorbed.

During this time there was also bloodshed between two factions of the Italian mob fighting for the dictatorship. One was dominated by a younger group of American-born Italians. The other was led by immigrants, many of whom either talked no English or had trouble speaking it. With this group, however, were a few American-born Italians, natural allies because they had been born and brought up in Italian-speaking districts of Brooklyn, Manhattan and Chicago, and thought along old-country lines. The Italian-speaking group won out. Chicago's underworld—as well as the underworlds of all cities in the United States—is now dominated by mobsters with a direct tie to the old country.

Presently to become dominant in the Chicago picture were

the notorious Fischetti brothers, cousins of the Capones, also from Brooklyn. There are three—Charles, the oldest, who is the boss; Rocco, the "vice president," and Joe, a younger brother without a criminal record, who is the apple of his older brothers' eyes, a spoiled young man who is glamor-struck and associates with stage stars and screen beauties.

The present day setup of the National Crime Syndicate and how it operates in Chicago will be described in the next chapter. That is, if we live to write it.

23. THE CRIME CARTEL

CHICAGO'S underworld Syndicate cannot be understood, let alone believed, without a broader view of the nation-wide and world-wide organization of which it is a part. That is the Mafia, the Unione Siciliano, the super-government which now has tentacles reaching into the Cabinet and the White House itself, almost every state capital, huge Wall Street interests, and connections in Canada, Latin America, England, France, Italy, Turkey, Greece, China and Outer Mongolia, and even through the Iron Curtain into Soviet Russia.

Repeatedly, crime investigations, interstate violations and tax, immigration and dope dealings have been established with sufficient proof to convict by the hundreds. In every instance since Mayor O'Dwyer, as Kings County District Attorney, convicted the heads of Murder, Inc., the New York-Brooklyn commercial murderers, and Governor Dewey, then New York D. A., convicted Luciano and Jimmy Hines, every investigation that reaches figures of consequence in the Syndicate has been called off and stymied, including findings of the F.B.I., except as to the big movie extortioners, all of whom got preferential privileges.

When the guns stopped belching, when Prohibition ended and the older and wiser case-hardened mob leaders decided to affiliate instead of assassinate, they had to come to the Unione Siciliano. That society had long before perfected an organization, was rich, had established its political forces first with men of their race, whom they had elected or appointed wherever they could, and then through them with officials whom they could influence and also through Italians who had become political and official powers. One instance under oath in New York established that Frank Costello had hand-made Magistrate Thomas Aurelio a high judge. Italian mayors were elected in many of the principal cities, which also sent Italians to Congress. Almost every one of these was in heavy debt to the organized underworld, by its deliberate design.

Already rich from rum-running, these rapacious adventurers set about calmly and ruthlessly to take over every form of illegitimate enterprise. To catalogue what they own and who protects them, as a result not of human gratitude, but of definite pre-arranged pledges and reciprocal rewards, would take more type than appears in this book.

Their most profitable single source of income now is the monopoly on manufacture and distribution of narcotics. This is more lucrative than illicit liquor ever was, because dope is comparatively easy to handle, requires no such tremendous man power as was engaged in running breweries, merchandising bulky booze in bottles and cases, chartering and owning ocean-going ships, financing speakeasies and fixing hordes of federal, state, county and city officials, and police, and burying their dead.

There is no competition to break prices and the final pushers work on commissions, earning only out of what is already in hand.

Though the American Syndicate is run from above, with reigning headquarters in Italy and American headquarters in New York, Chicago is the point of top importance because there the Mafia has effected its highest degree of immunity after a half century of the machinations of Colosimo, Capone and the men they raised to carry on their work.

But above them, as the cartel expanded, there grew an executive setup, like that of any great commercial corporation, of men who will be named here, who are not necessarily principal stockholders or by any means majority owners.

Even above Luciano, who is the international chief of the Syndicate and of the Unione Siciliano; above the Costellos and the Fischettis, is the board of directors of the Mafia, the Grand Council. They are the supreme arbiters of the works. With the exception of Paul Ricca, of Chicago, all these councillors are unknown to the public and few law-enforcement officers, including many who carry out their every order, have ever heard their names. This is the first time they have ever been printed:

The chairman of the board or Grand Councillor, as he is called, is Vincent Mangano, alias James Costa of Brooklyn.

Other councillors are Philip Mangano, Joseph Profaci, and Vincenzo Traina, all of Brooklyn; Paul "The Waiter," Ricca of Chicago; Stefano Margardino of Niagara Falls, New York; Albert "Big Al" Polizzi of Cleveland; and Frank Milano of Akron, Ohio. Meetings of the Grand Council are held in Cleveland.

The intermediary who delivers orders back and forth between the secret Grand Council and such executives as Costello, Fischetti, et al, is that other unsung, unpublicized and generally unheard-of character whom we had occasion to mention briefly in the preceding chapter. His name is Gaetano Ricci, but he is known to the underworld as Tony Ricci or Tony Goebels.

He lives in Brooklyn, but from his apartment at 125 Ocean Parkway he transmits orders to the huge and sprawling Chicago underworld. No decision of any importance is taken without contacting Goebels, who is known in underworld worship as "The King."

The authors of this book have a list of phone calls made by Goebels. They prove conclusively that before any important step of any kind is taken he is contacted for orders, and he in turn contacts others. The records show that during the period when wires were being pulled to effect the release of the convicted movie extortionists from the Federal penitentiary, Goebels was constantly on the long-distance phone to Chicago.

During the time of the parole scandal in 1947, Goebels was in communication with members of the Campagna family (Campagna is one of the prisoners), including Frank Koch, 2927 Maple Avenue, Berwyn, Illinois, son-in-law of Louis and Charlotte Campagna.

In that year he was also in contact with Owney Madden, mentioned above.

From time to time, Goebels and a woman registered in Chicago hotels as "Mr. and Mrs. Ricci, 125 Ocean Parkway, Brooklyn." At those times he was in conference with the Fischettis in their luxurious triplex penthouse at 3100 Sheridan Road, and with Jake Guzik in a midtown hotel suite. He also had conferences at the Owl Club, a gambling joint believed to be owned by Tony Accardo, in Calumet City. He further was in touch with Francis Curry, a bookmaker and slot-machine operator of Joliet, and for a long time was one of the most important contacts for Paul DeLucia, who is known as Paul "The Waiter" Ricca. He has been in constant touch with Pete and Ollie Arnstein, 19 E. Ohio Street, previously mentioned as the ringleaders of organized vice on the near North Side.

Goebels also was observed visiting the home of "Enforcer" Frank Nitti shortly before the day Nitti committed suicide.

There was another flurry of activity on his phone with calls to Chicago and Las Vegas, before the murder of Bugsy Siegel, in Beverly Hills, California, in 1947.

Goebels also continually phones a captain of the Chicago police force, calling him on a private and unlisted phone number in a Loop hotel. This captain, who is the real political boss of the police department, has long been suspected of being an integral member of the Syndicate.

This is the same Goebels described in a preceding chapter, who, during the years between 1928 and 1932, ran back and forth between Chicago and New York with orders from Capone to take over New York for the Italians.

Chicagoans, who have a fierce local pride, even like to think of their gangsters as the most important in the country. So it will come as a shock to learn that their powerful Fischetti and Capone brothers receive their orders through a man in Brooklyn. As a sop to local pride, however, Chicagoans may be assured that this was decreed by their famous mobster, Al Capone, when he still meant something.

Who is this man who transmits their orders to the kings of Chicago's crime? Also known as "Bobo," he was born in Ciesta, Italy, on January 1, 1893. He is about six-feet-three and weighs 210 pounds. He was once married to a woman whose first name was Florence and they had three children.

In 1934 Goebels filed a petition for citizenship which was withdrawn in 1940 because of some question about his cohabitation with a Brooklyn woman, not his wife. She was the widow of a wealthy manufacturer and presumably had a considerable amount of money. Goebels' petition for citizenship was renewed in the latter part of 1940, and he was naturalized November 20, 1944. At that time he gave his address as 296 Adelphi Street, Brooklyn. The association of Goebels and this woman goes back as far as 1934. During that period, the robbery of the Rubel Ice Company took place. It was one of New York's most notorious crimes. An automobile used in the robbery was owned by her, but had been reported stolen a few hours previously.

Neither Goebels nor his girl friend was implicated in the robbery, though it is now common knowledge in the underworld that their car was purposely stolen by the robbers to "finger" Goebels and get him out of the way before he was able to complete his absorption of New York for the Italian mob.

In his early days, Goebels was connected with what was known as the Division Street gang, and was then an associate of Joseph Dato ("Joe Adonis"), head of the Italian lottery in Brooklyn, an intimate lieutenant of Frank Costello.

One example of how Goebels makes the Chicago underworld tick will be given here:

Dominick "Libby" Nuccio was the leader of the North Side Syndicate gang. A phone call came from Brooklyn to Paul Ricca, local councillor of the Unione Siciliano. The call was from Goebels, who ordered that Nuccio be deposed and one Tony Mack, another Sicilian, be given the North Side leadership. In the old days, before the tight organization, this would have meant gunplay. Now it was accomplished like a change in the personnel of a branch office of a chain store.

Ricca told Nuccio he was through, after which Mack, Ralph Pierce, Willie Groves and a man known as Caesar took over the huge wire room at 104 East Walton Street, and Mack opened up his offices in a three-story building in the 800 block on North State Street.

Reverting to the organizational setup of the underworld Syndicate, we find on the one hand a board of directors, representing the far-flung Unione Siciliano in the analagous position of stockholders of the corporation.

This brings us to the executive setup.

It must be borne in mind that the Syndicate must in some ways remain complicated. There is no way of knowing always which are partnership operations and which are individual ones. For instance, A may be the owner of a gambling joint by himself, and in partnership in a neighboring bawdy-house with B. B, himself, may own several enterprises and be in partnership with C and D and E in others. E also could have some holdings all his own.

But in the final showdown, though A and E own nothing in common, they are allies and come to each other's aid if need be, to pull political wires when necessary and provide cash in emergencies.

Some of these enterprises may also be operated by A or B or C for the account of the Syndicate, the real owner. In cases like that, A is a district manager and gets a cut of the receipts for his efforts.

Many boys further down the line who have been useful in one capacity or another, as torpedoes, fixers, or collectors or front men, may be staked out with minor rackets such as neighborhood gambling or whore houses, saloons, gas stations or hat check concessions, which they then own themselves, but at all times are members of the Syndicate and can call on it for assistance.

Thus, though the Syndicate is set up loosely, it is ruled with stern precision and anyone who gets too far out of line is quickly disposed of, as was Siegel.

In many ways the Syndicate reminds one of a giant international trust or cartel. It is somewhat like, say, the Standard Oil Company, which is divided into subsidiary companies, such as Standard of New Jersey, Standard of Indiana, of New York, of California, etc., and other operating units like Vacuum Oil, cosmetic companies, pipe lines, railroads and gasoline filling station chains. Many of these Standard affiliates are by now so loosely connected that they compete vigorously against each other.

The key figure in the executive setup is the notorious and infamous panderer, Charles "Lucky" Luciano, deported to Italy on his release from Dannemora, where he had been sent by District Attorney Dewey and pardoned by Governor Dewey. "Lucky" was and is the president of the International Crime Cartel.

The president of the American Crime Corporation is Frank Costello, of New York, who was Lucky's chief aide in the old days and has now inherited that spot, since Lucky's involuntary departure and enforced absence from the operational field.

Costello is not only the president of a company doing business all over the United States, which he conducts for the benefit of the entire Syndicate, but he also is the boss of local territories which are staked out for his own account. In addition to the Eastern seaboard, Costello also runs Louisiana and controls the entire slot-machine industry in the United States.

These enterprises are operated for him by assistants.

For instance, Joe Adonis is the deputy chief in the East for Costello, and also runs numerous gambling layouts. Adonis also personally owns all the gambling in northern New Jersey, and several nightclubs and brothels in Chicago's near North Side.

The vice president of the American corporation and the second most powerful figure in the American underworld is Charles Fischetti, Chicago's prominent citizen. He is nicknamed "Trigger Happy." Fischetti, as national vice president, shares with Costello the conduct of all underworld affairs in the United States and has his fingers in the pie in every city.

In addition to being the vice president of the national company, he, like Costello, also has individual holdings, with subordinates to superintend them. Thus Fischetti is the president of the Illinois subsidiary, which he owns with many partners. He is a part owner in the St. Louis operation, and the sole owner of Kansas City, which, as will be explained later, is gradually making him the top man in the nation's racket picture, possibly even more important than Costello.

Charlie Fischetti, a man in his 50's, is a dude and a snob. He platinas his gray hair to give it a platinum blond effect and wears elevator shoes to make himself taller.

He usually uses the name of "Dr. Fisher," and sometimes "Fish," and gives his occupation as an art collector. Collector is right, but not art. With his two brothers, Rocco and Joe, he lives in Chicago's most luxurious triplex penthouse, atop the building at 3100 North Sheridan Road, which he is reputed to own. This sky-nest was once occupied by mayors Thompson and Cermak, and was regarded as Chicago's executive mansion. Fischetti moved in as the logical successor, for he has more say in Chicago's affairs than does City Hall.

Rocco Fischetti, the middle brother, is nicknamed "Money Bags," because he likes to flash dough. He is one of the top men of the local branch of the Syndicate, but seldom sits in on the affairs of the national organization.

The youngest brother, Joseph Fischetti, nicknamed "Stingy," is the baby of the family, pampered by his two older brothers. He has no criminal record, having reached manhood after the family fortunes and position were already established through Cousin Al Capone's heritage and his brothers' sagacity, energy and artillery.

All three Fischettis are nuts about show-girls and entertain a harem of them in the huge three-story apartment. Chicago is the only city in the country where gangsters are still looked up to. Many Chicago glamor-girls are thrilled to be seen in their company, though there are no records of any Fischetti ever spending liberally on one.

Joe's most recent conquest is Peggy Maley, blonde movie and stage starlet, who forsook the Marquess of Milford-Haven for him.

Rocco Fischetti beat up a former "Miss Chicago" who had been living in his penthouse. He tired of her and when she didn't want to leave, he helped her make up her mind.

Three years ago when they flew from Miami to Havana to attend on Lucky Luciano, hiding out there after his expulsion from the United States, the Fischettis sent down a plane load of Miami call-girls for his and their delectation.

They also transported $2,000,000 of his accumulated dividends, in currency.

The Fischettis always winter in Florida, where they have big gambling interests, and at this writing, are planning to take over hotel gaming in Cuba.

Joe Fischetti has a boat and likes to brag about his deep-sea fishing, but it is noticed that he never comes back from his excursions into the Gulf Stream with a sunburn. Feds believe he is setting up a spot on a lonely Florida or West Indies island, to smuggle Lucky back into the States.

As overlords of the Chicago mob, the Fischettis were and still are extremely important in Hollywood's movie industry. A shocking criminal trial exposed how Chicago extortionists had gotten complete control of this huge industry. However, the sentencing of some of the figureheads of the ring did not by any means end the underworld's hold on Hollywood.

Because of the airtight tie-up between vice and politics there, the Chicago branch of the Syndicate is not only one of the most profitable, but is probably the most powerful.

As has been seen, there has always been an unholy affiliation between crime and politics in Chicago, as far back as 1871.

But that was long on only a local level, between neighborhood gangsters and ward leaders. Quite often, the tie-in reached City Hall, but usually only through the proper district channels. In other words, if you wanted anything fixed you went to your ward or legislative leader, who then approached the mayor, who talked to the police chief. The district leaders were the most powerful figures in the city.

But it remained for the Capone mob, bent on organization on a new scale to take over all Chicago, and later take over the entire state and the entire nation, to break through directly to the top, by-passing the whole succession of intermediaries.

After the first election of Franklin D. Roosevelt, the Kelly-Nash-Arvey machine of Chicago made a deal directly with Washington, *quid pro quo,* which meant "votes for favors."

Capone was sent to the penitentiary and his gang had temporarily dispersed during the administration of Herbert Hoover. From 1933 on, with the exception of the prosecution of the movie extortion ring, which will be explained at some lengths as a special case, there have been few Federal prosecutions of Syndicate gangsters—and in Chicago none.

Of the three major politico-criminal prosecutions conducted by Uncle Whiskers in other parts of the country, one was that of Enoch "Nucky" Johnson of Atlantic City, the Republican leader of his county, at loggerheads with Frank Hague, then Democratic National Committeeman and White House insider.

Another was the crackdown on the Huey Long mob in New Orleans, which came only after the Kingpin's break with the administration when he became ambitious to succeed F.D.R.

The third, that of Boss Pendergast of Kansas City, who was

Truman's political godfather, was conducted by an intransigent, independent and fearless U. S. Attorney, Maurice Milligan, who was fired for having sent the Democratic leader to the penitentiary as the first act of President Harry S. Truman.

The only other major underworld prosecutions of this generation were those against Waxey Gordon, in Federal Court, during a Republican administration; Lucky Luciano and Jimmy Hines, by Republican Tom Dewey, in New York State Courts, and Brooklyn's Murder, Inc., by ambitious Bill O'Dwyer, who was called off before he got too hot, by being promoted upstairs, first as a Brigadier General in the Army, and then Mayor of New York.

The Fischetti penthouse is the nerve-center of the Chicago underworld, where its plots are hatched.

Charles Fischetti came up through the ranks, starting as bodyguard for his cousin, Al Capone. He built up strong political connections, which stood him in good stead when he had brushes with the law for everything from murder to white slavery.

On November 6, 1933, Detectives John Howe and Drury arrested Charlie Fischetti and ten other members of the Syndicate's upper circle in their offices at 1 N. LaSalle Street, on charges of trying to interfere with an election.

They found guns on Fischetti, Murray ("The Camel") Humphries, and William (Three-Fingered Jack) White.

The three were convicted by juries and given one-year prison sentences.

Fischetti later estimated it cost him $50,000 to fight the case through the Illinois Supreme Court, until the gangsters won reversals.

Charlie and his brothers met prosperity around the corner when they got control of all the rich North Shore gambling places. They found Lake County authorities cooperative and, as a result, practically took over Deerfield. Special trains and buses hauled the suckers to the "games of chance."

Police even arranged to set up road-blocks, so that when the signal was flashed that a Fischetti casino had been held up, rival hoodlums could be apprehended while making a getaway.

The brothers, who once dominated the theatrical union, hobnobbed with Hollywood and New York screen, stage and café society satellites. Further proof of Charlie Fischetti's exalted position in the underworld was the fact that it was he, on orders from Tony Goebels, who arranged the surrender of Louis ("Lepke") Buchalter.

Buchalter, most hunted man since the Lindbergh kidnapping, was wanted in New York for eighty murders, while J. Edgar Hoover's F.B.I. wanted him for narcotics and income tax cases. Fischetti promised the fugitive the gang would see he only did a few years if he would give up to Hoover, through the latter's friend, Walter Winchell.

But Fischetti was blowing the wind. He had been promised nothing. Buchalter was executed March 4, 1944, in Sing Sing's electric chair.

This was the Italian Syndicate's way of getting rid of Lepke at the State's expense and without risk. Lepke threatened to the last hour to "blow the roof off," but died mum.

The sumptuous Fischetti penthouse is the scene of frequent gatherings of underworld leaders from all over the country. Many times important politicians are also entertained there.

Under Charles Fischetti, the national vice president, and also the executive in complete control of the Midwest Syndicate, there is a staff of important managers, each in control of various phases of crime and vice in Chicago and surrounding territories.

Each of the four Capone brothers has been staked out with juicy subdivisions. Paul Ricca, the Unione Siciliano councillor, also has a big chunk of the gravy train.

Two of the principal Fischetti lieutenants are not Italians, though they are now working members of the Unione Siciliano. They are Jack Guzik, a Polish Jew, and Murray Humphries, an Irishman. Guzik is a brother of Harry Guzik, who joined the Capone mob instead of fighting it and became the paymaster for the outfit. Humphries came into the Syndicate in much the same fashion. It was a question of killing him or buying him off, and the boys figured that more of their own lives would be spared if they made a peaceful deal.

Guzik is vice president in charge of prostitution and dope. Humphries is the boss of gambling.

Guzik's interest in prostitution came naturally, as his brother, Harry, was famous as a dive-operator in the old Levee, and Jack Guzik worked up under him. Lait knew Harry well when he ran his cesspool on 21st Street. His place was usually Lait's last port of call on his beat when he was doing night police in that district of untrammeled vice, crime and debauchery. He signed his name "Cusick" then. Lait wrote many stories about him and that spelling was never disputed. His since-notorious brother, Jack, was then his waiter.

Harry, the direct cause of the inception and passage of the Mann Act, was chosen to be the first man to be arrested under the new law. Assigned to the case were Bill Dannenberg, local agent in charge of the old F.B.I. and Secret Service agents Pete Dratzberg (later a famous private detective) and Larry Ricci, later the secretary to President Hoover.

But the historic anecdote that came out of Harry's whorehouse gave a fantastic origin to the term "white slave" as it became and is now applied.

A girl named Mona Marshall, one of Harry's inmates, who roomed upstairs, got doped up one night, and, morose and melodramatic, wrote a note on which she stated, "I am a white slave."

She signed her name. She attached the paper to her room key and threw it out of the window, to the street, one floor below.

She was no slave in truth. She spent half her days and nights on the street level, with open doors. She strolled and solicited on the sidewalk in hot weather, though that was forbidden even then. She had a night off every week and went out.

But an honest milkman came along in the gray dusk just before sunrise. He saw the note, picked it and the key up, and read the lurid lament. He galloped to the 22nd Street police station with it. Some men were sent back with him. Mona, to her immense surprise, and Harry, to his intense indignation, were hauled into custody.

The Assistant State's Attorney at the police court for the area was an earnest young man named Clifford Roe. He took the thing seriously, let loose an oration against sin, the whole nefarious district and connivance of the city authorities in it all. Though Mona, in a confused manner, mumbled that she didn't remember writing the note, Roe insisted she had sounded a great truth.

"This empire of vice does enslave weaklings like her," he cried. "The doors may be open to them, but the decent world is closed against them. They may not be enslaved by bars and whips, but they are bound by the fetters of a colossal system of money, political power, corruption of the law and desecration of divine commands. This unfortunate girl did not know how true were her words, but her subconscious soul did as it dictated them!"

This and a lot more, Roe declaimed.

Of course, he was a county Republican haranguing against city Democratic rule. And he didn't get very far. But—

His flaming oratory was published. Ministers, women's clubs, reform societies took up his charges. The practitioners against the proscribed profession raised a standard and Roe carried it. Such a commotion did he stir up that he was deluged with invitations to address congregations and civic organizations. He soon resigned his office and made a career of lecturing on the topic with which he had become identified.

(This had happened before Mann introduced the law for which he is still remembered, and that was often referred to as the "White Slave Act.")

Mona returned to her serfdom, despite all the furor. Harry returned to his dirty traffic and bore her no grudge.

All this was in the reign of "Big Jim" Colosimo, long before he engaged Johnny Torrio, who brought on Al Capone. Jim was boss of the badlands. He was in the same trade as Harry's, among his many interests. Harry didn't behave like a thug. He was as mild-mannered, genial and easygoing as any black-hearted dealer in his unspeakable racket. He would never be picked as "most likely to succeed" under so ruthless an outlaw as Capone—for one thing, he was too fat!

Charlie Fischetti, like his confrere in New York, Frank Costello, is thin-skinned to publicity. He does not like to be called a gangster. He prefers to think of himself as a man of the world and as a dilettante art connoisseur.

In the old days, gangsters weren't touchy. You could print

anything you wanted to about Colosimo or Capone. They considered it a hazard of the business. Many of their kind loved it, were as vain about their "notices" as are actors.

On the other hand, the Fischettis go to great extremes to deflect unfavorable publicity from themselves. It is generally agreed in Chicago that all unfavorable mentions should describe the underworld as the Guzik-Ricca-Capone Syndicate, without mentioning the Fischettis at all. The Fischettis fraternize with some newspapermen in an effort to convince them they are sadly misunderstood citizens. They say they have "paid their debt to society" for their youthful slips, and are now respectable businessmen. These bleeding hearts have actually convinced the more susceptible reporters and editors. Only infrequently do you see their names linked to sinister subjects. Meanwhile, Guzik and Humphries are the whipping boys. They are from the old school and don't mind much, as it makes them big shots in the only circle where they would be welcome.

As these reporters briefly explained in their previous book *New York Confidential,* when the gangland wars were over, the Syndicate went into honest businesses on a big scale. They have untold wealth. So much that its very existence became perilous to them. The loot from rum-running, prostitution, narcotics, gambling and other forms of crime almost was valueless when hidden in safe-deposit vaults. They could not spend such money in quantity because it would attract the attention of Internal Revenue Agents and make them liable for income tax violations, civilly and criminally. They did not declare these huge sums. Being thieves at heart, they could not find it within themselves to make a fair income tax return. They were advised by astute attorneys whom they employed by the year, at princely fees, that if they did make declarations about their illegal businesses they might be turned over to certain law enforcement bureaus.

It is a popular misconception that information contained in income tax returns is sacred and cannot be referred to any other government agency. The popular belief is that if you fairly and truly tell where you got the money and then give Uncle Sam his cut, the government will keep your confidence. This is not completely true.

Internal Revenue usually will not give the information to

state authorities or to other departments of the government. But if it finds any violation of Treasury laws of any kind, that will be transferred to the coordinating officer, who will then route it to the proper investigative agency. And, inasmuch as the Treasury enforces the Narcotics Act, through violation of which a major portion of the underworld bankroll is made, it is easy to see why the boys can't turn in honest reports of dishonest profits.

The Syndicate also goes in in a big way for smuggling and counterfeiting, which also come under the Treasury, and is deep in dealings with alcoholic beverages, both bootleg and legal, and the enforcement agency there is the Alcoholic Tax Unit, another branch of the Treasury. The A.T.U. also enforces the Federal Small Arms Act covering Tommy guns and sawed-off shotguns, tools of the gangster's trade.

Gangland's overlords hired the most expensive legal and accounting advice. They were told that the only way they might get any use out of their money was surreptitiously to invest it in legal enterprises and that then, after a while, they could enjoy the spending of the legal dividends which these investments paid. Thereupon the underworld began to make tremendous investments in a variety of legitimate undertakings. Some were made directly by Costello and the Fischettis in their own names. Others were made for their accounts.

By far the greatest part of the gangsters' holdings in legitimate business are made through highly regarded investment houses, trust companies, real estate agencies and hotel management companies. It is more than possible that many of these agents do not exactly know in whose account they are buying property. A bank does not turn down a stranger who comes in with a million dollars in cash and asks the bank to invest it for him.

When the Syndicate selects these agents, it sends go-betweens, possibly ten times removed from the main source. By setting up a maze of holding companies and interlocking directorates and private corporations—as many as a thousand—it is almost impossible to trace to its source ownership of any property in which they are interested.

The Intelligence Unit of the Treasury Department, which

is the hush-hush super-police agency assigned to break cases which are beyond the capabilities of other government cops, is well aware of the magnitude of the investments of the underworld. Getting enough evidence to prove it beyond a reasonable doubt to a jury of twelve men is another thing. It took the Intelligence Unit years to unravel Al Capone's complicated structure before sending him up, and that was simple compared to today's labyrinthian task. Capone was a local boss. The Syndicate is world-wide.

The Syndicate owns a controlling interest in three of the most important hotel chains in the country. It owns two of the largest clothing chains in the nation. It is interested in a department store group. It owns hundreds of blocks of prime real estate in major cities, including skyscrapers on Wall Street and 5th Avenue in New York, valuable frontage on Michigan Boulevard, State Street and Lake Shore Drive in Chicago, and some of the cream of Los Angeles and Beverly Hills property.

Listed under individual ownership but all belonging to the mob are fifty residential hotels in Chicago's North Side. The world Syndicate owns a trans-Atlantic steamship line of foreign registry and is busily engaged building hotels and guest-houses throughout Latin America, some already opened. It has great holdings of movie stock and owns many film theatres.

In many cities, the laundry business is controlled by the Syndicate. One of its most prolific operations is automobile dealer franchises, in many key cities. It owns chains of gasoline stations, restaurants, taxi companies, bus lines, and has broken into the railroad business. The Syndicate has bundles of stock in the Hudson and Manhattan Tubes which connect New York and New Jersey and owns the valuable twin Hudson Terminal Buildings in New York's financial district.

Along the line, the Syndicate is interested in the operation of nightclubs, many because of their tie-up with gambling casinos and others because the boys like to be big shots, boss chorus girls around and get prime ringside tables.

With all these holdings, the Syndicate leaders still find they are embarrassed by having too much cash. They take it in too quickly to invest it wisely.

When Jack Guzik was arrested on suspicion of the murder of James M. Ragen, rival racetrack wire service operator, Guzik said to the cops who pinched him, "I've got more cash than Rockefeller and there's twenty of us with more than I have. No one's going to push us around."

Your authors repeated that statement to a Treasury Department official who has been studying the workings of the underworld. He said that while Guzik is inclined to boast, he is certain "Greasy Thumb" has as much as $150,000,000 in currency in Chicago safe deposit vaults.

And Guzik is way down in the hierarchy.

With the Fischettis, Capones, Ricca, Guzik and Humphries on the top of the Chicago picture, the setup fans out down the line, into several tributary territories.

For instance, the top Mafia boss of the West Side is Tony Capezio. The South Side boss is Sam "Golfbag" Hunt, an Italian high up in the local Mafia. Hunt is so nicknamed because he carried his machine-gun in a golfbag. The North Side boss is Dominick Nuccio, back in power again. Eddie Vogel controls the county territory outside the city limits and is also in charge of all slot machines bought in Chicago.

The fabulously wealthy Loop is owned by Guzik. Sam Gincana of the old 42 Mob is coming up fast in that area.

Meanwhile Pete Fosco inherited the First Ward political leadership from Hinky Dink and the Bath. Fosco is not to be confused with Joe Fusco, last arrested in 1934, who now dominates the sale of liquor downtown. Many of the best cocktail lounges in the Loop are operated by Frank Harmon who held a mortgage on Al Capone's palatial Miami Beach island home.

Operating through these men and their associates and lieutenants, the Mafia controls every illegitimate activity in the city and much that is on the square.

There the boys own many laundries that service nightclubs and hotels and have big interests in practically every kind of company that does business with these enterprises. Whether your restaurant or hotel is mob-owned or not, it usually buys its linens, tableware, soft drink setups, beer and whiskey, as well as its food, from some firm in which the mobsters have a piece.

Many of Chicago's unions are gangster-controlled and are openly operated by the mob.

The contractor who repairs police cars is Babe Baron, the associate of gamblers. The most popular beer in Chicago is Canadian Ace. During Prohibition the brewery was operated by Johnny Torrio and Dion O'Banion for the Syndicate, and later by Capone. Its present "owner of record" is one Louis Greenberg, who also owns the Seneca Hotel on the near North Side, where, it was testified before a Congressional Committee, many gangsters reside.

The New York State Liquor Authority recently refused a license to Canadian Ace because of the unsavory background of its stockholders.

Under oath, Greenberg admitted knowing many of the underworld's aristocrats. He is also friendly with Cook County Democratic leader Jake Arvey.

Arvey's son, Buddy, maintains his ex-wife, Sunny Ainsworth, and child in Greenberg's Seneca. Miss Ainsworth was also briefly married to Tommy Manville. Young Arvey's current protégée, blonde Lila Leeds, who was convicted with movie star Robert Mitchum in the Hollywood reefer scandal, and who was later in a Los Angeles call girl investigation, also resides in the Seneca. Young Arvey advertises in theatrical trade papers that he is Lila's manager. The gossip columnists insist that he is more than that.

When a meeting of the board of directors of the Standard Oil Company of New York is called, it is held in offices at No. 26 Broadway. But this bandit empire, perhaps richer than Standard Oil, can do no such thing. Its big shots must hold their meetings on the fly. They are afraid to trust public communication systems for really important matters.

To make personal contacts, they are embarrassed by the fact that if they set up regular headquarters it would be possible for any suspicious dicks to watch them going in and out and thus tie up all gangsters with each other. Furthermore, there are laws, though seldom enforced, which make it a crime for two or more known criminals to consort. A reform administration, intent on breaking the mobsters en masse, could throw the book at them on this alone.

The Illinois Vagrancy Law provides that if two or more

known gangsters are seen consorting, they can be sent away for six months. State's Attorney Boyle, the incumbent, before his election wrote a letter which we have seen, in which he solemnly promised to drive the hoodlums out of town through the use of this weapon.

At this writing it has not been used once. And when queried by a newspaperman, the official asked plaintively, "Why do you try to embarrass me?"

Gangsters' favorite properties are nightclubs, though few of them ever pay a profit. By this means they are able to contact their allies and yet not arouse suspicion. For instance, it will be known that Joe Fischetti can be found at a certain cabaret every Wednesday night, at 11. So anyone needing to deliver a message to the Fischettis comes into the club, sits at another table, then bumps into Fischetti "accidentally." In emergencies, notes or word can be left with owners or head waiters. But it might incite suspicion if the same gangster were seen in the same nightclub every night, so they contrive to have more than one hangout. These may be nightclubs, restaurants, gymnasiums, Loop hotel rooms or offices. A rigid schedule, which is known to all concerned, is set up so that it is always possible at any hour of the day or night to find any important gangster.

The following are some of the places in Chicago where the underworld bosses are frequently seen:

St. Hubert's Grill on Federal Street, half a block from the old Post Office. It is "owned" and operated by Tom Kelly, a pal of Jake Guzik. Many Federal judges and assistant prosecutors eat here. Some are on terms of intimacy with the not-so-respectable customers.

The Syndicate maintains a suite of offices under an assumed name in the State-Lake Building.

The boys gather to play cards and confer on the second floor, over a bar and grill at State and Van Buren (Silver Bar, 400 South State Street). This is Ralph Pierce's headquarters. Pierce is an old-time Capone henchman who bossed whore houses for him. Though not an Italian, he is a valued member of the Syndicate because of his smoothness, experience and high-grade intelligence.

Another gathering place for the elite of the crime Syndicate is in a basement card-room under a fine restaurant near State and Lake.

The mob meets also in the penthouse of a Loop commercial hotel.

Ricca's hangout is in another Loop hotel. Guzik can be found daily at a gymnasium on Monroe Street.

The mob eats regularly at one of four Loop and near North Side restaurants and also in the swank dining room of a near North Side hotel.

We told earlier how the Syndicate decided to tighten its political tie-ups some fifteen or eighteen years ago.

Frank Costello and Jimmy Hines came to Chicago in 1932 for the Democratic Convention which nominated Roosevelt. Their suite in the Drake Hotel was the dynamo-room for the undercover campaign to knock off all anti-Roosevelt strength.

The underworld then began to perfect its tie-ups with big city political machines. Wherever the dominant party was Republican the mob was Republican. Where it was Democratic you could be mighty sure the boys were good Democrats. In New York, when the American Labor Party was at its strongest, the underworld played footsie with the Reds, fine proletarians all.

After the Democrats moved into Washington the boys had a line practically into the White House through their connections with the New York, Chicago, Jersey City, Kansas City, Rhode Island, Memphis and New Orleans machines.

From that time on, as was seen, major prosecutions of important underworld leaders practically ceased, except in cases where the mob itself initiated the action for revenge or "tightening the lines." Or, as in the case of the movie extortion plot, where the extortion got out of hand and ran into forces that had pull and power.

Meanwhile, the Chicago mob extended its influence into Kansas City, where the death of Tom Pendergast left a hole. Charlie Fischetti's lieutenant, Tony Gizzo, went down there and took over the Kansas City graft, politics and crime machine. At the same time, one Charles Binaggio, a ward-heeler, shot up with the speed of a meteor as a political leader. It has been charged in Congress that the Fischetti mob was throwing immense sums of money into his local campaigns and providing him with strong-arm boys from all over the country to get out the vote.

After Boss Pendergast's conviction, and later his death, his outfit, of which President Truman was a paid-up member, began to have rough sledding. Last year Binaggio took over the entire Jackson County Democratic Committee, which now makes Charles Fischetti the undisputed overlord of the local organization.

That there has long been a tie-up between Missouri politics and the underworld was seen in testimony before a Congressional Committee linking the President's military aide, General Harry Vaughn, with Frank Costello. Certain Missouri politicians with entree to the President were suspiciously involved in the scandal accompanying the parole of the movie extortionists, as will be here detailed.

In many ways the Syndicate resembles the setup of Fascist and Communist fifth columns, with cells reaching into all vital spots, except that there is no misplaced ideology behind it.

These mobsters become more brazen and more open every day. Their money has purchased immunity from the law. Time and again honest Federal agents find evidence against them, but regardless of who is sitting in the main offices, no prosecution gets past the barriers of dough and drag.

The unique, baffling Chicago situation is that there is no "opposition." In every other machine-manipulated municipality there is an aggressive minority party, an active "reform" movement of some proportions. In Chicago there is none. The Republicans, who long owned the county and state, now depend for sustenance on reciprocal deals; mustn't offend our foes, because we'll need them, so we'll keep it peaceful; no mud now boys, or we get nothing.

The Crime Commission is stymied. While its standing is unchallenged, its end results are nullified by public apathy and organized monopoly.

Corruption and mob-managed whitewashing seem to be sustained when anything at all gets out of hand lower down. There just is no recourse against injustice. There is no place, no person to whom the helpless who would appeal can go. The blind alley of politics-gangdom-graft ends in a solid wall which none may crack or vault.

24. MAFIA ROSE

THERE IS probably no one who has created more hot "copy," around whom more misinformation has been published, than that column-created legendary figure known to newspaper readers as Virginia Hill.

No one could look less like the gun-moll of film and fiction than this young, attractive, affable brunette now again living in Chicago, where she first turned up about fifteen years ago, when she was very young, well-rounded, bristling with sex appeal.

She is of Polish or Slovak origin, from the factory town of Bessemer, Alabama. She was one of a large family with many brothers and sisters and an elderly mother, and she set out for the North with undefined but determined intentions of making money so she could raise the standard of her family's living.

She soon became a party girl, and as such met one Joe Epstein. He was a big-shot gambler and, though not a key figure in the Syndicate and not an Italian, he had connections. He showed her a new world in which men in $250 suits tossed $1,000 bills around as though they were cigar-store coupons. Virginia soon turned up in fine clothes, furs and jewels. But she wanted more.

Epstein, smooth and polished, taught her cosmopolitan manners. He displayed her proudly to his friends, including those to whom he looked up. They found her a revelation of charm, humor and quick perception. They could use a girl like that. The fantastic climb which was to make her a factotum in the underworld began with some errands as a messenger and go-between. It has been noted that in some affairs telephones, telegrams and mails are not trusted. She talked the language and was always desirable as a "date," therefore she could do delicate work where a man or a battle-axe would arouse primary suspicion.

Charlie Fischetti, oldest of the three brothers, now the kingpin of the Chicago mob, was already on the ascendancy. He saw in Virginia a valuable business asset. No one thought that strange, because Charlie always has gone in for dazzling dames. Whether the general belief that she was his sweetheart was planned and planted, or was true, that accepted relationship made her a priceless blind. Fischetti had transactions in New York. There Virginia illuminated the scene and was welcomed as the girl friend of Joe Adonis, which meant that she frequently conversed, probably conferred, with Costello.

Virginia burst on a hospitable Broadway like an explosion. No one had ever seen a spender like her. She threw fabulous sums of money away every night in cafés. She explained its source by saying she was the daughter of a rich and aristocratic Southern family and that four times she had been married to and divorced from millionaires, all of whom had made handsome settlements.

The town fell for her story. Even the society editors called her "the rich Southern blueblood."

Back of her checkbook was the underworld. No one in modern times openly spent like she did. It was customary for her to bring twenty or thirty people to nightclubs every night, and before the evening was over she had gone "on the nut" for $1,000, $2,000, and up.

She liked to rumba and occasionally had raving romances with Cuban bandleaders. She was briefly married to one.

A couple of Broadway promoters suggested that, inasmuch as she was spending a good $10,000 a week in nightclubs, it might be a good idea for her to buy her own, where she'd be the boss and which she could support by patronizing it herself. Virginia liked that idea. She came up with $60,000 to open the old Hurricane Restaurant, at 49th Street and Broadway. She was there the first and second nights, but by the third had grown lonesome for the other rumba joints. So she was soon spending as much elsewhere as she always had.

After two weeks she tired of the whole idea and tossed the stock certificates for the Hurricane over to the promoters and said, "Here boys, you can have the place—a present from Virginia!"

The Syndicate was now extending its sway into Hollywood, where, as stated, it attempted to take over the movie industry. Meanwhile, some of the top guys from the Eastern mob found it expedient for their continued good health to go to California to escape scrutiny by Dewey and O'Dwyer. One of these was Benjamin "Bugsy" Siegel.

Siegel was an old-time East Side killer, a partner of Meyer Lansky. Meyer is still Frank Costello's close associate and one of the few Jews remaining in top positions in the Syndicate. Their old gang had been called the "Bug and Meyer Mob" and its members, including Siegel, were among the most feared and reckless killers the city had ever spewed forth. They were torpedoes for Lucky Luciano, one of the silk-lined savages who had risen to the top as a panderer and murderer.

When Siegel went into exile, the supposed-to-be smart Broadwayites were finding out that Virginia was no society girl at all, but a gang-moll. They had taken her for Joe Adonis' girl friend, which was the same malarky that had been used in connection with her previous underworld "sweethearts." When Siegel and many others were sentenced to California, it became necessary to set up a means of liaison between New York, Chicago and the West Coast. Virginia was the answer. She began to make frequent trips between New York, Chicago and Hollywood.

Soon myopic gossip columnists giggled about what they said was a double-cross in the underworld. They printed the plausible story that Adonis had written to his old friend Siegel in California, asking him to show his girl, Virginia, around, and that Siegel had stolen her. This made snappy reading, based on no more fact than the earlier tales.

Virginia continued to commute between the three big cities, and during the season she followed the boys to Miami, Havana, Saratoga and other playgrounds and workshops of the underworld aristocracy.

Virginia kept on with her fantastic blowouts in California. If anything, she went further. There she lived in lavishly furnished homes, entertained regally and spent with an abandon that startled Hollywood, where $10,000-a-week movie stars frugally pinch pennies and pay 80 per cent in income taxes.

Virginia brought her mother and brothers and sisters to Hollywood and supported them as though the family had really been born to ancestral millions.

She was likable, friendly, sympathetic and genuinely big-hearted. No appeal for help ever went unanswered. She over-did her charities in a community crawling with chiselers and moochers.

She was a welcome visitor to any nightclub, because she meant $100 tips to headwaiters and magnums of imported vintage champagne. Many times she'd look around the room, then tell the manager to give her the tabs of any acquaintances she saw there.

One example of her compassion is shown by an example of what happened on New Year's Eve, at dawn of 1946, a few months after the war. Virginia was entertaining a big year-end party in Hollywood's swank Mocambo Restaurant. Setting off the main dining room where the elite of Hollywood was making gay with wine and noise contraptions, was a rope which kept the bar riffraff at a respectable distance from the Olympians. The bar was crowded with tourists and gawkers, who had come to see how the gods play.

At the bar stood a group of five young men in Army uniforms. They were boys of Japanese descent en route from Italy to their homes in Hawaii. They were frightened and shy, afraid of the elegance, the wealth and the glamor. They knew well that Japanese were not greeted with open arms in California.

Virginia saw them standing forlornly. She went out and brought them to her table, where she introduced them to movie stars and gangsters, and one of your reporters, who were sitting with her. Then she ordered champagne for all. One of the boys noticed Yvonne De Carlo with Turhan Bey. Virginia thought it would be a nice gesture for the two actors to pose with the young Jap soldiers. A waiter, who was sent to ask them if they would, reported they were too busy with each other to consider it.

So Virginia sent Siegel's side-kick, Al Smiley, to them. It was now no longer a request. It was an order. The movie-players were very glad to pose with the soldiers. Weren't they heroes?

In 1946, Virginia was introduced by Mortimer to Carl Laemmle, Jr., son of the late founder of Universal Pictures. Laemmle, in his late 30's, is a bachelor, reputed to be one of the wealthiest in Hollywood. Laemmle fell madly in love with Virginia. Despite having known thousands of screen beauties and having remained single, he proposed marriage. Virginia liked him. But, apparently, his honest millions were not enough to take her away from the excitement and danger of her underworld associations—or her bosses wouldn't stand for her quitting and going square.

At the close of the war, Siegel had conceived the idea of building the Flamingo Hotel and gambling casino in Las Vegas, Nevada. This was to be in the most luxurious resort in the West, and it required substantial capital. He invited his partners in the Syndicate to take stock in the deal, and as the setup was finally organized it was owned by New York, New Jersey and Chicago mobster interests, with Siegel officiating as the front man and director. When Siegel moved into Las Vegas he found that the Syndicate had already apportioned all the concessions to other hoodlums. Gambling is legal in Nevada, but you've got to have an okay from the boys before a wheel can spin. However, Siegel's grandiose dream was something superspecial and he was assigned a spot in the gambling picture.

The enterprise soon proved to be a costly white elephant. Siegel was living far beyond his means. He was a chump for movie stars and had openly lived with one for years. He threw fabulous sums away on them and on other luxuries. He played with actual nobility and held up his end with $500,000-a-year moguls.

Meanwhile, his income was falling off because his social life interfered with his business.

Among the enterprises he had cooked up was heavy smuggling of, and thus untaxed, perfume from France, one of the most lucrative of the avenues open to the underworld; he was a key figure in narcotics in Southern California; he also had an interest in the California racing wire, and, of course, had his fingers in every other illegitimate racket in the territory.

His attempt to be a social figure—he was on intimate terms with all the borderline society and busted royalty thereabouts—cost him plenty.

The Flamingo soon got into trouble. Siegel constantly kept

calling on his associates for more ready cash. They had huge investments in it and quickly came through. There is one record of a $300,000 telegraphic transmittal from the Fischettis in Chicago to Bugsy.

When the Flamingo was $6,500,000 in the hole, the Syndicate decided to step in and see what could be done. A committee composed of representatives of the New York, New Jersey and Chicago mobs came to Las Vegas and inspected the enterprise. They told Siegel they would continue to support it on one condition—that he withdraw as its active head and let them put in an experienced hotel man.

Siegel haughtily refused. He loved to stand in the lobby with a carnation in his buttonhole and play big shot to the wide-eyed worshipers from Hollywood. He entertained them in one of the two lavish penthouses of the building. The other was reserved for Virginia Hill.

Siegel was insulted. He phoned Frank Costello in New York and Charlie Fischetti in Chicago, and told them he wouldn't stand for it. He called Luciano, who was then in Havana, and got tough with the toughest boss. Siegel had delusions of grandeur. That was one reason for his having been called Bugsy from earliest childhood. He pictured himself a movie-type gangster, dressed and acted like one. He looked like George Raft and lived like Raft played.

He told Luciano that unless the boys quickly came up with some more money he would "blow the whistle." People don't talk that way to Lucky. But the mob leader knew Benny had a hot temper and considered it an idle threat between friends. Siegel sent word up and down the Las Vegas Strip that he was taking over everything in town. This was against all rules. The territory had been staked out by the Syndicate and all who got in were loyal henchmen.

By this time Luciano was back in Italy. There were many conferences back and forth between Fischetti in Chicago and Goebels and Costello in New York. It was decided that Siegel had to be disposed of.

Virginia Hill knew all about it. She went to Europe ostensibly to see Lucky and ask him to spare the life of her "boy friend."

Lucky ordered Siegel's execution. He was put on the spot

in Virginia's tropical mansion in Beverly Hills. It should be noted that Virginia had carefully removed herself 6,000 miles from the scene of the execution and was dancing in Paris while Bugsy was exterminated in her living room.

Siegel had flown in from Las Vegas that evening with Al Smiley and gone to Virginia's home, where he kept his wardrobe, to change clothes. Smiley, who was in his confidence, sat on a couch and Siegel sat beside him. As he reached the cushion a blast from a carbine came through the window and shot half of Bugsy's head off. There was only one seat in the room which could be seen by the killer who was hidden in bushes on the adjoining lot. That was Siegel's.

A half hour before Siegel was executed, four hoodlums from other Las Vegas gambling casinos converged on the lobby of the Flamingo and sat silently smoking and watching the clock. At the exact moment of Siegel's last breath, 400 miles away, these gangsters walked over to the manager of the Flamingo and announced that they were taking over.

Now the boys in Chicago and New York sent new bankrolls. The place was reorganized. It still failed to pay. The New York hoodlums began to tire of their expensive toy. While these pages were being written the Fischettis had arranged to assume the whole shebang and the Flamingo is now being operated directly from Chicago.

The underworld tried to make Siegel's killing look like a private affair, even intimated that one of Virginia's brothers had engineered it because he disapproved of Siegel's association with his sister.

The fact is, the shot was fired by a marksman imported from Chicago with a carbine probably lifted from the Las Vegas city or county police arsenal. It is believed that a Nevada peace-officer, formerly a member of the Los Angeles force before he was fired, was also on hand. More than fifty ex-Los Angeles cops and deputy sheriffs are employed as protectors and bouncers in and near Las Vegas.

Virginia never returned to Beverly Hills. Police Chief Clinton Anderson would not have her. She went into exile in Mexico, where she continued her sensational spending. From time to time there were reports that she had attempted suicide. She would be taken to a hospital suffering from an overdose of sleeping-pills. Chumps surmised she wanted to end it all, was afraid of the mob, or of the cops.

None of this was true. She did not attempt suicide. But whenever a remittance from the Syndicate failed to arrive on time, she took just enough sedatives to put her into a heavy slumber. Virginia, as we have intimated, was a very keen cookie. She knew what had happened to other gangsters' girls when their usefulness ran out or the romantic flame had died. Those who knew too much disappeared mysteriously, sometimes in a barrel of cement dropped to the bottom of the river.

So Virginia made sure to let her friends in Chicago and New York know that she had planted enough evidence to send the twenty top leaders of the mob to the electric chair or the gas chamber in a safe deposit vault in an unnamed bank, with instructions that on her death it be sent to Chief Anderson, to the United States Bureau of Narcotics and to the F.B.I.

Whenever the boys read that Virginia had "attempted suicide" they sent the dough immediately, by wire.

Virginia got tired of Mexico. She wanted to come back to the States. She is basically honest and hates the mobsters with whom she is tied up. Virginia would willingly "tell all," but after that she would be killed. Knowing and not telling is her guarantee of existence. So Virginia contacted Luciano instead and told him she was coming back and she was going to pick up where she had left off—and that she wanted a cut-in on all the take.

As these words are being typed, Virginia has returned to her old haunts in Chicago and lives in a luxurious suite in a near North Side hotel. She made the rounds of the city with old pal Joe Epstein and revisited the sights that had thrilled her when she came there, young and hungry, but willing and able.

She also checked up on her own extensive Chicago holdings, which include several North Side cocktail lounges and their interests in the 26 games, and considerable real estate.

That is the inspiring success story of one simple American girl with modest aspirations.

25. IT'S WHO YOU KNOW

THIS REMINDS US of the old legal trade-story of the stranger, arrested in a small town and thrown into the hoosegow. The lockup-keeper recommended a lawyer. When the client asked the attorney if he was sure he knew the law, the lawyer said, "No, but I'm sure I know the judge."

Most of this chapter is not confidential. It is from the record. It is used here because it so comprehensively proves the arrogant power and complacent confidence of the Syndicate in its immunity when the single recent instance transpired to convict and imprison some of the top thieves and thugs of the Chicago hierarchy.

It echoes the boundless resources behind these criminals, in money, influence, amazing favoritism, subversion of government practices and links with fixers whose tentacles were familiar with the inner walls of the Cabinet, the White House and whatever Federal machinery they sought to manipulate.

That there were perjury, bribery, impudent chicanery, short cuts across law and government regulations, cannot be doubted. That things were slanted shamelessly for these convicted freebooters is palpable. That none of it could have been accomplished without amazing pull and cash and corruption is obvious.

No more thorough picture could be presented of a rich, entrenched organization moving boldly to upset justice, thumbing its nose at public opinion, overruling honest officials, pushing aside the rules and precedents, to "spring" as filthy a crew of racketeers as ever had grown and flourished in a civilized community.

Here is the noxious tale, all from hearings before Congressional Committees:

Two faithless labor union leaders, George Browne, president of the International Alliance of Theatrical and Stage Employes, and William Bioff, his special representative, a convicted panderer on the lam, worked up a soft, heavy touch, shaking down employers.

The underworld overlooks nothing. When word got out that big money was being made by these union racketeers, the Unione Siciliano moved in and Browne and Bioff moved over. They became employes of the Syndicate.

Now, with gangland's guns and gold behind them, Browne and Bioff started out to "organize" and control the entire theatrical industry of the United States. They were successful, assuming great power in Hollywood, where Bioff threatened to tie up the film business with a nationwide strike that he could keep going indefinitely.

Large sums were paid him to call it off. Two important motion picture company executives were later sent to the penitentiary for falsifying on their income tax returns blackmail bribes to Browne and Bioff as legitimate expenses.

In the spring of 1941, Bioff and Browne were indicted in New York City for violation of the Federal anti-racketeering statute. The prosecution was carried on in New York because the home offices of all major film companies are in that city, not in Hollywood.

In November, 1941, they were sentenced; Browne to serve eight years, Bioff to serve ten, and each was fined $20,000. The fines were paid.

After their convictions, both turned informer and assisted the government in convicting the Mafia leaders, who, they said, were the real bosses of the racket. In payment for their services the court subsequently released them from prison, in December, 1944, because they had "turned state's evidence."

After Bioff and Browne sang, the U. S. Grand Jury for the Southern District of New York indicted Louis Campagna, Philip D'Andrea, Charles Gioe, Paul De Lucia, alias Ricca, and five others: Frank Nitto, alias Nitti, whom we referred to before as "The Enforcer," Francis Maritote, Ralph Pierce, John Roselli, and Louis Kaufman, all of Chicago. They were all charged with conspiring to extort $1,000,000 from Loew's, 20th Century-Fox and Warner Brothers. Shortly after the indictment was returned, Nitti committed suicide, probably on orders.

On December 31, 1943, the other defendants, except Pierce,

in whose favor the court directed a verdict, were convicted. Kaufman was sentenced to seven years and a $10,000 fine. The others were each sentenced to ten years and fines of $20,000.

A second indictment had been returned on March 8, 1943, charging the same defendants, except Kaufman, with fraudulent use of the mails. It alleged that by a 2 per cent assessment against union members, the defendants had obtained another million dollars from employes of the motion picture industries, who were members of the unions controlled by Browne and Bioff.

Attorneys for Campagna, Gioe, Ricca and D'Andrea pleaded for light sentences on the grounds that on the records of their clients each would probably have to serve the full term imposed on him, and never qualify for parole. The defendants' chief counsel said, "Your honor may know that they will probably serve every day of the sentence that your honor imposes." Another lawyer for the defendants said: "I say to the court that with the reputation that goes in for these men, there is not one chance in a thousand they will be paroled when they first become eligible."

Mind you, these were statements in open court of the defendants' own attorneys. They knew their clients were criminal gangsters. Their experience at the bar led them to believe no parole board or executive would commute their prison terms.

On imposition of the ten-year sentences, the convicted men were sent to the Federal penitentiary in Atlanta, Georgia. That prison, under Warden Sanford, had the reputation of requiring stricter discipline than other Federal jugs.

In May, 1945, alleging that they wished to be transferred to a prison where their families and relatives could more conveniently visit them, Campagna, D'Andrea, Gioe and Ricca applied to be shipped to the prison at Leavenworth, Kansas.

The warden in Atlanta opposed this. He wrote the following memorandum:

"From information received, it is quite evident that money is being paid to obtain the transfer of these men to Leavenworth, and I do not believe they should be transferred at this time for this reason. I, of course, would have no objection, but there will be problems at Leavenworth in respect to the above, the same as here. Also, I do not believe they should, if approved for transfer, be transported by rail under any circumstances. I know that you realize that if these men are transferred because of residence, requests will be immediately made by the other co-defendants."

Despite this opposition, the prisoners were transferred to Leavenworth. Later, Chicago was startled to hear they were paroled!

A committee of Congress investigated. Early in the hearings, the committee, headed by Rep. Clare E. Hoffman, of Michigan, requested the F.B.I. to give it information—not the source of the information—gathered by its agents while they were investigating the granting of the paroles.

The F.B.I. refused, on the grounds that it was an agency of the Department of Justice and acting under instructions from the Attorney General, and could not and would not comply with the request.

A similar request to Attorney General Tom Clark, now an associate justice of the U. S. Supreme Court, also met with a refusal. No reason was given other than that the information was "confidential" and that the refusal was in compliance with an executive order issued by President Truman.

Subsequently, a report from the Department of Justice was filed with the committee. According to Rep. Hoffman, it did not contain any information of value. The committee report said, "It was negative in character, carried rumor and gossip, and some of the statements given to the Federal Bureau of Investigation and quoted in the report were an obvious attempt to discredit some who had been instrumental in giving publicity to the granting of the paroles."

The applications for parole had been made in 1947. The parolees had answered Question Six on the application blanks, "Previous record of arrests and dispositions," as follows:

Campagna: "In Illinois, I committed a felony about the latter part of 1918, pleaded guilty and paid my debt to society."

D'Andrea: "1916—Chicago, Illinois, suspicion, discharged. 1931—Chicago, Illinois, contempt of court, six months county jail. 1932–Chicago, Illinois, gambling raid, discharged."

Ricca: "This is my first conviction. Have been arrested few times just on suspicion and released."

Gioe: "February, 1936, Des Moines, Iowa, failure to have proper credentials for automobile. Dismissed. 1928–Chicago, dismissed."

Boris Kostelanetz, special assistant to the Attorney General, who had prosecuted the parolees, made the following recommendation at the time of application for parole:

"Campagna was one of the leaders of a gang in Chicago commonly known as the Syndicate, and which succeeded to the power of Al Capone. He and his confederates extorted by threats of force, violence, and coercion over $1,000,000 from the motion picture industry. He, together with others, was the physical recipient of over two-thirds of $1,000,000 in extorted funds. Parole is opposed."

Judge Bright, who sentenced them, said: "I would oppose the parole of the above named defendants. . . . I know of no better way to suppress these kinds of activities than severe punishment."

All of the foregoing was available to the U. S. Parole Board. It acted contrary to all these recommendations.

The Board, following its usual procedure, designated one of its three members to interview the applicants personally, in prison. The record shows that the parolees were examined in a perfunctory manner. Under Federal procedure, parolees are not to be released until a report has been received from the local probation officer in the prisoner's home town, showing that a near friend or sponsor has qualified.

On August 12, 1947, a day after the paroles were approved, and a day before they were to become effective, these and other records required to effect the release of the prisoners had not been completed. To expedite their completion, a long distance phone call was made from Fort Leavenworth to the probation officer in Chicago, and immediately thereafter Chicago wired the warden at Leavenworth, "Parole release approved." For others the papers go by mail and take weeks to process.

At the first hearing in Chicago, testimony showed that at least two of the parolees had been charged with income tax evasion, failing to pay some $400,000 owed the government.

The subcommittee was unable to learn whence came the funds to settle these tax claims.

Attorney Eugene Bernstein, of Chicago, testified that unidentified individuals came to his office, sometimes when he was present, sometimes when he was away, and "left" various sums of money, which totaled $78,000, with the statement that it should be used to "help Louis." The lawyer characterized his own testimony on this matter as "fantastic."

Both Campagna and his wife told the committee they did not know who the contributors were and had no knowledge of the contributions.

Paul Dillon, a St. Louis attorney, was one of those instrumental in obtaining the transfer of the parolees from Atlanta to Leavenworth. He also appeared before the Parole Board in Washington in their behalf. Dillon insisted that when he so appeared it was because of a desire for revenge. He told Chairman Hoffman that he was there because "Browne I wouldn't believe on oath and Bioff was a panderer and a pimp." These sweet characters had helped convict Dillon's sweet clients.

Dillon, who later received $10,000 from Mrs. Campagna, (plus his "revenge"), boasted at Chicago hearings that he was a personal friend of President Truman, had managed the President's Missouri senatorial campaign on two occasions, and that "when he came to Washington, he felt free to call at the White House without an invitation." However, he denied that he "used his influence" with the President in connection with the parole.

He also stated he had been on social and friendly terms with the chairman of the Parole Board, and that he and his family had dined with him at his home.

Another attorney for the parolees was A. Bradley Eben, whose mother still was at the time of the Congressional hearing an employee at the White House. Eben received a fee of $15,000.

The argument of the Parole Board before the hearing was that it had the right to equalize the penalties imposed on all those convicted of a violation of the anti-racketeering statute.

In other words, they said that inasmuch as Bioff and Browne had been given time off for helping the government send the parolees to jail, the Board was justifying the same time off to the parolees.

Some time before paroles were granted, Maury Hughes, a Dallas, Texas, attorney and a boyhood friend of then Attorney General Clark, was also retained by the parolees. It appeared that before the paroles could be granted, it was necessary to effectuate the dismissal of the other indictment, charging fraudulent use of the mails. These indictments finally were vacated on the general proposition that they grew out of the same circumstances for which the defendants had already been convicted.

However, there was evidence that the parolees and their associates, all habitual gangsters and criminals, had obtained other large sums of money, not only from the movie industry, for which they were being punished, but also from the employes of that industry, which was another and distinct crime. Because it was the practice to refuse paroles when an indictment for another offense was pending, it was necessary that the indictment for the mail fraud be dismissed before these men, who had such busy lawyers, could get out.

Hughes testified that an individual, introduced to him only as "Mike Ryan," and whom he had not previously met, in Chicago paid him $1,000 of a $15,000 fee; that, later, in New York, the balance of $14,000 was paid by Ryan. He said he had never met Ryan after the final payment, and did not know his identity or his place of residence. The money was paid in cash and converted in his presence into a cashier's bank check.

One of the more sensational facts disclosed at the hearing was that Murray Humphries and Tony Accardo, top Chicago gangsters, had repeatedly visited some of the prisoners in Fort Leavenworth for the purpose of carrying out routine business of the Syndicate. Note that one of them, Paul "The Waiter" Ricca is a Grand Councillor of the Unione Siciliano.

When Humphries and Accardo called on the convicts, one always used the name of Joseph Imburzio Bulger. Bulger was Ricca's attorney of record. The other posed as an associate. It was testified that the real Bulger had never visited his client in the penitentiary, therefore his face was unknown to prison attachés.

Bulger is president of the Italo-American Union, which he admitted was formerly the social branch of the Unione Siciliano, which is now purely fraternal.

Bulger's brother, known as "the Hindu," operated the Italian Village at the World's Fair, in partnership with Ricca.

Further evidence that the Camorra was not concerned with political party lines was demonstrated when Vito Marcantonio, sole American Laborite in Congress, was retained by one of the defendants after his conviction—not before, mind you. This was in the days when the Democrats openly slept with Vito's left-wingers, and they had plenty of power, both in New York and in Washington.

The hearings disclosed that the parolees, with the possible exception of Gioe, had made perjurious answers to Question Six in their applications, in that they had failed to disclose truthfully by the answers previous arrests and the result of those arrests. Neither the parolees nor their attorneys made any effort to show that any, other than Gioe, had ever been engaged in legitimate business for livelihood. Ricca openly stated he was a gambler and had been for years.

One of the most shocking aspects of the whole case was in connection with the settlement by the Treasury Department of deficiency tax assessments against some of the parolees.

Though it was common knowledge that they were immensely wealthy and that one owned vast and valuable farmland in his own name, the government did not levy attachments on his property.

Income tax liens against two of the gangsters, which might have been a bar to their parole, were reduced from approximately $670,000 to $128,000, and the Treasury accepted the smaller sum in full settlement of the income taxes of two men whom a former Attorney General of the United States had proclaimed to be boss and treasurer of the notorious Capone gang. The two men, Ricca and Campagna, had the effrontery to tell the subcommittee they "did not know" who furnished the $128,000.

Rep. Fred E. Busbey, a member of the subcommittee stated

that rumors were rife in Chicago that the Capone gang had paid $500,000 to effect the release from prison of the four parolees. Though the parole board tried to justify its decision and refused to be pinned down on whether the paroles would or could be revoked, the action was so raw that a reconstituted Parole Board did revoke the "passes" and ordered the men back to Atlanta to serve their full terms.

Ricca was picked up in Chicago, but his attorney, John Scott Stewart, chief-of-staff of the underworlders' legal battery, immediately applied for and obtained a writ of habeas corpus from Federal Judge Michael Igoe, long a Chicago politician.

U. S. marshals were luckier with two of the other parolees, Campagna and Gioe, whom they were able to lock up in Atlanta before they could apply for writs in Chicago.

Hearings in their cases were held before Judge Marvin E. Underwood, in Atlanta. He ordered them released. The government's appeal from Underwood's order was quickly heard by the Fifth Circuit Court of Appeals, in New Orleans, which ordered them back to prison. At this writing they are out on bail, subject to a rehearing and appeal to the U. S. Supreme Court.

But the U. S. Circuit Court of Appeals in Chicago, which heard the government's appeal from Igoe's order freeing Ricca, ruled otherwise than did the court of parallel jurisdiction in New Orleans.

The three-man court agreed unanimously that when the Parole Board revoked Ricca's parole in June, 1948, it did so with "no information of any violations." The court found several vague "distinctions" between the boss racketeer's case and that of the two minor henchmen.

The government had argued that under the law an alleged parole violator is not entitled to a hearing until after he is returned to prison. The courts ruled, however, that the felons have "civil rights."

No attempt was made to reincarcerate the fourth, D'Andrea, said to be seriously ill.

26. CAFÉ SOCIETY

HOME-GROWN big shots never mean as much as the imported variety. The autograph nuts wouldn't cross the street for the signature of Chicago's most famous; but a Hollywood bit-player is worth standing in the rain for. Anyway, Chicago is painfully short of local celebrities. Those who fancy the favored must depend on transients from New York or Los Angeles between trains.

Native VIPs who can afford the flossy resorts are mostly gamblers and gangsters, or well-heeled merchants and their fraus or sweeties. The real bluebloods seldom patronize public dining or dancing establishments. These people entertain and are entertained in their homes and private clubs.

The glamor joints are thus forced to exist on the pickings from mobocracy and slobocracy.

The Windy City, once a great nightlife town, is now *spurlos verschwindt* after dark.

Save for the famed Chez Paree, most of the major supper-clubs were shuttered at this writing. Rush Street, on the near North Side, once the home of one hundred luxury cabarets, is atomized. You can buy almost any night club at your own price, which is too much.

The yokelry, which comes in force to visit fairs and conventions, are just finks from the tall corn. You can count them out as café society prospects. A few who can remain awake after 8 o'clock and who have a few bucks want shockers they can brag about back home in Indiana and Iowa. For them there's West Madison Street and the other locations with cheap and cheesy saloons presenting burlesque shows on raised platforms behind the bars.

No admission. No cover charge. No minimum. No good.

You pays your four bits for a beer and sees Maisie the Magnificent Model peel all. The dopes from the alfalfa go for it big, but the quality of the beer, the dives, and Maisie is so low it nauseates decent Chicagoans and respectable tourists.

That, in a nutshell, is the story of what happened to café

society in this burg that once set itself up as the Paris of the Western World.

On the other hand, Chicago is a great hotel-going town, a habit it shares with many other cities, but which is *passé* in New York, where only out-of-towners visit the hotel-grills and roof-gardens. Probably the swankiest room in town is the Mayfair, of the Blackstone Hotel. Visitors and householders go to the Empire Room of the Palmer House and the College Inn to see floor-shows with chorus girls. The Edgewater Beach has a beautiful lake-front room.

There are several rather tony eating-places on the near North Side, which try desperately for Parisian atmosphere while they incongruously cater to rich and fat wholesale grocers. Chicago was once famed for eating places. Few fine ones now exist. Henrici's is rich in Chicago tradition. Though it resembles a bakery shop, which it is, and service is by waitresses, Henrici's is and long has been the nearest thing to a cosmopolitan gathering-place. It is patronized by politicians, show people and other smart characters.

Mike Fritzel's Chop House, at State and Lake, is big-time, too. It reminds one of a cross between Mike Romanoff's in Hollywood and Toots Shor's in New York, with the accent on Hollywood décor. This restaurant is open day and night. Its customers are sporting and theatrical figures and important businessmen.

The most highly publicized feed emporium in town is the Pump Room, in the Hotel Ambassador East, a favorite stopping-over place for the so-called glamor set. The sophisticate who patronizes it is a peasant who overdresses himself and his blonde and shoots the roll in the place, which is decked up as garishly as both of them.

To the tourist mind this splendiferous retreat is a sort of combination Buckingham Palace and El Morocco. But the Easterner sees many of its patrons as corn-fed Main Street dandies playing at being big town. The pièce-de-résistance is a steak on a flaming sword, served by flunkies gotten up like Roxy ushers. In Gotham, flaming swords go with the $1.15 table d'hôte in Rooshian tea-rooms heavy with atmosphere, Gypsy fortune-tellers and hot tea in glasses.

The gracious old Blackstone, overlooking the beautiful

lake-front, still retains a stately air, one of the few spots in the city that does.

Here the wayfarer en route from New York to Hollywood, who is held over for a few hours between trains—even in these days of through travel—stops by for lunch. The Manhattanite forced to sojourn overnight finds it almost like home. Its Mayfair Room is the town's smart rendezvous, featuring stars in the $7,500-a-week bracket.

Most Chicago nightclubs go in for large dance-floors, instead of the small ones of New York and Hollywood. Chicagoans love to dance. But the rumba and other sacroiliac-displacers have failed to achieve wide popularity. Some of the bigger spots employ Latin bands, but the locals torture themselves doing fox-trots to Cuban rhythms.

Sunday, which is a slow night in other towns, and a closed night in some, is the biggest of the week in Chicago. The Chez Paree is booked up for weeks ahead for every Sunday. Even the hotels put on floor-shows on Sunday nights, a practice not observed in any other city in the country. Tuesday is the slowest night. Many clubs close. Others operate with relief bands and no entertainment.

Chicagoans are heavy drinkers and like their liquor authoritative. Only since the war, when it got hard to get, have any wanted Scotch. In the old days Scotch was only for Englishmen and fairies. When a Chicagoan asked for whiskey he got rye or bourbon. Bourbon is still popular with the old-timers and those who don't feel the need to pose.

Few places, except the toniest, stock imported champagne or wines. Domestic wines are in demand because of the price differential.

Chicagoans are faddists. They go in for new fashions, customs, recipes and concoctions with enthusiasm. A favorite at this writing, which is almost obligatory as an order if you want to appear "smart," is "Moscow Mule." This drink is a mixture of vodka and ginger beer, served in an iced copper cup—a corny concoction we found it. Already they are changing the name to "American Mule." A foretaste of things to come?

Almost every saloon and eating-place has a piano-player who interminably pounds and sings torches off-key.

The College Inn has had a glamorous past. Its beginnings

go back to 1901, when Joseph Byfield took over the Sherman Hotel and opened a German Rathskeller in the basement. In 1909, while the old hotel was being rebuilt, the restaurant was temporarily removed but came back with a new Inn in 1910, the year Byfield's son, Dr. Albert Byfield, graduated from medical school. In his honor it was renamed the College Inn and opened with a grand flourish on New Year's Eve in 1910, to the waltz music of Gypsy Rigo and his violin.

Under such famed headwaiters as Gabe Gilderbeck, Blondie Thomas, Billy Erenson and Rober, it stepped out to become one of the best-known in the country. Those were the days when America was becoming dance-team conscious. The College Inn presented the Castles, Maurice and Walton, and Mae Murray and Enrico Muris.

Meanwhile, Joe's son, Eugene, who had become somewhat of a Chicago celebrity, took over the management of the Sherman, which he shared with Frank Bering, still one of America's best-known and best-loved hotel men. The Inn went in for big-name bands, introducing some of America's most famous orchestra leaders.

Prohibition not only ruined the great room, but put the hotel itself on the financial rocks. In the early 1930's, with repeal in sight, the Inn came back bigger and better and pioneered the celebrity night, which was to become so popular in New York.

The best-known after-dark spot in Chicago, one of the few first-rate ones in the entire country, is the Chez Paree, on the near North Side. This is a big glitter-and-glamor room, seating 500 and presenting floor-shows of the first magnitude with $10,000-a-week name stars and dancing girls.

The Chez was started in the early 30's by Mike Fritzel, an old-timer in the cabaret business, and Joey Jacobson. In January, 1950, the club was sold to a syndicate headed by Dingy Halper and Babe Baron, mentioned elsewhere in this tome.

Mike Fritzel started out with a joint on West Madison Street, called the Arsonia.

"Arsonia" might mean a place where they set fires. Mike and his brother "Dutch," who died recently, did keep a hot dive, but that wasn't how it got its name.

It was first called the Ansonia. But the New York hotel of

that name sued and won. So the frères Fritzel found it more economical to repaint one letter on the sign, and not even that; they just blotted out the tail of the lower-case "n" and that left "r."

Mike was quite a character in the roughneck days of the West Side, when the Desplaines Street police station was the official center of the wild section of a very wild town. He ran all night so the Arsonia was a handy and hospitable port of call for newspapermen who did the late police trick, and they all knew and liked Mike.

As the years went by, he grew and spread. He became the proprietor of a saloon downtown, in the shadow of the Loop, on Van Buren Street. The housewarming was in the Arsonia tradition and the place prospered.

During Prohibition, Mike ran the notorious Frolics in East 22nd Street, an all-night spot with sixteen chorines and dancing until dawn, where all the notables hung out.

Now the Chez is the nearest thing to New York, west of the Hudson River. Its patrons include everyone who amounts to anything in Chicago, and all overnight important people in transit. Fritzel and Jacobson, remarkable hosts, made it that way.

Generally speaking, Chicago, once the wonderful night-life town, is down and out and in the dumps after dark. An important reason is the deadly competition of the brutal burlesque-bars, the subject of previous study in this work.

Chop suey restaurants in most other towns are patronized by thrifty people who find the gooey food cheap and filling. In Chicago some are celebrity hangouts, and a visit is an occasion. Chief among these are the Beachcomber, also owned by the Fritzel-Jacobson combination, the Singapore and the Shangri La. They sell carloads of barbecued ribs and you've got to know the headwaiter to get in. How tony can you get—reservations required for fried rice and egg rolls!

Cafés go in for the darnedest names. Get a load of The Last Chance, Pub and Prow, Shaky Jake's, The Ruptured Duck, The Sewer, The Screw Ball, Myrtle's Turtle and Barge Inn.

* * *

A WISE GUY'S CLIP PROTECTION: When the flower gal tries to sock you for posies, say you have hay fever. When the photo gal wants to take your picture, state you're a professional model and charge ten bucks to pose. When the cigarette gal tries to sell butts at inflated prices, ask if she handles reefers. When the B girl asks you to buy her a drink, state you are a member of the United Drys.

27. STOCKYARD SOCIETY

CHICAGO as the habitat of Society seems incongruous. Discarding the accepted snobbery of that unofficial designation in a country which has no blooded or feudal aristocracy, there is no phase of human association which does not in time separate the goats from the sheep; and goats and sheep and hogs and cattle in Chicago determine largely the distribution of wealth, which is perhaps the major factor in American social superiority.

Every little burg has its little paper which reports the doings of the banker's wife and the department store owner's daughter, and calls it Society. But in Chicago a true upper class came into being through the personality of one figure, Bertha Honore Palmer, who put the city on the international map. Bertha Honore, born in Kentucky, was petite, with deep brown eyes and a regal bearing, a congenital gift of her French and Irish forbears. She married Potter Palmer, who was much older, one of the score of men who rose with the city; who became a partner of Marshall Field and Levi Leiter; who was an ironmaster; who built the original Palmer House and rebuilt it after the fire of '71. He adored his bride and established her in the stone mansion on the Drive, an architectural bastard version of an English palace.

Mrs. Palmer moved gracefully and unopposed into the position of social leader, and by unanimous consent she headed the Board of Lady Managers for the World's Fair of 1893. That made her Chicago's official hostess. Among the representatives of foreign nations who came to dedicate their buildings at the exposition was Princess Eulalie of the Royal House of Spain. When she was apprised that she would be welcomed by Mrs. Palmer, she haughtily refused. "I will not meet an innkeeper's wife," she ruled.

She did meet the innkeeper's wife. But the story had gone around the world. Mrs. Palmer had been spending her summers in Europe and she had so charmed Queen Victoria that she had an open invitation, not to visit Buckingham Palace, but to live there. All America rose in indignation against the rudeness of royalty and the press of the nation swarmed to see her and was captivated. It was the first that America knew of Chicago in the social aspect.

Thereafter the city's Society schedule was Mrs. Potter Palmer's schedule. No one could make plans until she had announced her fall and winter program, because any affair she sponsored canceled out any that any other woman contemplated. The grand climax was her annual Charity Ball, in the Auditorium, when a dancing floor was laid over the seats, and private Pullman cars from New York and everywhere were parked in the freight yards for the event.

Mrs. Palmer rode lightly. She was the reporters' darling. She gave the boys a break and whatever she said was copy. Her husband rarely appeared in formal dress, except on her state occasions, but preferred to lean his six-foot-two frame on a sidewalk chair against the front of his hotel, wearing a hickory shirt and a Pawnee Bill hat, no necktie, and cowboy boots, greeting the commoners by their first names as they went by.

Years after the Fair, some Council committee fell across numerous miscellaneous bronze and plaster statues which had been made for the Fair and afterwards dumped into a municipal storage house.

It was thereupon solemnly resolved that this—in a town where four-bit inkwells in City Hall had gone down on the records at $250 each—was pure waste. And it was further resolved that the statuary be dusted off and set up in various public parks. Lorado Taft was the sculptor-art connoisseur who dominated the esthetic domain of Chicago. He visited the parks, scrutinized the retrieved statuary, threw his slender hands toward the heavens and cried out that these banal pieces were atrocities, which they were. The elegant Taft yammered in his agony: "That rubbish is not Art!"

The reporters descended on Mrs. Palmer, who had headed the committee which, with a bit of pressure from some aldermen who had friends in the business, had passed lightly on the statues. The boys wanted to know whether or not they were Art. And Mrs. Palmer, who received them, shrugged and asked them, "What is Art?" The newsmen, who had been hurriedly rounded up from the East Chicago Avenue police station, which was handiest, were not authorities on the subject. Mrs. Palmer disclaimed any specialized information on the technical definition, and the nearest dictionary was vague and indecisive.

"I cannot argue with Mr. Taft who is a pundit," she said. "But in my limited conception it is the work of some genius graced with extraordinary proclivities not given to ordinary mortals. Speaking of Art—my husband can spit over a freight car!"

Mrs. Palmer's sister married Frederic Dent Grant, son of the man who saved the nation and became its President. Her brother Adrian, who was as handsome as she was beautiful, never married and didn't have to; the ladies swooned over him. He was a judge and became Bertha's escort after she was widowed. She never remarried, though King Leopold of Belgium wanted to make her his consort. She had two sons, Potter, Jr., and Honore. Potter wounded his mother when he married Pauline Kohlsaat, of a fine Germanic family, but whose father had grown rich with a chain of bakeries and beaneries. She couldn't even be rightfully designated as an innkeeper's daughter. Honore did better when he married Grace Brown, of the Baltimore clan, descended from the Carrolls of Carrolltown. Neither son revealed great business capacity and the family fortune dwindled. Her niece, Julia Dent Grant, was one of the first Chicagoans to land a title when she married Prince Cantacuzene, of high Russian pedigree and great wealth. Their children, Prince Michael and Princesses Julia and Bertha, made a spectacular escape from Moscow as the Bolsheviks moved in, and with the Prince moved to Chicago, where Julia divorced him. Bertha is now Mrs. Oakley Thorne, of Boston, devoted to Christian Science and petit point rug-making, and Julia is Lady Hanbury-Williams, of London. Prince Mike, after one unfortunate marriage, took on an undistinguished widow and they are quite happy on little money and many friends.

As these lines were being set, the engagement in London was announced of Lady Hanbury-Williams' daughter Barbara, 20, to her second cousin, Prince Michael Cantacuzene, known also as Count Speransky. The younger Prince Mike, who is

35, is employed as a sales manager by a French rayon concern. His father, Serge, is a first cousin of the American Michael.

With the passing of the social queen her mantle descended on the slender shoulders of Mrs. Edith Rockefeller McCormick, oldest daughter of John D., the wife of Harold F. McCormick, the son of Cyrus, the inventor and business prodigy who revolutionized American farming with his machinery. The McCormick match was predicated on love, though Edith had little physical charm except an irresistible smile, tiny feet and exquisite ankles. She did much to bring culture to Chicago, was interested in youth, all good works and fine music. For years she and Harold spent millions to give Chicago the finest in opera. When her romance chilled, her name was often bandied about with that of Campanini, the immortal conductor. Harold fell for the Polish siren, Ganna-Walska, who had an obsession for rich husbands and an operatic career, of which only the first item was realized.

Harold was partial to Mary Garden, who never married, and to whom he turned over the management of the Chicago Opera Company. When he became bedazzled with Ganna-Walska, he divorced Rockefeller's daughter, got himself a monkey-gland operation, and took the would-be diva away from a rich carpet manufacturer of Yonkers. Of course that didn't last, and in time he married his nurse, Adah Wilson. Their son Fowler married Fifi Stillman, divorced from Jim Stillman, the New York money magnate, after a historic scandal. Fowler was young enough to have been her third or fourth son. They are still together, living at 1500 Lake Shore Drive, where the late George Woodruff built his million-dollar penthouse.

Cyrus McCormick's daughter, Mrs. Anita Blaine, now 84, like many frustrated patricians with too much patrimony, including far younger heirs, turned radical. She supported Henry Wallace for President and is backing an extreme and expensive left-wing daily in New York.

She gave $1,000,000 outright to the World Government movement. But her standing is unassailable. She is too rich to be too wrong.

Sam Insull, who had started as the secretary, in England, of the great Thomas A. Edison, rose to the top of Chicago

Society though he cared nothing for it. His wife, a pretty ex-actress, was ambitious, and when he came into the big chips she induced him to subsidize Grand Opera, which was always an entrée. He built the new opera home and subsidized the operatic bottomless pit until his financial crash. That was the last of the big sing stuff as a Chicago civic institution.

The Harold McCormicks had lived in the mansion on the Drive which covered a block from Oak Street to Bellevue Place, originally built by General Torrens. After the divorce, she went abroad and returned from Switzerland years later as a devotee of Freud and Jung intermingled with occultism, and accompanied by a blond young man named Edward Krenn, who had been a hairdresser and her private secretary. They promulgated a tremendous project for founding an ideal suburban community, and Krenn, who knew nothing of such things, superintended it as she financed it. The Utopia didn't utope, and it all went back to seed with her death of cancer, not in the McCormick home, which is now a private school, but in the Drake Hotel, nearby.

At her bedside were Krenn and McCormick. She who was the daughter of the world's richest man, who loved beauty and exquisite things, lay on hotel linen and dined from hotel dishes until her daughter, Muriel Hubbard, brought her some befitting napery and china.

The Insulls, who never commanded anything like the social reverence paid to Mrs. Palmer or Mrs. McCormick, retreated from the field when his utilities empire blew up and he fled for a while to Athens. He was acquitted shortly before he died. Mrs. Insull lives at good hotels here and there and is no longer a figure. So there is no Society leader now by common consent, though the wealth of several families, almost all living in the suburbs, still provides reading-matter for the women's pages.

Perhaps the greatest social prizes were grabbed up by the children of Leiter, who had once tramped the rural roads with a peddler's pack on his back. His three daughters married British titles and Mary, the oldest girl, sat on the throne of India as the Vicereine, wife of Lord Curzon. Joe, the son, who once tried to corner the world wheat market and almost broke the old man, was long a bachelor and had his fill of affairs before he married Juliette Williams, daughter of a colonel.

Most of the mighty mansions on Prairie, Drexel, Calumet and Michigan Avenues, where six-course breakfasts were the rule, are now occupied by Negroes. The last survivor of that era was Arthur Meeker, who valiantly wore his top hat in the Easter parades to the last. He came into being as the handy-man for J. Ogden Armour, oldest son of Philip D. Armour, the founder of the packing dynasty, who bragged to his dying day that he had shoved a wheelbarrow with his own hands and had made Chicago's first industry with those hands and his fast brain and commercial acumen.

J. Ogden Armour, whom the stockyards reporters in the press building nicknamed "J. Hogpen Armour," was a rather dour and hard-working executive with only a few of the characteristics which made his father a tremendous person. He married beautiful Lola Sheldon, of Connecticut, and they had one child, Lolita, who was born with a pelvic deformity. The famous bloodless surgeon, Dr. Lorenz of Vienna, was brought at fabulous expense for an operation which was partially successful. He also worked on Betty Hoyt, daughter of the Phelps Hoyts, who married T. Philip Swift of the second largest butchering family.

J. Ogden Armour, though he lived out his life with his wife, was also enamored of Mary Garden. Mrs. Armour held her head high and is still beautiful and proud at seventy. Mellody Farm, the Lake Forest showplace, built with the blood and guts of the original Armour fortune, and where Lolita married John J. Mitchell, Jr., son of the head of the Chicago Trust and Savings Bank, was sold and it, too, became a school. John and Lolita were divorced after they had adopted two children. John married a non-Society girl and they have two children and live in California, as does Lolita, who wed a Wilder—perhaps as a sop to her pride. But it didn't pan out and she leads a lonesome and rather obscure existence.

Early Chicago Society marked its path with ideographs in the form of houses. Every rich man built himself a residence to express his success. So much was the baronial dwelling a part of the great family that Helen Swift Morris Nielson, in whose name you read the combined blood of the pork, lard, bacon and by-product history of Chicago, left a testament commanding that her home be torn down after her death. She was the daughter of the "Yankee of the Yards," Gustavus Swift. She married Eddie Morris, the son of Nelson Morris. Her son Ed married Helen Conover, of another packing-house strain, and Nelson, named for his uncle, became ambassador to Sweden and was decorated by many European monarchs.

When the widow Morris married Francis Nielson, who had been a clergyman and Member of Parliament in England, there was a loud cry of "fortune-hunter!" But he turned out to be a man with brains and breeding, made the beautiful Helen happy, and induced her to write a couple of books of reminiscences. Their home was a landmark, but she ordered it demolished on her passing, so that no stranger might violate the nest where she had been so happy.

There are good clubs which have withstood all the changes. The Saddle and Cycle Club, which nestles like a little cow-barn in the shadow of the Edgewater Beach Hotel, where it was built on reclaimed land, has survived many decades and is still smart. On the South Side the Saddle and Sirloin Club, which was the private gathering-place of the meat tycoons, is kept up, principally through the interest of Thomas E. Wilson, the packer. Hundreds of thousands from all over the world visit there for the International Live Stock Shows. The Wilsons still retain their South Side home, but live mostly on the Ed-Ellen farms, near Lake Bluff, where they raise pedigreed stock.

The Arts Club is a soigné institution begun humbly in the old Harvester Building, now homeless because it has been driven out of the South Wrigley Building by broadcasting companies. The late Mrs. John Alden Carpenter I, of French descent, and Mrs. C. B. (Bobsy) Goodspeed, did a sincere job of décor, and artists, writers and musicians were drawn to hobnob with Society. Dues were low and the moving spirits kept it functioning at a loss. Among the directors is Fanny Butcher Bokum, one of the city's rare gifted newspaper-women. The Chauncey McCormicks, John Shaws, Mary Hastings Bradley and other warm advocates of fine things, upheld it in a spirit of art appreciation far from a talent for spitting over freight-cars.

The Casino was another dream of Mrs. Carpenter's. It has lowered its bars a bit, what with taxes. A small, squat building that looks like an exaggerated beetle, it has an oval modernistic lounge and about the best food in town, with rigorous rules to enforce the main idea.

The Racquet Club, residential, is on North Dearborn Street, favored by superior suburbanites coming in for the theatre. The Armours, Blairs, Mitchells and the other Lake Foresters consider it a second home.

The Tavern Club, of which Ernie Byfield was a ranking founder, is just south of the Tribune Tower, tall, with a tier of terraces. Its principal reason for existence is the fact that the Cliff Dwellers, one of the established arty organizations, admits no one of the Jewish race. But the majority of Tavern Club members are not Jewish and one of its guiding original stars was the blue-blooded Eames Mac Veagh. Its secretary is Charles Collins, the distinguished veteran editorial-page columnist of the *Tribune*.

Mac Veagh was a prominent citizen, a vestryman at the fashionable St. James Episcopal Church, and the son of Franklin Mac Veagh, who had been Secretary of the Treasury. Though he became enmeshed in a suit brought by a former Swedish manicurist, who claimed that they had a son, he lost nothing of his standing with the best people. Where that "son" is and who he is still remains a perennial Chicago mystery. Mac Veagh married Zelie Bartholomay, daughter of a French consul. He and Tom Chalmers and Frank Hibbard were famous cronies. Tom was the son of "Puss" Pinkerton, daughter of William A., hereditary head of the famed detective agency. After its owners died, Lady Duff-Gordon bought the Mac Veagh residence for her dressmaking shop, and it later was torn down leaving an ugly weed-filled hole in the Drive.

The Chicago Golf Club, in Wheaton, and the Onwentsia, in Lake Forest, contest for the honor of having the best courses. Golf was made respectable by Mrs. Hobart Chatfield Chatfield-Taylor, who was the daughter of John V. Farwell, another of the ex-Marshall Field partners. Taylor was perhaps Chicago's outstanding literateur and highborn Chesterfieldian. The story is that his childless uncle, Chatfield, gave him a million dollars to incorporate and hyphenate the Chatfield name into his, so it would not die.

Mrs. Chatfield-Taylor was one of the most beautiful Chicago brides and tremendous picture copy because she introduced the knee-length golf-skirt, and when she swung her beautiful legs were revealed, making exciting "cheesecake" portraits, legitimatized by an impeccable name.

It is not the purpose of this book to enumerate all who have claims on social distinction. Chicago developed a surprising number of true American aristocrats, and if some of them had a little cattle-blood under their fingernails they were still of that bedrock stock which dominates all accomplishment in our national history, descendants of men who would have been earls in the mother country.

It appears to be the destiny of mankind that heirs and successors can rarely preserve the accomplishments of the original constructors who hacked success with toil and character out of adversity and primeval soil. In this respect Chicago resembles the stuck-up East with its current generation of idlers who collect the proceeds of the fortunes founded by their immigrant great-grandfathers, many of whom came to power through piratical methods.

The Chicago packer has been a standard laughing-stock in fiction and musical comedy. But he made a mighty metropolis and brought the world to his gates. His breed still flourishes, though it has been thinned out with paler elements —from the veins of weaklings.

28. THE PEOPLE'S FRIENDS

THEY SAY Mayor Kennelly is always smiling, but he doesn't know what about.

The mayor, a novice in politics, was elected on a "reform" ticket. A bachelor, he was long active in philanthropic affairs and wartime patriotic drives. He was said to be a good businessman and a great organizer.

Former Mayor Kelly, sensing "machines" were on the skids, voluntarily retired and selected "Clean" Kennelly as his successor.

According to the Chicago *Tribune,* Mayor Kennelly is the "goingest" mayor Chicago has ever had. He is the antithesis of the little man who wasn't there. He responds to invitations to weddings, lunches, dinners, conventions, sports events, club and church meetings, like the proverbial fire-horse to the gong. The *Trib* says:

"In addition to his mayoral duties, Kennelly has attended 201 functions in the last 109 days, which would be some sort of a record for someone else, but for the city's genial top executive it was a breeze, as the saying goes. He attended 52 banquets and receptions, 19 luncheons, 10 conventions, three parades, eight weddings, 21 wakes, 16 hospitals and churches, eight neighborhood and civic groups, 29 picnics, outings, baseball and football benefit games, 15 radio and television broadcasts, five meetings outside his office, and he visited 13 sites."

"Martin has been going to wakes and weddings all his life," a friend of his remarked. "He visits the sick and buries the dead."

But the mayor has a serious reason behind all this gadding about. "Most residents learn nothing about their city government except during a campaign," he stated. "I want to get people interested. I enjoy getting out to the neighborhoods and talking to them. I've been doing it since I took over the mayor's job. It's almost like a continuous campaign, but there's nothing political about it."

It is charitable to say that Mayor Kennelly is naïve. Nowhere else on earth is there as tight a tie-up between politics and the underworld. In Chicago they are indivisible. It has been that way most of the time since the Fire of 1871. Any mayor who tries to fight the system, soon finds it cannot be done. Several who did could not get renominated.

The alliance begins in the gutter grades and works all the way to the top. On the ward level it is the local hoodlum, who is tied up with the committeeman, who controls the district police captain. On the city and county scale, the Fischettis, Capones and Guziks do business with the top political leaders, and thus have direct contact with the police commissioner, mayor, sheriff, state's attorney, or even governor, regardless of what party is in office.

Through tie-ups already mentioned, the underworld has a pipeline even into the White House.

An opposition legislature in Springfield can do little or nothing to curb criminal conditions in Chicago. Through a unique system evolved by the Illinois bosses, a certain number of favored legislators are kept in office permanently and they cannot be displaced.

Among them are a group of fifteen servants of the Mafia, who are able to stop all legislation meant to strengthen crime law enforcement.

Of the 153 members of the present Illinois House of Representatives, 78 are in on "passes," which permitted them to be elected without contests, by prearranged deals.

With a guise of legality, so-called Senatorial Committeemen hand out the "passes" from these no-contest districts.

This is how it works:

Each of the state's 51 Senatorial Districts elects three Democratic and three Republican Senatorial Committeemen at the primaries. These are small-fry ward-heelers, completely under dominance of the major political organizations. Any time after election they can meet and determine whether one, two or three candidates for representatives will be nominated by their party at the next primary. Once their decision has been made, no one can overrule it. If there are two vacancies to be filled, and if the Republicans nominate only one man and the Democrats two, it stands to reason one Democrat must be elected, regardless. If there are three vacancies and the Republicans nominate one and the Democrats two, then all nominees must be elected. The ratio between parties is determined in back rooms.

The examples of underworld-political "coincidences" are endless.

Federal Judge Michael Igoe, a Roosevelt appointee, was honorary pall-bearer at the funeral of "Big Jim" Colosimo and was attorney for the late Dennis Cooney, chief whoremaster under Capone.

Col. Jacob Arvey, Democratic boss of the state and County Commissioner, is a fervent New Dealer. Among his associates, open and surreptitious, are kingpins of the underworld.

That Arvey does not hesitate to use his political connections for his private gain was demonstrated as these pages were going to press in a startling story in the nominally Democratic *Chicago Sun-Times.*

Search of the records proved that Arvey and an associate had secretly acquired large land holdings which they knew were soon to be condemned for the Congress Street throughway. Profit on the turn-over ran over $300,000.

Arvey, who admitted the transaction, said it was merely a normal business deal. He said he had been bankrolled by Col. Crown, local building contractor, who had put up the $3,000,000 for Conrad Hilton to purchase the Waldorf-Astoria.

Known instances of graft are too numerous, and always have been, to mention in a book of this size. A classic case is:

Some years ago, an effort was made to keep Chicago's streets clean. The City Council appropriated a sum for garbage-boxes at every corner. Instead of having the sensible kind employed in other cities, with a swinging cover through which waste and refuse can be dropped without effort, Chicago purchased unwieldy iron boxes with lids so heavy, it is practically impossible to lift them. Apparently, some alderman's brother was manufacturing the boxes.

A novel political racket was uncovered recently in the coroner's office. Motorists whose cars were involved in fatal accidents, in which the driver was not to blame, were shaken down by some deputy coroners with the veiled threat that if they didn't pay, the coroner's jury might not return a verdict of "accidental death," and the motorist might be held for manslaughter. Two deputies resigned, but were given other political jobs. A third was demoted.

It seems that in some of the Municipal Courts, after the defendants had pleaded guilty and had paid their fines and left, the judges remanded all sentences and the money was then divided up among beneficiaries not yet named. After considerable buck-passing it was decided the judges and court attachés were blameless.

Underworld bosses contribute heavily to political campaign funds, with immunity to arrest as the pay-off.

These cases are merely cited as examples. For every one mentioned here, there are hundreds unreported.

Mayor Kennelly, who claims he has completely cleaned up the city, will probably be surprised to learn that a gambling-house is operating full-blast next door to one of the storage warehouses which bear his name.

On every occasion when the mayor is questioned by reporters regarding the crime Syndicate, he asks "What Syndicate?" Mayor Kennelly consistently denies there is organized vice or crime in the city. But, recently, the swank Edgewater Beach Apartments, on the North Side, in which he lives, was offered for sale by Federal Court order.

After hectic bidding, a group of residents in the hotel organized and bought the property from the trustees.

Mayor Kennelly said out loud, "We had to do it to stop the Syndicate from getting it."

What Syndicate, Mr. Mayor?

29. THE BRAVE BULLS

THE GENERAL impression seems to have gone forth that wicked, wild Chicago has gone sissy, has an efficient "business" administration, and has cleaned house by shelving a machine mayor and electing a member of the Chamber of Commerce who has the freedom and the know-how to run the city for the city's good. Don't you believe it.

Chicago, whether Mayor Kennelly knows it or not, whether he knows it and likes it that way, or whether he knows it and his hands are tied, is the heaven and the haven of mobsters, gamblers, thieves, killers and salesmen of every human sin. City Hall is dismally dumb or completely complacent or hog-tied.

The city of Chicago is right now officially, formally, expensively and blatantly fighting not the corruptors and the hoodlums, but the two square, fearless police officers who so misunderstood their city that they had the temerity actually to arrest the chief paymaster-collector for the Fischetti mob, on a murder rap.

Captain Thomas E. Connelly and Lieutenant William Drury, with more than forty-eight years of service between them in the department through which they rose, gangster-haters in their hearts, nabbed Jack Guzik. James M. Ragen had been assassinated on the street because he wouldn't hand his racing news service to the Syndicate. Connelly and Drury nabbed Guzik. Then a lot of things happened—but not to Guzik.

He was freed within two hours. But Connelly and Drury were indicted!

The charges against them were bizarre—that these officers were depriving Guzik, the ex-convict, panderer, cash-register for the world's most rapacious mob, of his civil rights! Guzik told them they would be busted, and they were—they still are.

Three of Guzik's torpedoes had been identified as Ragen's murderers and were under indictment for the murder. You can see the processes working in the results: two of the eye-witnesses recanted; the third was bumped off. Then the indictment was dropped.

Connelly and Drury were summoned before the Grand Jury. They were handed immunity waivers to sign, which they refused to do unless so ordered by Police Commissioner Prendergast—and he did not order. Their knowledge of Chicago prompted them to believe that the purpose was to find out how much they knew. They refused to lay themselves open to a procedure they felt was designed to have them tip their mitts.

Testimony under oath later alleged that State's Attorney Tuohey had "pressured" the jury into indicting Connelly and Drury after that body had returned a no-bill. Sworn allegations also were that Tuohey had third-degreed the witnesses against the alleged murderers (not the accused) in an effort to have them withdraw their positive identification of Guzik's men.

First Assistant State's Attorney Wilbert F. Crowley admitted under oath that he had gone night-clubbing and to the races with George Bieber, attorney for Guzik, and had entertained him in his home. It was Bieber who had rushed in with a writ of habeas corpus to free Guzik soon after his arrest by Connelly and Drury. Do you think Crowley resigned after that? You're right. He did—when he was nominated for a judgeship. And he was elected!

After the Ragen murder indictments had been quashed, came Connelly's and Drury's indictment on charges of "conspiring to obtain a fraudulent indictment." The two officers demanded trial, the State stalled with postponements, and finally nolled the charges.

Meanwhile, Prendergast brought Connelly and Drury before the Civil Service Commission, alleging conduct unbecoming of officers, because they had refused to sign waivers—the waivers he had refused to order them to sign. Such department prosecution is customarily presented by the corporation counsel. But in the case of the two cops, who had dared arrest Greasy Thumb Guzik, a special high-pressure prosecutor from the state's attorney's office fought them. They were dismissed from the force.

Connelly and Drury sued. Judge Sbarbaro heard the case

and ordered them reinstated forthwith, including full rank and back pay. But the "reform administration" appealed. The case went to the Illinois Supreme Court, which did not overturn Judge Sbarbaro's decision. But again the city, which was supposedly for clean government and against gangsters, refused to accept the higher verdict.

The city, which had already spent more than $30,000 keeping Connelly and Drury jobless, found a technicality on which another appeal could be brought before the Appellate Court. There Guzik's threat to break them was made good. Two jurists "heartily approved the wholesome decision of the Civil Service Commission."

And that was notice to Chicago's 7,000 policemen that the racketeers and their assassins must not be disturbed. None has been since—not up to now.

The ousted officers, having spent their small savings in legal battles, went to work for the Chicago *Herald-American* as reporters-investigators. They published the inside story of their persecution and considerable of what they knew of the underworld through long earlier experiences while trying to fight it. This didn't change or dent anything. They were later dropped from the paper when they appealed their cases and were turned down.

The Illinois Supreme Court, appealed to again, refused without comment to rehear the case. Without their powerful newspaper connections the two ex-policemen were now friendless. But this same bench had repeatedly heard appeals brought by Charlie Fischetti, Jake Guzik and Murray Humphries, and had upheld their "civil rights" not to be disturbed while carrying concealed weapons on their persons.

Connelly and Drury now have a new lawyer, who is going to carry their case to the United States Supreme Court without fee.

Drury, in 1930, had arrested Harry Guzik, also in connection with a murder. That fat Capone vassal was sprung immediately then, also. A prosecutor at that time called Drury, who was admired by thousands for his courage, aside and whispered in his ear that that was no way for a young man to get along on the Chicago force.

The men stated that when they nabbed Jack Guzik in 1947, Prendergast shook his head and said, "They won't like it!" There was no need to ask who "they" were.

The detectives say that when they brought Jack Guzik in the last time they dared him to take a lie detector test, and that the gangster's dark jowls turned green as he muttered: "If I took a test twenty of Chicago's biggest men would jump out of windows." Guzik refused a drink of water, fearing it might contain truth serum.

We know Connelly and Drury. We know Guzik. And we know Chicago.

Since the modern Syndicate system became powerful it has won many a victory over decency, honesty and the law. But the victory over Connelly and Drury was its greatest. Finally the courts had officially ruled that the organized mobsters are untouchable.

Connelly and Drury have an amazing record of having frequently mussed up these characters with their bare fists. That type of cowardly gunman has an inbred fear of brave enemies. Whenever one of them meets these deposed officers of the law, even now, he pales and takes the other side of the street.

Drury, purposely, every day, to and from downtown, passes the swank building on Sheridan Road atop which the Fischettis dwell in their luxuriant triplex penthouse palace. He always slows down so they can see him and blows his horn so they can hear him.

City Hall doesn't dare reinstate these two and get them out of its hair by transferring them to some remote Siberia, because the mob and the administration know they would spend their free time at their hobby—tracking and hounding hoodlums. This they did as newspapermen, a trade at which they were tyros, but to which they brought a wealth of knowledge and experience and a fortune in guts and enthusiasm for their cause.

The average young man who joins a police force is usually sincere.

Whether he will go straight or become a crook depends on outside influences. Police departments can be honest. The

F.B.I., Scotland Yard, the Canadian Mounted and most New York cops are examples. Inevitably there are bound to be some dishonest men, but the great majority will not take raw graft and will despise fellow officers who besmirch the force.

The awakening comes when police discover their superiors are on the take, or that special interests control the machinery of the law. When privileged criminals are sprung as soon as arrested, the force quickly loses its morale. Young cops say to themselves, "What's the use? I might as well be in on it myself."

Chicago's crime and corruption could not exist without the knowledge of and the approval of its police authorities. There is no such thing as a cop being unaware of any happening on his beat. If he doesn't know, he's asleep on his feet.

The morale of Chicago's police department is purposely kept low with poor salaries and penurious pension systems. The powers refuse to give the police high enough wages to immunize them against temptation. Underpaid police can be bribed more easily. Chicago's police department bosses are always long on alibis. If plain lies don't help, they sometimes fake the figures to make them indicate crime is being cleaned up.

In recent years, according to Virgil W. Peterson, the Chicago Crime Commission has viewed with skepticism the police department's own statistics. Criminal figures, at best, are incomplete, due to numerous offenses that are never officially reported, especially when committed by persons with the right connections.

As far back as 1929, the Crime Commission discovered that thousands of criminal offenses never appeared on official records. Crime figures are utilized by candidates in almost every campaign, and the temptation is always there to reduce crime through doctored statistics.

"The manipulation of figures on criminal offenses is not difficult when a police department is under political control. Unfortunately, the reduction in the number of offenses affords no protection to the public if the decrease rests solely on bookkeeping methods," Peterson charges.

Discipline, as well as morale, is low on the Chicago police

force. From time to time, the Crime Commission makes available to the Commissioner of Police the results of careful investigation by its staff.

These reports have frequently reflected deplorable lawbreaking conditions prevailing in certain districts. They have provided names of police officers engaged in misconduct, together with names and addresses of notorious characters who have been violating the law with impunity. The tenor of many such reports would clearly indicate the desirability of an independent personnel investigation which might form the basis for disciplinary action on corroboration of evidence made available by the Crime Commission. Instead, it has frequently been the practice to forward reports of this nature to the commanding officer of the district involved. In effect, he is asked to investigate himself! And it is not surprising that he is invariably "unable to substantiate" information which would show himself up.

The Chicago Crime Commission reported to the Commissioner of Police that a notorious illegal establishment was being operated with immunity at a designated address by one of the best-known hoodlums in that area. Obviously, he could not keep going without protection. The personnel investigation was referred to the captain of the district, who submitted a report in which it was stated that he interviewed the hoodlum, who denied the illegal operation. This was accepted at face value. A few weeks later a man was shot and seriously injured in the same establishment. Who denied that one?

Inadequate police protection in some areas is directly traceable to the absence of proper supervision over policemen. Repeatedly the Crime Commission has conducted investigations regarding prevalence of burglaries in certain business districts. In some instances it was found that police officers were missing for hours at a time from their assigned posts of duty, in which burglaries were regularly occurring. A spot check showed that on a single night fifty cops had failed to make the required pulls of police-boxes on their posts of duty.

It has been common knowledge for years that collusion exists between many policemen and switchboard operators. For a monthly payment to the switchboard men the hourly pulls of officers are recorded automatically. This arrangement permits police to leave their posts at will and stay away as long as they choose.

The methods of selection of Chicago police candidates are haphazard. Men have been enrolled who had been convicted of felonies or high misdemeanors. The department reasoned that since such convictions had occurred years before, there was no disqualification for service in the force sworn to fight crime.

There are many instances of policemen, who, as officers, committed these offenses for which they were convicted: murder, robbery and larceny.

Commissioner Prendergast himself, indicted on Federal Prohibition charges in the 1920's while he was a police captain commanding the district in which Capone's empire had its headquarters, obtained a long postponement and took a year's leave of absence during which some others named in the same true bill were convicted. On his return the indictment against Prendergast was nolle prossed.

Department training methods and law enforcement equipment are deficient and outmoded. The city, otherwise so princely with its expenditures, is notoriously niggardly toward the law-enforcement department.

But political interference is the chief reason for Chicago police inefficiency. Many officers are originally selected by political considerations. The ward committeeman is more powerful than the police district captain. Frequently, officers who do good work are bawled out by ward committeemen, and are forced to change their testimony or be fired, as were Connelly and Drury.

One of the cutest methods for collection of graft ever devised is going on merrily in Chicago. This is the "tip jar," a minor gambling device. The story was first brought out by the Crime Commission when a uniformed police agent and a patrolman raided a neighborhood hamburger shop, conducted by a couple of good reputation who had been induced to display a punchboard.

The sergeant told the owners that the police had received a serious complaint about the board, and he'd have to take them to jail; the place would be closed for two or three days and they would be fined at least $100. But, said the sergeant, the official records could be changed and the complaint dropped for $25. The $25 was passed over.

Two men entered the shop a few minutes later, placed a tip jar on the counter and told the Nelsons they were privileged to display the jar and sell chances. He also told them it was he who had caused the police to seize the punchboard, as the owners were not "authorized" and were moving in on his exclusive territory. To convince the shopkeepers, the man called the district police station and put the proprietor on the phone. The police station spokesman assured the shopkeeper that what the man had said was right.

When those facts were duly reported in writing to the proper officials by the Crime Commission, the sergeant was suspended, pending trial by the Civil Service Commission. That body, after hearing testimony, ruled in favor of the police officer and restored him to duty. He had not arrested Guzik.

Existence of a vice ring was brought to the attention of the Crime Commission by a girl of eighteen, who named the wives of two policemen as being engaged in dealing with commercialized vice. The girl had been brutally beaten by her procurer. The Crime Commission followed the case through every step and worked up the evidence that caused the arrest of every one connected with the ring. The testimony showed that the apartment of Patrolman Vernon Smith, on South Parkway, was maintained as a bawdy-house and that this had been more than once reported to high ranking officials of the police department. Further investigation by the Crime Commission revealed that the girl complainant had been an active participant in spectacles of sexual perversion. Questioning her disclosed that several of the degrading acts were not only performed with knowledge of Patrolman Smith, but that at least once he was present with other persons during the staging of one of the "shows."

Captain Dan Gilbert, of the Chicago police department, assigned as chief investigator of the state's attorney's office, is said to be the richest policeman in the country. During Congressional hearings into the manipulation of grain on the Board of Trade, it was testified that he owned hundreds of thousands of bushels. He admitted in an interview with the Chicago *Tribune* that he owned 18,000 shares of Royal Crown Cola and had extensive utility holdings.

Before the last election, prominent citizens asked candidates of both parties for state's attorney to commit themselves on whether they would keep Gilbert if returned or elected to office. But when Boyle, the Democrat, won, he reneged and said he would fire Gilbert only with Mayor Kennelly's approval, which was not forthcoming.

Gilbert maintains a room, 1901, in the Sherman Hotel, where he transacts his private business.

Though Chicago's population is roughly half of New York's, its police force has only one-third as many men. It is kept understaffed because the crime Syndicate wants it that way.

Whenever the newspapers demand police action the cops get busy—enforcing traffic regulations. Right now, 1,400 of the 7,000 cops are on traffic duty. The men assigned to that work are youngsters, fresh out of the armed services, and are the cream of the department. They should be in the field, fighting crime, but they haven't been around long enough to be "trustworthy."

The setup of the police department is further complicated by the fact that there is another, an independent, police force in Chicago, consisting of 700 men, with full official power in the parks and on the boulevards and contiguous territory. This contingent is not connected in any way with the city police. It is bossed by the Park Commission, which is the personal property of Democratic Committeeman Jake Arvey.

The city flatfoots are ruled by a council of elder statesmen known to all cops as the "Big Four."

At this writing the top man is Captain Dan "Tubbo" Gilbert. Commissioner John "Shakey" Prendergast stands second. The No. 3 man is Captain Ray "Midnight" Crane, former Mayor Kelly's bodyguard.

The fourth member of the inside ring is Captain Walter G. "Peaches" Storm, an ex-chief of detectives. Storm was transferred from that post when things got too hot. But he bosses the present chief of detectives, Tim O'Connor.

Captain Gilbert, in charge of the 100 detectives assigned to the state's attorney's office, is the most important cop in the county. He was in union labor politics before he joined the force. It was testified under oath that all his records in the police department files are missing. It has also been published that Gilbert has been seen frequently with Owney Madden at Hot Springs.

Former Circuit Court Judge Oscar F. Nelson ran for state's attorney against Thomas E. Courtney in 1940. During the campaign, he publicly accused Captain Gilbert, who had been chief investigator for the state's attorney's office since 1932 (by appointment of Courtney), as follows:

(1) Gilbert at one time was indicted on a charge of "assault with intent to kill" in a labor war. The indictment was suspended with leave to reinstate. Subsequently, the records disappeared from the Criminal Court files.

(2) On May 6, 7, and 8 in 1939, Gilbert was seen with gang boss Frank Nitti in the lobby of the Arlington Hotel in Hot Springs, Arkansas, and on the golf course there. Courtney was ostensibly looking for Nitti at that time.

(3) Gilbert used gold-plated golf sticks at Hot Springs, presumably given him by Nitti.

(4) Law enforcement in Cook County was on a "fix-it" basis with Gilbert as boss. Nitti gambling joints were virtually immune.

The campaign charges were denied by Courtney and Gilbert as a "pack of lies." They accused Nelson of being a close associate of Scalise. Nelson admitted knowing Scalise "only slightly," since he had been attorney for many labor unions. Nelson was beaten by Courtney.

Nelson is now dead. Nitti was indicted in the movie-extortion case which led to the conviction of Paul Ricca, et al, and killed himself on the eve of the trial. Courtney is now a judge.

In December, 1949, Gilbert was nominated by the Arvey-ruled county committee for sheriff of Cook County, the over-all top law enforcement job. Arvey had proclaimed that "party loyalty" was a paramount qualification for the post.

The Chicago *Tribune* scathingly protested; it stated that, in 1941, it had come into possession of some records of the Syndicate; that Jack Guzik had carelessly left the papers in a cold oven when he moved out of a flat; that these records summarized profits and protection money on one month's gambling in suburban Cook County.

The *Tribune* editorial stated:

> "On the page which constituted a monthly payoff record appeared one item set forth as 'Tub . . . $4,000.' It was never publicly established who 'Tub' was. Captain Gilbert said, privately, that it certainly wasn't he. His friends, he explained, didn't call him 'Tub.' They sometimes called him 'Tubbo.' The records were turned over to State's Attorney Courtney, for whom the captain was chief investigator. Nothing came of them.
>
> "The fact remains that for 16 years Captain Gilbert has been the chief investigator for three Democratic state's attorneys. During that period gambling has flourished almost without interruption in suburban Cook County, in spite of occasional threats to indict municipal officers in whose bailiwicks it is found. . . ."

In January, Gilbert took a temporary leave from the police department for the duration of the campaign.

Arthur Madden, agent in charge of the U. S. Treasury Intelligence in Chicago—who sent Capone to jail—says at least forty police captains are worth at least a million dollars each. A few years ago he instigated an investigation, trying to trace these sums. He said, "Cash in safe deposit vaults doesn't leave any trail." For that reason it was practically impossible to get anything on most of the captains, though three or four were made to cough up.

With such situations it is no wonder Chicago has the most appalling crime record of any city in the world.

Whenever charges such as these are made, the higher officials pass the buck or deny they exist. An example came to hand while these pages were being written.

Police advised Mayor Kennelly that, following complaints in newspapers, they had arrested 2,317 men and two women in a drive to clean up Skid Row. A report from Captain Joseph Hartnett said there is no open gambling or prostitution in the district, though documented articles in the Chicago *Daily News* and Crime Commission statements gave names and addresses. Following the old Chicago custom of allowing police officials to investigate themselves, Mayor Kennelly read a section of Hartnett's report and said, "The facts disprove such reports."

When no other way is found to buy off cops, and when they refuse to be intimidated by their superiors, they are told they are silly to bother making arrests, because the cases "probably won't stand on appeal."

Gangsters are permitted to tote guns with immunity, but when actor Chester Morris, appearing in the Chicago company of the play *Detective Story,* applied for permission to carry an unloaded pistol on stage, the cops sternly refused.

Crooks place so low an estimate on the Chicago police department that recently a burglar broke into police headquarters, stole $15,000 worth of property from the custodian's office—and the uniformed chief's extra suit of clothes!

30.—AND ROBBERS

ANYTHING goes in Chicago, including murder.

In previous chapters we told of the unholy alliance between the protectors of organized crime and the politicians. This chapter is concerned with the working of crime, itself.

It must be borne in mind that not all law-breakers are members of the Syndicate. By far the largest number function on their own. They have no political pull and no protection.

When a lone wolf breaks the law in Chicago he gets pinched and is put away. The cops are virtuous when it comes to locking up law-breakers who have no pull. This builds up figures, shows they are on their toes and know how to make an arrest and put over a conviction.

Chicago's crime record is doubly depressing because, in addition to the organized rackets, it is a natural and geographical center to which bad eggs from all over the country converge. Through the underworld grapevine they know that the Illinois criminal statutes, which have purposely been set up to make law violation easy for the organized underworld, will also work to the advantage of the man who takes a chance on his own.

There are other contributing factors. One is the cockeyed Illinois law which forbids branch banking. This statute goes back to pioneer days, when the early residents feared Wall Street and centralized banking control. They were afraid that if banks were allowed to open branches, one or two large institutions might corral all the money and credit in the state, which has happened in California, where the Bank of America has mushroomed into every town and hamlet.

The practical result of this archaic law in modern times is that outlying neighborhoods are denied banking facilities. Each big commercial bank has but one office, downtown in the financial district. A few small banks operate in some of the more important outlying neighborhoods. But there is not a bank every few blocks, as in other cities where branches are permitted. It takes considerable capital to organize an individual, independent bank.

Meanwhile, local merchants, deprived of banking facilities, have found a makeshift. This is a new kind of business, built on the idea of the check-cashing service. These agencies, and you will find scores in every part of town, do much more than cash checks.

Some have safe deposit vaults. They draw money for your payroll from your bank and deliver it to your premises. They pick up your daily receipts and transmit them for deposit. They sell money-orders, and cashier's checks. They deal in foreign exchange. Some, without legal sanction, make loans by the simple expedient of cashing post-dated checks for fees big enough to include interest. These agencies are a natural for bank robbers, because there is no danger of the F.B.I. being called in.

Under Federal law, the F.B.I. takes over whenever a national bank, a member of the Federal Reserve System, or a bank insured by the Federal Government, is cracked. That category includes 98 per cent of the banking institutions in the country, but not check-cashing services.

Bank robbers from all over the map gravitate to Chicago. Some of the most spectacular crimes of the last few years were stickups of these places, some of which cost the lives of brave guards and policemen.

Another inducement to crime in Chicago is failure to fingerprint those who work in cafés. Thus jewel thieves are able to get their finger-men into the swankier restaurants, to get leads on patrons who wear worthwhile jewelry. Many waiters in the good cafés are ex-cons.

Criminals work openly and brazenly in Chicago. It was found necessary to install a burglar alarm in City Hall after footpads walked out with an expensive miniature reproduction of an antique which decorated its corridors.

Chicago lays itself open to much "private" crime because most blocks are intersected, both ways, with alleys. These are seldom lighted, even in the heart of the Loop. In those passageways, narrow and sinister, lurk rape and robbery, assault and murder. Their entrances and exits are naturals for highwaymen lying in wait, where they can see out but cannot be seen. And they provide ideal getaways, the more so because they are lined with low fences past which are dark yards with other exits, into streets not visible from the alleys.

Another factor that accounts for the tremendous amount of crime in Chicago is lack of proper coordination between the police, the prosecutor and the courts. Ineffective police work can make a successful prosecution impossible. Good police work can be nullified when the courts fail to support the police.

A classic example is the record of Steve Tomoras, age 25. He was brought to trial following the holdup of the "Louie the Hatter" store, on Archer Avenue. Police testified that when they arrived on the scene they saw a dark-colored car in front of the store. Its right side door was open. A spotlight was focused into the vestibule of the store and the cops saw two men carrying bundles of clothing.

At this time the car, driven by a third man, started to move and turned directly in front of the squad car. One burglar threw his bundle of clothing into the moving car; the second dropped his and leaped to the running-board. The cops fired at the fleeing vehicle and the man on the running-board fell to the street. He immediately got up and started to run. A cop gave chase and caught him a few blocks away. The officer testified he never lost sight of the fugitive. The captured man was Steve Tomoras.

Tomoras' defense consisted solely of his own testimony that he had met a girl at Randolph and State Streets earlier that night. He could give no name for the girl other than Eileen. He said he took her home and let her out of his car around the corner from where the crime was committed. She wouldn't tell him where she lived. He said he was following her up Archer Avenue when he noticed a crowd of people. The next thing he knew, the police arrested him.

Tomoras was represented by George Bieber, of the firm of Brodkin and Bieber, which specializes in underworld law. Notwithstanding the fact that the sole defense consisted of the defendant's uncorroborated fairy-tale, Judge Frank Bicek took the decision away from the jury and directed a not-guilty verdict.

The phenomenal success of Steve Tomoras in gaining acquittals in Cook County criminal courts, as well as Chicago municipal courts, has not been limited to this one case. Tomoras was arrested thirty minutes after burglars had robbed a radio store. Seven stolen radios were in Tomoras' car. Under Illinois law, persons found in possession of merchandise recently stolen are presumed to have committed the theft, unless possession is satisfactorily explained. Tomoras' sole explanation of how he got the stolen radios was that he was sitting in a restaurant and his friend, Carl Fiorito, asked him if he had $20 on him. It appeared that a few minutes before, at 4:20 A.M., Fiorito had bought seven radios from two men, whose names he didn't know, and had paid them $205 in cash, and needed $20 more to complete the deal. Tomoras did not have the money, so they drove around at 4:25 in the morning, trying to borrow it. That was when the police chased them and they were apprehended. Judge Roberts found Tomoras not guilty.

This Steve Tomoras, who is tied up with such hoodlums as Paul Labriola and Marty the Ox—who died in bed early in 1950—affiliates of the Capone gang, is the alibi kid. Between June 23, 1938, and May 11, 1949, he was arrested thirty-seven times, but, apparently, never served a jail sentence. Among the charges were grand larceny, sex offenses, burglary and other felonies. In the few cases where he was convicted, he was put on probation.

The Chicago Crime Commission, in connection with the Tomoras case, submitted the foregoing facts to the Chicago Bar Association. The association exonerated the judges.

Crime costs Chicago one-third of a billion dollars a year in actual cash, and no one knows how much more in such unmeasurable things as the corruption of juveniles and the driving away of legitimate business. But this sum is only a small fraction of the total amount of money handled illegally by criminals in Chicago.

Because of its favorable climate for hoods and its geographical location, it is the natural center for most of the big interstate rackets. The headquarters for the stolen-car ring is in Chicago as is the national headquarters for fencing stolen jewelry.

The front for the latter is a jewelry store on Adams Street, owned indirectly by the Fischettis.

The theft of jewelry is a very complicated and highly organized business, which demands a large and trained organization. Before the actual "heist," finger-men must locate the stuff, must determine the best time to make the haul and must ascertain when police are least likely to be about. After the actual "lift" the pieces, especially if they are rare and valuable and known to the jewelry trade, must be quickly transported to another town, and, if they are to be marketed immediately, must be broken up beyond recognition by skilled workmen.

Then comes the "outlet," which, if the stuff isn't "fenced," will return it to the insurance companies through shady private detectives, for the reward money or part of its value.

The huge increase in the number of important jewel stick-ups in the last few years was brought about by the incursion of the Syndicate into this business. The boys were not only able to provide the national organization, but considerable protection as well. It is believed many of the spectacular jewel thefts committed recently on the French Riviera were engineered by the Big Mob. The stolen gems were immediately transported to the U. S. through the smuggling channels already set up to get illicit narcotics into the country.

Another nationwide racket which has its headquarters in Chicago is the hijacking of men's high-priced clothing. After a typical gangland slaying in the rear of a confectionery store, police found more than 300 suits and topcoats, valued at more than $10,000. These were traced to burglarized stores in New York, Pittsburgh, Washington and other cities.

This business is believed to have run into more than a million dollars a year. The suits, many of which were made to retail for $150, are resold by the fences to small merchants throughout the country who believe they are getting such bargains because the suits come from "broken stock."

Chicago still abounds with petty neighborhood crooks who go in for protection on a small scale. Some neighborhood merchants are taxed as little as $1 a week to be let alone, but if they don't pay, vandals smash their windows by hurling bricks from speeding cars.

Illinois' antiquated laws, which cannot be revised because of the opposition of some members of the legislature who are ever zealous for the Syndicate, make the future look no better.

Honest prosecutors find their hands tied because of the ridiculous perjury law. It is impossible to get a conviction for perjury unless it can be proved that the untruthful testimony would—in itself—have resulted in a conviction.

Criminals are also protected by the fact that in Cook County alone, of all of the state's counties, the grand jury must not sit for more than thirty days, and cannot be extended, as in all other jurisdictions, state and federal. This means there can be no such thing as an efficient grand jury investigation or a "runaway" grand jury.

The Chicago Crime Commission attempted to secure passage of a bill which would have put Cook County grand juries on a parity with others in the state. The organized bitter fight against this bill, as well as others suggested by the Commission, was led by certain representatives and senators from the old "bloody 20th" and adjoining wards, at one time a stamping ground for many important Capone mobsters.

Voting against the proposed legislation were Representatives Andrew A. Euzzino, Peter C. Granata, John D'Arco and James J. Adduci. State Senator Roland B. Libonati opposed all the bills. In the 1930's a photo was published showing Libonati at a public function with Al Capone, Machine Gun Jack McGurn and their bodyguard.

James Adduci, a pal of mobster "Dago" Lawrence Mangano, was picked up with Willie Bioff in 1933, but was elected to the Legislature in 1934. Ably assisting these legislators in opposing the grand jury bill was the law firm of Brodkin and Bieber, attorneys for Jack Guzik and many other mobsters.

Even good citizens fear to testify against criminals. It does not "pay" to be an innocent bystander. Those not intimidated are frequently murdered or often jailed and held incommunicado while the felons go free.

31. IT COULD HAPPEN ONLY IN CHICAGO

JACK LAIT hit a peak on the Chicago *Herald,* where he knocked out a daily column titled "1,001 Chicago Nights." He later joined the Chicago *Tribune,* where he did the column, "In the Wake of the News," which still runs in other hands. Lait was drafted for New York. There he continued and still continues to specialize in Chicago stories.

This book is not a rewrite. There will be no recital of his pet stories, including his eye-witness account of the shooting of John Dillinger in Chicago, for which he flew there on a blind tip, and which has gone into many anthologies; this is no anthology. But here are a few confidential interesting bits about people, some now living, and their Chicago backgrounds:

Saga of the Four Dorothys

When Harry Richman got big enough to engage a personal press agent he took on an attractive young woman named Dorothy Gulman. She had become a publicity specialist at the age of thirteen, after starting a fan club for orchestra-leader Paul Ash, when he was a fixture at the Chicago Theatre, the first of the bobby-soxers' swoon idols. When she took Richman's account she was already promoting some of Chicago's big nightspots and hotels, including the Terrace Room of Hotel Morrison.

A Ziegfeld show was in town and Richman introduced her to Dorothy No. 2, beautiful and talented Dorothy Dell, who had been Ruth Etting's understudy and had taken her role on the road, where she was sensational with the song, *Was I Drunk, Was He Handsome!* The two Dorothys became pals. Dorothy No. 1 got Dorothy No. 2 national attention, through which she skyrocketed to a Hollywood contract.

Dorothy Dell was from Louisiana. She told Dorothy Gulman of a friend from down South, who was in town and broke. That was Dorothy Lamour, the No. 3. She had won a beauty contest in New Orleans and had come to Chicago to cash in on it, as many other contest beauties have done, entering by that revolving door which usually spills them out as soon as the first bloom of early maturity passes. Dorothy No. 2 told Dorothy No. 1 that Dorothy No. 3 hadn't been able to enter that door, and was reduced to running an elevator in Marshall Field's department store.

No. 1 took a ride in the elevator, looked over No. 3, and decided something might be done. She invited her to the Terrace Room for the next Sunday night, and, if she could sing a song, some agent might be interested. She flopped and left weeping. But No. 1 was not so easily licked. She ordered her to come back the following Sunday, and meanwhile she phoned Herbie Kay, rising local bandleader, to come, too. Kay saw her and heard her, was entranced and engaged her as a vocalist. She didn't get very far with audiences, came to New York, took a screen test, which was junked. But Dorothy Gulman had never lost faith in the possibilities of the girl she had seen push the department-store elevator levers. She encouraged her to get to Hollywood. The rest everyone knows.

Lovely Dorothy Dell died in a motor accident when she was at her loveliest and best.

Some years later, Harry Richman was starring at the Hollywood Restaurant, in New York. He was displeased with his press work and suggested to Joe Moss, his employer, that he bring on Dorothy Gulman. Miss Gulman came. In the chorus-line at the Hollywood was a cute little brunette, Dorothy Darrell, Dorothy No. 4. She was in love with Richman, and after he went to London she followed him there, with no luck. But Dorothy No. 1 had become a star press agent, handling Leon and Eddie's, Jack Dempsey's and many individuals, including Richman, Gertrude Niesen and Dorothy Lamour. To her Dorothy Darrell came and pleaded, "Get me something outside New York. I want to get away."

Dorothy No. 1 wired the Chez Paree, in Chicago, and sent Dorothy No. 4 there. Within two weeks lightning struck. Producer Joe Pasternak, who had discovered Deanna Durbin, saw Dorothy No. 4. He signed her and in Hollywood he married her. So the box-score of the four Dorothys stands:

For one, movie stardom. For another, tragic death. For a third, love and wealth. For the original, the *status quo,* still a great press agent.

Pretty Peggy

Peggy Hopkins was playing the Studebaker Theatre, as a great dramatic star, no less, under the personal and interested management of Lee Shubert. Her engagement closed on a Saturday night and she was leaving the next morning for a rest in Colorado Springs. After the show she was invited to supper at the Blackstone by Francine Larrimore. At an adjoining table sat Lait with David Belasco. They all knew each other and they joined parties.

Lait had gone to school with the young multi-millionaire Stanley Joyce. They never got thick, because Joyce was rich and Lait was working his way, having obtained a scholarship because he was a good ballplayer. But when Joyce caught a glimpse of the radiant blonde he suddenly discovered that he had always liked Lait, came over and greeted him with bubbling effusion. This made an introduction peremptory.

Peggy took her train next morning and Joyce took the one right after. Peggy Hopkins has been held forth as a notorious gold digger. She did anything but dig Joyce, who was by then worth fifty million dollars, as his share of the family lumber fortune. She refused to have anything to do with him and decidedly declined to marry him. He pursued her to New York, drowned her with flowers, pelted her with furs and diamonds, all of which she sent back. One day she long-distanced Lait, who was still living in Chicago, and said, "You pushed this on me, now get it off me!" Lait, instead, advised her to marry the guy, who was young, good-looking and had the rest of what it took.

It was a mistake. Joyce drove her frantic with jealousy, had her followed, on their honeymoon, by private detectives, and after he had to leave her in Paris and come back for two weeks, he sued her for divorce and named eight co-respondents. That made Peggy mad and she came back and sued him, dared him to prove anything, which he couldn't, and she divorced him and got a bundle, enough so she never had to "dig."

She forgave Lait, and never married any of her other five husbands without having him meet them, pass on them and give the nod. He never failed. But all the marriages did.

The Great Getaway

Frank Buck has become famous for bringing them back alive as a safari man, a jungle explorer and showman.

One of your reporters knew him in the wilds of the Virginia Hotel, when Frank was a bellboy. He also knew Amy Leslie, the even then venerable ex-soubrette who had become dramatic critic of the erudite Chicago *Daily News*. Amy was a widow, as big around as she was up and down, but late in her life came love in the person of the handsome bellboy.

Amy was a person of great consequence. She had an excellent income and had been a Gilbert and Sullivan star. She said she wanted to marry Buck. Lait was not nodding this time. He told her she had lost her mind. But she took Buck out of uniform and to her bosom. Of course, it was ridiculous. Buck stood as much of it as he could, and then started off to get as far away from Amy as the surface of the globe permitted. She chased him pantingly and he kept running. That was how and why Frank Buck first saw a jungle.

All Chicago insiders knew the story, and Lait wrote a column burlesquing it, which, condensed, was about as follows:

There was a young man so attractive to women that he got fed up and started to escape from the whole sex. But wherever he sought sanctuary, a woman sought him. He fled to Africa, and there the dark ones made a grab for him. He escaped into the almost impenetrable interior, and even there he was afraid, so he climbed the highest tree. There he rested and sighed, "At last, safe from snakes and women!"

He fell asleep but awoke suddenly—a female giraffe was kissing him!

Beery-Swanson

Gloria Swanson was a chorus-girl at the Essanay Picture Studio, on Argyle Street. Louella Parsons was scenario-editor. Wallace Beery was one of the stars. Gloria was gorgeous, as she still is, thirty years later. But Beery, though successfully sued in his last year of life in a paternity case, was a strangely lone person. He dined solo, he lived alone, he never turned his head to look at a girl.

Gloria had plenty of men wild over her and she wasn't smitten with Beery, didn't even worship him as a star. But she got him to look, he looked hard, and he married her.

The chief interest in Beery's life until then had been a custom-made, low-slung open Stutz Bearcat roadster. He wouldn't let anyone else in it. The marriage was big news, and the published deduction was that Gloria had married Beery to get a ride in that car.

The Torcheroo!

Chicago never saw two prettier blondes than the Sykes sisters, Dama and Gladys. Their father was a photographer of beautiful women, but he could do nothing for them that nature had not already endowed them with lavishly.

Dama married Billie Halligan, who was a beefy entertainer in Freddy Train's dive, in the Levee, where also sang and danced a dumb dish who was never known by any name except Baby Doll. The piano-player was Bernie Adler, whose wife was interested with Harry Guzik in McCarthy and DuVal's, the trading-post for prostitutes which brought about the Mann Act. Dama divorced Halligan after a few hectic years, moved to New York and became the wife of a businessman.

Gladys, who was tall and icy and stately and queenly, married the handsomest man in Chicago, the daredevil auto-racing driver, boulevardier and son of wealth and aristocracy, Arthur Greiner. Arthur was the prince of the College Inn, the city's best-known man-about-town, manna for the columnists, Romeo multiplied, a fist-fighter and the companion of all the live locals, the visiting actors and sports celebrities.

He and Gladys settled down in a Hotel Sherman suite. He adored her, but the girls wouldn't let him alone. Gladys took as much of that as she could swallow, left him and went East to live with Dama. Greiner frantically telegraphed and telephoned, but she wouldn't yield. Jack Lait was their intimate, had been the best man at their wedding. Art came to him in despair. He was not given to tears, but he shed them as he sobbed, "You must get Gladys back for me. Go to New York. Tell her I love her. Tell her I can't live without her. Tell her I'll kill myself if I can't have her."

Lait went. He argued, he pleaded, he pulled out all the stops, and finally Gladys melted. She said she would go back if Art would come and get her. Lait wired the happy news, returned, and was embraced with joy. Greiner got a stateroom on the 20th Century that afternoon. Lait went to see him off. In the stateroom he saw a fluffy little brunette number, settled in a fluffy gown.

Lait drew Greiner into the corridor and demanded, "What the hell are you doing with a woman in your room, when you're going to bring Gladys back?"

"Oh," said Greiner, "the train can't take me fast enough . . . but why waste a night?"

The Gimp

There was a little basement cabaret on South State Street with a chorus of eight, all young, all green and all pretty. One was Helen Morgan, who went to fame and an early death as the torch-singer on the piano and a star of Ziegfeld shows. Another was a kid from a village in Nebraska, named Ruth Etting. Ruth wasn't eighteen when she married Moe (Gimp) Snyder, a limping gunman and labor-slugger.

For twenty years, during which she reached and held the heights in the theatre, on the radio and in pictures, Snyder was her "manager." If there had ever been any affection, it had early been replaced by fear. Snyder was with her everywhere day and night, and in order to justify his "occupation" he brawled with producers and sponsors and directors. But he kept her working. He fought for bigger billing and higher pay. His ambitions for her were celestial.

They bought a home in Beverly Hills out of her sumptuous earnings, which at times reached $7,500 a week.

On Vine Street, near Hollywood Boulevard, is a hangout for gamblers, mostly New York and Chicago expatriates. Snyder could not resist the place and for a few daylight hours he relaxed his vigilance over Ruth. At a radio rehearsal she met a young composer-pianist, Merle Alderman. He was gentle and her heart went out to him. Snyder had contacts with show people and he heard that his property was in jeopardy.

He found his wife with Alderman, not in a "compromising position," but he pulled an automatic and shot the musician. From jail he sent her word that if she didn't return to him he would drive her out of show business. Snyder did a year in a lofty county jail cell in Los Angeles, during which Ruth divorced him on cruelty charges.

He didn't have to drive her out.

Though she had to give him his share of the "community property," with what she had left she quit, bought a little roadhouse in a mountain pass in Colorado, and was never again heard from as a performer except in one attempt at a comeback in Copacabana in New York. But she had lost her spirit.

It was Trilby without Svengali!

Flirting Flirters

Chicago had a police chief named Francis O'Neill, a deeply religious and moral man. What shenanigans he had to overlook he shut out of his mind. But he became perturbed over "mashers," male and female, in the public streets.

He sent for Jack Rohan, the best-looking flatfoot in the department, whose usual assignment was guarding the swells at charity balls and the opera, and acting as close bodyguard to men like J. Pierpont Morgan when they stopped over. O'Neill ordered him to walk the streets, let himself be seen, and bring in any female that attempted to flirt with him—except on Quincy Street, where the perambulating pros were permitted to ply their trade.

He then called for Alice Clements, a dashing policewoman who had newly been added to his force. He sent her out to pinch any man who made a pass at her.

If you don't know the answer, we won't stretch it out with dialogue. But Rohan and Alice arrested each other—for mashing on Randolph Street.

PART THREE

THE LOWDOWN
(*Confidential!*)

32. TIPS ON THE TOWN

Booze

DRINKING is a personal habit. We don't have to tell you what or how much you should take. But we know our Chicago saloons—incidentally, don't call them saloons. By law they're taverns! If you're not sure of the place, always demand to see the bottle first. Even this won't protect you if you're in a dive that refills 'em. It's always a good idea no matter where you are, to ask for the liquor in a separate glass, before mixing, and do the mixing yourself. Few places in Chicago comply unless you demand it.

Legal boozing age for minors is eighteen for girls and twenty-one for boys. Why the discrimination? Don't men have equal rights with women?

Cabaret Info

Most nightclubs and hotel grills present two floor shows nightly at 8:30 and 12:00. The Chez Paree, Vine Gardens and a few others do a third show at 2:00. Burlesque bars run continuous from opening throughout the night.

Few Chicago nightclubs have a cover charge, though most hotels have. There's a nominal one at the Chez Paree. Minimums in cabarets range from $1 to $3 a head. There is never a minimum or cover at burlesque bars.

Though it's against the law and the rules of the American Guild of Variety Artists to permit female entertainers to sit at tables with male guests, this is winked at, except by hotels. No matter who you are, you can't get that second cutie from the left out to your table, in the Palmer House Empire Room.

The top supper clubs won't permit girls to mix with strangers, but if you are a regular customer or a liberal tipper, the headwaiter will see what he can do for you. At all other clubs and at the burleycues, the girls have to mix.

Clip Joints

A friend of ours who does this kind of research as a hobby counted 165 such in a square mile on the near North Side. The victim is steered by runners who are usually cab drivers and sometimes even cops. They may be in semi-private brownstone houses, or a cocktail lounge or tavern or burlesque bar that apparently runs openly and aboveboard. The bait is always the same—"women." The chump finds his bill brutally padded, his checks raised, and his drinks loaded with knockout drops. If he's lucky, he may wake up alive.

Curfew

The law says taverns must go boom-boom at 2:00, while those that pay extra for a late license may remain open until 4:00 on weekdays, with an hour's grace for both on Saturday nights. Practically speaking, there is no such thing as a curfew. Any place with enough customers to make it profitable to run after closing does so.

If you don't know where to find drinks during the so-called closed hours, ask any cop, cab driver or bellboy. Not that you will need such advice. It is difficult not to find booze, whatever the hour.

Dames

We don't know what your tastes are, whether you go in for tall or short, fat or skinny ones, blondes, redheads or brunettes. We don't know whether you like pushovers, or those hard to get, or whether your intentions are honorable or the usual. That's strictly your business.

But it's our business to tell you (confidential) vital facts about the town.

We are assuming that you do not hanker for the professionals. If you do, you don't need our advice.

But if you're a stranger in town and are looking for a date and don't know how to get one, follow this advice.

Call the bell captain.

Refer to Appendix for list of escort services.

Walk up to any girl you see in the hotel lobby or cocktail bar.

Try the manicurist.

Get yourself a big, vicious dog and walk along the street. The cuties will stop to admire it.

It's not considered the least bit rude to offer a lift to a girl waiting for a bus or streetcar. If you've got a smart convertible, she'll probably take you up.

If it's summer, get yourself a bathing suit and go to one of the many fine beaches along the lake front. But we only recommend this if you look like Tarzan.

Visit a dance hall. See Appendix. It is perfectly okay for you to ask any girl to dance. But first make sure she isn't there with a bruiser.

(*Inside stuff:* Don't talk to girls sitting at bars in Rush Street cocktail lounges. They are "hookers" or maybe girl friends of tough guys, waiting to be called for.)

If you are really hard up, you can always join a church or the "Y". Young female hayseeds off the farms usually head directly for such places in Chicago.

The above pointers are only applicable if you are free and over twenty-one. If you're married and your ball and chain is with you, you will have to figure out how to get rid of her. That's up to you. If you're under twenty-one, we won't give you our advice, and you will know more than we do.

Dancing

Dancing is a popular indoor sport in Chicago, but one which requires considerable energy. The Lindy Hop is still in vogue in some places, and unless you can jive you just don't belong, socially.

Even the smart spots that have gone in for the rumba find few takers. If you are the sleek Latin type, and know how to wiggle your hips properly, you shouldn't have any trouble doing okay with the dames. They're all mad to learn.

At this writing, the only big place we can find that goes in for matinee dancing in the Loop is the Glass Hat, at the Congress Hotel.

At night you won't have any difficulty finding where to show off. Every hotel and night club features extra large dance floors, some with two dance bands to provide continuous music.

The cocktail lounges are popular because there is no 20 per cent Federal amusements tax.

Hotels which feature dancing usually knock off for the night at 2 A.M. The big night clubs present dance music until closing. Dance halls also close at 2.

If you don't know how to dance, consult the classified phone directory under "Dancing Instruction." You will find four pages of listings of dance schools. And some actually teach you how to dance.

If you like to dance, but can't afford inflated night club prices, you can find plenty of it free at churches and "Y's." And during the summer, the city fathers present free dancing in some of the parks. Consult the daily newspapers.

Dining

Food, like liquor, is also a personal subject. We are not going to recommend any restaurants here, though a list of Chicago's best-known places can be found by consulting the Appendix. After all, we don't know what your tastes are or how much you have in your purse.

The price of food appears to be somewhat less in Chicago than in other big cities, and the quality of the meat better, due, no doubt, to the stockyards.

There are restaurants for all, from a complete meal for two bits on West Madison, to $25 a head on the near North Side.

Few top restaurants remain in the Loop. Most of the better ones are on the North Side. If you go in for atmosphere and exotic stuff, you will want to get off the beaten track.

You will find that considerable class distinction takes place in the eating department in Chicago. While the highly publicized expensive dining rooms on the North Side cater to theatrical people, gangsters, and recently rich merchants, you will seldom, if ever, see any blue bloods from the society pages. The non-sporty element avoids the feeding grounds of the *nouveau riche.*

Aristocrats eat in private dining clubs, some open only to businessmen for lunch. Some serve in the evening, an accommodation to members and their wives when they are in from Lake Forest to attend the theatre.

Among the swank private dining clubs are: The Tavern, 333 North Michigan; The Attic, 135 South LaSalle; and the Casino Club, on Delaware Place.

Few who read this book will ever get inside. But it is possible for you to eat at the Imperial House and L'Aiglon, if you look presentable and have enough money to pay the bills. It is suggested you make reservations in advance. (See Appendix.) If you are not known to the headwaiter, be sure to tip him liberally when you come in.

Divorce

The causes for divorce in Illinois are many. Cruelty is always easy to prove. Other grounds are adultery, desertion, alcoholism, conviction of a felony, impotency, violence, loathsome disease, and five years' separation. The law requires a year's residence in the state before beginning the action, but almost any lawyer knows how to beat this by cooking up affidavits that you have been there that long even though you just flew in that day. Divorces are granted the same day the case comes to court if there's no contest. Divorcees may remarry immediately.

Elevators

When the lift operator tells you to stand back, be sure and do it. For in case you have not noticed, Chicago's elevators have no safety doors inside. If you are too near the front, and someone gives you a shove from the rear while the car is traveling at high speed, you might get your arm cut off. The law requires buildings to install safety doors only if they've already had one serious accident. The Real Estate lobby, through generous contributions to the political machines, effectively prevents the passage of a sane elevator safety act.

Escort Service

If you're alone in Chicago and must attend a function that requires you to come with a companion, you can hire good-looking girls or presentable boys on an hourly fee basis. (See Appendix.) In the case of the girls, these escorts are not prostitutes, though many of the boys, if you can call them that, are in training to become gigolos.

In most cases, the girls are well-bred and often college students. Many, however, are in business for themselves, after hours.

It is customary after employing an escort, male or female, to tip liberally, depending upon the number of hours you've engaged their services. A minimum of $5 is suggested.

If the escort is a man who has been engaged to take a woman out, it will look better if before they start, she gives him the money to pay the bills so that she is not seen settling up.

A sandwich man outside the Palmer House hands out ads for one of the better escort services.

(*Inside stuff:* When old dolls foot the bill for young gigolos, they should slip the dough unobtrusively. But when old goats give $100 bills to young frills for cab fare it's O.K. to pass the cabbage over the table. It pays to advertise.)

Fines

We warned you that everything goes in Chicago, except traffic violations. They will crack down on you for the smallest infraction. For most offenses, however, it is not necessary to go to traffic court in person to pay fines. Many stationery, drug stores, hock shops and check-cashers provide a service which will appear in court for you and pay your fine for a slight fee—as low as 25 cents.

Another outfit follows traffic cops around and leaves cards on your car when you get a ticket for parking, advising you where to contact the service. Their fee, too, is only 25 cents.

It has been rumored that sometimes these groups work in cahoots with the traffic cop.

Flirting

In many cities, it is positively dangerous to flirt with strange women, especially in crowded business districts where you are in danger of being run in. In Chicago, however, the wenches seem flattered by these attentions, and will not resent them even though they may not necessarily take you up. As already mentioned, you can talk to any young thing, or older one, that you see in a hotel lobby or cocktail bar. You will not be thought forward if you offer a lift to a girl waiting for a ride. In fact, if you go by in an empty car and don't offer it, she'll think you're selfish.

Guns

You require a license to carry a concealed weapon, but there are no laws against keeping any kind of an arsenal in your home or even in your car. Cops can't pinch you, even on the street, without a search warrant. Chicago's pistol law is handmade for mobsters.

(*Inside stuff:* But the Federal Small-Arms Act, which is enforced by the Alcoholic Tax Unit of the U. S. Treasury, provides that anyone who transfers a machine gun, sawed-off shotgun, or carbine, must pay a $300 transfer tax. It further forbids any felon to carry a pistol.)

Guys

Some paragraphs back we told lonesome men how to meet dames, and now we are going to do the same for you femmes. If you are pretty, or even half-way attractive, you won't need this advice. In Chicago, all you have to do is stand on a street corner and you'll be swept off your feet, and not by the wind, either.

The same information that we gave the men goes for you, except that you are somewhat limited because there are no burlesque bars that employ B men and few bawdy houses with boys. However, Chicago even possesses those. But you've got to know where to find them and we don't.

What we said for men is to be applied in reverse by girls.

Hat Checks

Wherever you go, you will find that a cutie grabs your hat and coat before you are half in and hands you a pasteboard check in return. For this service you are expected to tip her at least a quarter. Dime tippers get a bad reputation. The girl, of course, does not keep this money. She works on a straight salary for a concessionaire. The concessionaire pays the café owner a yearly rental, usually in advance. Quite often this rental is the money that enables the club to open up in the first place.

If you are extra-liberal, you may be pleased to learn that a smart hat check girl soon learns how to steal from her boss. When business is good and the take is above average, she does not hesitate to pocket several dollars herself, though this requires considerable legerdermain, because the concession manager has eagle eyes.

Hat check girls are usually paid from $30 to $35 a week and the concession figures that they steal another $2 a day, which they don't yell about. If it's more they fire the girl.

Largest concessionaire in Chicago was Richards and Hassan, a New York firm. At this writing, it has been broken into two separate companies. Chicago manager is Jack "Blubber" Rosen, once a New York cab driver and slugger for the cab driver's union during the strike of 1934. Rosen used to work the cab-rank outside the old Paradise Restaurant on Broadway, and became known as "Cupid" when he evolved a system to provide packaged weddings for drunks.

When he saw an especially romantic couple come out of the club and get in his cab, he told them they ought to get married and then offered to drive them to a country town where he had an arrangement with the Village Clerk and the Justice of the Peace. The $25 charged included cab fare, license, judge's fee and wedding breakfast in a roadhouse.

Many Broadwayites were swept into marriage by this enthusiastic salesman, though records show none lasted more than a week.

When that business petered out, Blubber became an errand boy for the characters who ran the nightclub and soon found himself managing the hat check room. Then his future was assured. His climb was steady. Soon he was sent to take over Chicago. Blubber now drives a Cadillac convertible.

Hotels

When you arrive in Chicago, we presume you know where you want to go. Do not let the cab driver steer you elsewhere. If you haven't made hotel reservations, don't take his advice. Consult the Traveler's Aid Society.

You can find hotels in Chicago for every taste and pocketbook, though those suitable for the luxury trade are too few.

On the other hand, there are many "hotels" that you might want to patronize for stated reasons, but not to be a guest in. Many assignation houses still operate in the Loop and in surrounding territories.

If you want a family hotel where every woman is your wife, you will find them on the near North Side. It is reported that at some they ring a bell every morning at 7 so the guests can return to their own rooms.

Considering its location as a transportation center, Chicago does not have enough hotels. This is still the most important convention town in the country and it is always difficult to get a room. It is suggested that you make your reservation well in advance. If, however, you do arrive without a reservation, you can pull the old one like going up to the room clerk and asking if he's got a room for "Mr. Jones," meanwhile slipping him a ten spot.

Most hotels are broadminded and do not inquire too closely about the marital status of couples who check in with baggage. However, many are death on bringing unregistered girls to your room. This is not for moral reasons, but because the bell captain, the house detective and the room clerk have the call-girl concession and resent outside competition, amateur or not.

Application to the hotel credit manager will enable you to open a charge account at most, and have bills sent to your home or office in or out of town. You can cash checks, too. This service is especially desirable if you want a room for a few hours for the afternoon or evening. It saves embarrassment. You phone in, find out what room is assigned to you, and then pick up the key at the desk on your way up. The bill is sent to your office at the end of the month.

(*Inside stuff:* It is a specific offense to defraud a hotel of revenue. Maybe they won't pinch you because you've got a babe in the room, but they will go after you if you try to beat 'em out of the difference in rate between one and two guests. It is a crime to obtain lodging and food in a hotel with attempt to defraud, but hotels are obliged to serve all comers to their capacity.)

Guests may not be barred because of race or creed, but no hotel is required to serve intoxicated or disorderly persons.

The hotel bell captain is its most important functionary and you can't do without him. When everything else fails, he can get you tickets for shows or the ball game, rent you a limousine, find an all-night drug store, place a bet on a horse, or find a blonde. He expects to be rewarded lavishly for these services.

Limousines

The smart visitor or permanent resident always uses rented private limousines. You can look in the phone book or ask the hotel porter to get you a car and chauffeur or phone Thorne Anderson, LI 9-1790, or Gray Line, SA 2-4600. Except for the fact that the number on the license plate begins with the tell-tale taxi "O," it is indistinguishable from the millionaire's private car.

The chauffeurs are well-trained and uniformed. The cars are brand new Cadillacs or Packards. (*Inside stuff:* Many have draw shades over the rear windows so you can be in privacy.)

These limousines not only permit you to make an impression when you call on the dame, but they are downright handy and much better than cabs. Price is about $5 an hour, plus a minimum of $1 an hour tip.

Marriage

Don't think we're advising it, but if you do have to get married, Illinois laws require a Wassermann test before the ceremony. That's to give you a chance to change your mind, which might not be a bad idea.

However, if you're in such a hurry that you can't wait, or if you have doubts about your ability to pass, your bell captain will be sure to know of some hick-town judge who can be prevailed upon to fake the test and hitch you up regular, for a $25 fee.

Midwest Manners

Chicagoans are informal. During the summer it's O.K. to appear on the street or even in some smart cocktail lounges, without coat or tie.

Most Chicago men prefer to wear hats summer and winter. The straw hat is extremely popular in Chicago and has not gone out as in Eastern cities. Either sailors or panamas are approved. No Chicagoan wears a felt hat in summer.

Whereas well-dressed Eastern men never have creases in their sleeves, the Chicagoan considers it necessary to show that he has had his suit pressed. Well, what do you send it to the tailor for?

Chicago's homey informality is seen in the cut and style of gents' clothes. Such trimmings as belts in the back and pleats in the coats are passable, but not recommended, especially if you plan to travel East.

Chicago women dress by extremes. It's slouchy house dresses and slacks, or beyond-the-minute Parisian imports with ridiculous hats. A Chicago woman would rather be found nude than without a chapeau. In New York the best dressed never wear them.

Chicago refused to give in completely to the new look and now the smart gals are saying, "See, didn't we tell you?" The extra long skirt never did come in completely in Chicago, and now that it is getting shorter elsewhere, Chicago is beginning to catch up, or maybe fashion is catching up with Chicago.

* * *

You can tell what part of the country you're in by how they serve the salad and the coffee. In New York, salad is always a separate course after the roast and before dessert. Coffee is always served after the dessert, at the tail end of the meal.

In California, salad is served as an appetizer before the meal and coffee alongside the eats.

But in Chicago salad is a must with the roast, and most people drink their coffee during the main part of the meal.

* * *

When your babe goes to the ladies' room, always give her at least two bits as a tip for the pro, plus a nickel if she plans to phone another guy—be broadminded.

Money

If you haven't got it, we don't know how you can get it. And if you do have it, we're not going to tell you how to spend it. But if you have so much it troubles you, here are a few tips. Hotels are not responsible if it's stolen from your room, but they are required by law to keep it and your other valuables in the safe.

Many money exchanges are open at night and some all night. These do not do banking services, but will sell you travelers' checks or money orders which are perfectly safe, and can be refunded even if stolen.

Nudes

We don't know why we brought this subject up. Nudity is such a cheap commodity, you can tell us more about it than we can you.

But if you want to see more of the female form divine than is displayed on North Clark Street, we suggest you join a life class in the Art Institute, or if you can afford it, set up a studio near Bughouse Square, and pretend that you're an artist and call a model's agency. (See Appendix.) As for a girl to pose in the raw. Or if that's too tame, ask the bell captain or cab driver to steer you to a place on Rush Street where they have nude shows with tricks.

Shave Yourself

"You're next!" But not in Chicago. There's an angle to everything there, so tonsorial parlors are no exception. It's not how long you've been waiting, but who you know. If you're a regular customer, the barber always slips you in ahead of strangers. The chumps are told the interloper had "an appointment."

The big shops in the best hotels are the worst offenders. Mortimer waited for an hour in the Drake barber shop while five "appointments" went ahead, out of regular turn. He finally left unshaven. Others, not favored, also did the same.

Taxi Talk

The two big fleets, Yellow and Checker, are under allied ownership. Most independent cabbies are veterans. Many hackmen are newcomers on the job and know less about Chicago than do tourists. Be sure your driver knows where your destination is before he starts his meter. (*Inside stuff:* The law says he's got to take you wherever you want to go in the city limits. If he refuses call a cop.) Flat rates are not permitted, and more than one party is not allowed. (Many South Side independents cheat.) Regular hackmen get paid $1.00 by some cafés for every party they bring. Remember this next time your driver tries to tout you off the place you want to go.

The way to tell if a cab is empty—at night—is to watch the light on the roof over the driver's seat. If it's on, he has no fare.

It's pretty tough to get a cab in the Loop during the late afternoon homeward-bound rush-hour. If you're stranded between 5 and 6 P.M., try the Randolph and Clark entrance of the Sherman, or the Wabash Avenue side of the Palmer House. Cabs are constantly discharging passengers at these hotels. Another good place to snag a taxi is in front of Fritzels, State and Lake, where diners begin to arrive early. Be sure to let the doorman know you intend to tip liberally.

Tipping

Of course, if you're a muzhik who doesn't care what they think of you and will never be back again, anyway, it doesn't matter how you tip. But if you expect to return often, it pays to be liberal.

Remember that 10 per cent is no longer sufficient for a waiter. He ought to get 15 to 20 per cent.

If you want a ringside table, the headwaiter turns up his nose at anything less than two, and will probably figure that you should have given him five.

The captain who takes your order and presides at your table should also get two. Don't forget the retiring room, the cigarette girl, the bus boy, the hatcheck girl and the doorman.

In other words, it's cheaper to stay at home.

Transportation

It is assumed that if you are making use of this book to learn about Chicago first-hand, you are already in the city or on the way.

Getting to Chicago is an easy business. In fact, once you board a train, either as a passenger in a Pullman, or a freeloader in a freight, it is almost impossible not to end up in Chicago.

We are not interested in why you came or how quickly you want to get out. If you travel the rods, you will not need this confidential advice. But if you arrived by train or by plane, we can save you time and trouble when you need it most, at the very beginning of your stay.

One of the most difficult things is to get a cab in a Chicago railroad station. The red caps are non-cooperative and will only haul your luggage as far as the loading platform. Chicago depot porters are white. Their union bars Negroes. Look for Porter No. 3 at La Salle Street. He can get you anything, anytime.

You can induce them to run to the head of the line and snag a taxi, by showing folding money. Smart travelers arrange in advance to be met by transportation, either by wiring friends if they have them or writing in advance to a motor livery service that rents limousines by the hour.

Chicago's airport is almost an hour from the Loop, near Cicero. When you arrive by plane, you will find that after you have waited an interminably long time for your baggage to be unloaded you will also have another long wait before it is transferred to the airline bus, and then again before the bus loads up with passengers and gets ready to shove off.

The smart traveler grabs a porter as soon as he debarks, gives him his baggage checks, and tells him to engage a cab at once. Then while the traveler waits in state in his cab, the porter pulls his luggage out ahead of the line. Suggested for this service is an extra dollar for each two bags.

It is comparatively easy nowadays to secure transportation in and out of Chicago, both by air and by train, although such swank trains as the 20th Century, the Chief, the Golden State and the U.P. Streamliners often are booked up ahead.

If you know no one who has an "in" with the railroad, you usually can get an accommodation on one of these trains by a little judicious bribing. It is against the law for employes of transportation companies to accept gratuities, but there is no law that forbids you to make them a bet of say $10 or $20, that they can't get you a ticket.

The New York Central's 20th Century Limited, which speeds between Chicago and New York in fifteen and a half hours, is the train you'll want to travel on if you care to make a splash.

This deluxe all-room train, which connects the nation's two largest cities, is more Chicago than New York. That is because few New Yorkers go to Chicago; but many Chicagoans go to New York. When you travel on her, you'll find that at least 75 per cent of the passengers are Chicagoans or look like Chicagoans. These are buyers bound to or from New York, executives off to directors' meetings, and wealthy folk tripping to Broadway to see the shows.

Outward bound from Chicago the Century is gay and gala. Its club cars are full of merry folk, dressed to kill, beginning an outing and getting properly drunk.

The return trip to Chicago is sombre.

Then the passengers are homeward-bound. The fun is over. They make a sad attempt to be happy, and quaff much liquor. But all the time they realize that when they arrive at La Salle Street Station at nine the next morning, they're back at work.

When you travel on good trains like the Century, don't forget to tip liberally and don't forget the dining car steward.

If you slip 'em a couple of bucks in advance you won't have to wait for a seat or to be served. If he knows you as a regular traveler, you can give him his gratuity at the end of the trip.

The good trains westbound from Chicago, like the Super-Chief and the Chief, exhibit another atmosphere. Whereas the Century is formal because it is going to New York, the extra-fare trains to the West take on the air of California as soon as they leave Dearborn Station. In the Century, you will want to wear dark clothes; but as soon as you get on the Chief, you go into sport-shirts and slacks, and no ties. The same rules about tipping hold good for the de luxe Western trains.

If you are traveling on Sundays, it is well to remember that dining and club cars can't serve liquor in such states as Indiana, Ohio, Pennsylvania, Iowa, Kansas, and many others. Bring your own booze.

Waiters' Rackets

All over the world waiters have their little tricks. But in Chicago they've invented a few of their own.

The thing to watch for is the switched check. He presents you with a larger check, originally written for another table, and possibly already paid. If you study it and see it doesn't belong to you, he'll apologize, say he gave you the wrong check, and then give you your own smaller one.

Padded checks are common, too, because the average person doesn't remember how many drinks he had.

This also applies to mistakes in addition in the waiter's favor. If you add it up and find it to be wrong, he makes a joke about his own poor adding.

Water

Most of our friends don't use water for anything except to wash in, but if you're one of the old-fashioned few who still drink it, you will be amazed and annoyed by the taste of the tapwater in Chicago when you first get there. It is so highly chlorinated it spoils your tea and coffee. Though you can get used to it after a fashion, you will find that most of the better dining places serve bottled water and that's a tip to you.

33. CONFIDENTIAL GUIDE TO CHICAGO

Alcoholism Treated: After a few weeks in Chicago you may need this. We did. Call Samaritan, RO 4-0981, or Halco, MO 4-0098, or look up "Sanitariums" in the classified phone directory.

Amusement Parks: You can kiss your gal friend in the privacy of the tunnel of love. If you haven't a girl friend, you can probably find one here. Riverview Park at Western and Belmont is one of the country's largest.

Artificial Eyes for Animals: We don't know why you'd be interested in this, but put it in just in case you are. Dorothy Flicek, 1151 West Grand, HA 1-1339.

Astrologers and Fortune Tellers: If you're wondering when that dark, handsome man will come into your life, or if you want to know what the stock market is going to do, call Algernon W. Asa, BA 1-8999 or Christina Dahl, KI 5-9477. Remember, we don't recommend this way of spending your money, but if you're a chump, that's your hard luck. (Wisdom of a Midwest Wolf: When your gal friend begins to get serious about astrology, comparing her birth date with yours, run, you poor fish, or you're hooked!)

Many tearooms also employ babes who read your tea leaves. There is no fee for this service. You're supposed to tip.

Some cocktail lounges and cabarets feature palmists, numerologists or handwriting experts. They work on a tip basis, too, and pay the club a certain amount weekly for the privilege.

Bail Bonds: We know our readers won't need this, but by looking up "bail bonds" in the classified phone book you can find an outfit that provides 24-hour service at all police stations and courts.

Bank, Auto Drive-in: In other towns you can drive into movies or soda fountains, but Chicago goes 'em one better. If you're out with an expensive blonde and suddenly find yourself short of cash, you don't have to get out of your car to get it. Central National Bank, 728 West Roosevelt.

Barber Shops, All Night and Sunday: If you get a quickie call at 2 A.M. and haven't a razor blade, you can get a shave 24 hours a day at Madison and Clark, Washington and Clark, and in the Morrison Hotel.

The barber shop in the Palmer House, as well as the Morrison, is open Sunday. In a real emergency, your bell captain can probably find a barber who'll come to your room. (*Inside stuff:* If you're used to looking at yourself in the mirror while the barber works on you, you'll be disappointed to learn that in Chicago they insist upon turning you away from the looking glass. Barbers have a strong union and don't want any advice from the customer.)

Baseball: Chicago has two famous teams which at this writing have been fighting it out for the cellar for many years. White Sox play at Comiskey Park, 35th and Archer Avenue, South Side. The Cubs appear at Wrigley Field, Addison and Sheffield, on the North Side. If you like novelty on the diamond, an all-girl league plays at Admiral Stadium, West Side.

Beauty Shops—All Night: Suppose your boy friend calls at three in the morning and says, "Come over, I'm lonesome," and what if your hair looks a sight? The Sultan Beauty Shop, 664 State Street, DE 7-9687 is open 24 hours a day.

Birth Certificates: We don't know why you'd want this, because if you weren't born it won't help, and if you were, you'll know all about it. But just in case you do want a certificate, whether you were registered at birth or not, try Alpha Press, PL 2-5739 or Louis Lange, DE 7-2229.

Blacksmiths: Practically everyone who comes to Chicago nowadays comes by plane, train or car, but if you're the old-fashioned type and prefer a surrey with a fringe on top, Chicago has horse manicurists. Try James Barber, 4230 South Emerald or Charles E. Larson, 2645 North Keeler.

Boating: This is for sailors on their days off. You can rent rowboats in any of the parks. Speedboat rides on Lake Michigan are available under the Michigan Avenue bridge. Excursion boats sail for Michigan points and Milwaukee during the summer. The latter are recommended as floating hotels. The cost is small.

Bridge Clubs: They don't call this gambling because it's supposed to take skill to play the game. The oldest bridge club in the West is in Room 705 of the Morrison Hotel. Bridge instruction obtainable from Helen Booth, MI 3-9530 or Mildred Cunningham, AM 2-5910.

Burlesque: Who brought that up?

Chiropractors: Illinois law permits these bonesetters to use the honorific "Doctor" in front of their names like real physicians and surgeons. If you go for that kind of cure, you'll find hundreds in the classified phone book.

Cleaners, One Day: If you've still got a suit left to be cleaned, after you've been taken at stud by the other one-day cleaners, you can get seven-hour service from "Same Day," BI 8-0333 or call for the valet in your hotel.

Comfort Stations: When you gotta go, you gotta go. It's for free in the Public Library and City Hall. You've gotta pay a nickel or a dime in most railroad stations and hotels. If you've got a lot of nerve, you can walk into any bar room, then walk out fast before the bartender sees you.

Detective Agency, Colored: In case you're looking for someone in Bronzeville, and you're afraid to go there yourself, call Bruseaux, DE 2-2515.

Dog Walkers: Maybe you don't use your pooch as a decoy for a pickup, in which case you will probably want a valet to take him out. Young men to walk or sit with dogs can be obtained by phoning the Moody Bible Institute, MI 2-1570 and ask for "Dog-walking Department."

Drug Addiction Treated: It's so easy to get the stuff in Chicago, this is a profitable business. If you're tired of flying high, and you don't like the idea of free treatments from Uncle Sam, call North Shore Health Resort, Dial Operator, WI 6-0211 or Dr. Weirick's Sanitarium, PA 5-2604.

Drug Stores, All Night: In case you forgot to buy something before midnight, or if you get sick, try Dearborn and Division or the Stevens Hotel.

Emergency Information: Birth Control Bureau of Information, 32 West Randolph, RA 6-8685 or Planned Parenthood Association, 203 North Wabash, DE 2-4856.

Escort Services: Attractive females and young men are supplied by Model's Escort Service, Inc., WE 9-5928, or else try At Your Service, Inc., AN 3-2747 or Kay Jarrett, DE 7-1408.

Fashion Shows: If your wife drags you along, at least you can lamp the pretty models. They have them Wednesdays and Fridays from 12:15 to 2 in Carson Pirie's eighth-floor Tea Room; Wednesdays and Saturdays, from 11:45 to 1:45 in Marshall Field's Walnut and Narcissus Rooms; and on Wednesdays at 3 at the Old Heidelberg.

Gambling: You should ask?

Guides: We hardly believe our customers are interested in seeing such sights as the stockyards, the Art Institute, and the Merchandise Mart. But if this gets into wrong hands, and you are the kind who goes for that, you can get a licensed guide—male or female—from Andrew T. Frain, WE 9-4318.

Horse and Carriage: New Parkway, 2155 North Clark, DI 8-6140, will provide you with a nag and driver for a ride through the park. This is the way some men of the world woo, but is it worth the trouble?

Horse Racing: You really don't have to go to the track to play the ponies in Chicago because you will find a bookmaker every ten feet and a horse room every 100. But if you want to watch your nag lose, the Chicago area has five running tracks, Arlington, Hawthorne, Lincoln Fields, Sportsman's Park and Washington Park, and one trotting track, Maywood Park. There are night trotters at Hawthorne, also. Ever since night harness racing came to the city, nightclub business has been lousy. All the folding money ends up in the pari-mutuel machines.

Hypnotism: When you've tried everything and the blonde still says no, take her to Hypnotism Institute of Chicago, 7 West Madison.

Investigations, Confidential: W. C. Dannenburg, former F.B.I. agent in charge of the Chicago district. Phone RA 6-4256. At night, LI 9-7961.

Lipstick Stain Removers: You don't have to leave home if the cutie smears makeup on your jacket. Try Ideal, HA 1-7935 or Spot Chek, WE 9-5821.

Maid Service: If your slavey quits without notice, refer to the classified phone book.

Manicurists: We don't have to tell the traveling salesman about this. The babes will file your nails, talk to you about politics, and maybe make a date. All hotels and barber shops or the bell captain can get one to come to your room —for manicuring, of course.

Manure: We slipped this in to see if you're reading. You can buy it by the truckload or shovelful from Gest's, 5820 South Western, or if in a hurry, call Midwest Mushroom Company, Dial Operator, Desplaines 3-017-W.

Marital and Sex Problems: If you still have same after reading this book, call American Clinical, RA 6-3570.

Marriage Tests: People have been getting married for millions of years, but now you've got to pass an examination like for driving a car. Two-hour tests from National, 30 West Washington, or try Uptown, LO 1-2934.

Midwives: After everything we've told you, some people insist on getting in that condition. There's a doctor on every corner, but if you're old-fashioned, you can find midwives listed in the classified phone directory.

Models' Agency: Maybe you want to become a model, or maybe you want to hire one. Try Patricia Stevens, 360 North Michigan, Patricia Vance, 6 North Michigan, Career Studios, 540 North Michigan Boulevard, 314 North Michigan, Connie Seaman, 75 East Wacker, or Sabie, 203 North Wabash.

Naprapaths: That's one we wrung in on you. We don't know what they are any more than you do, but there are plenty of them. See that heading in classified phone directory.

Naturopaths: Same goes as for above.

Nurseries, Day and Night: It's your own fault if you bring a brat with you. But if you have no one to leave him with at home, look in the classified phone book under "Day and Night Nurseries."

Osteopaths: These bone manipulators also are permitted to use the title "Doctor" in Illinois. You'll find them in the phone book.

Out of Town Newspapers: If you're lonesome for home so soon, try 37 West Monroe, or State and Randolph.

Post Office, All Night: In case you need money in a hurry, and Western Union won't trust you for a collect wire, you can buy stamps at Van Buren and Canal Streets—24 hours a day—if you have three cents.

Pregnancy Tests: It's your own fault if you get that way, but if you don't know, try Lincoln-Belmont, BU 1-5120, Uptown, BI 8-2088, or Chicago, HA 7-3359.

Psychologists: If you can't understand why you act so goofy (we know, you've read this book), call David Boder, LO 1-2684, Eva Bornstein, CE 6-6109, or Psychological Guidance Center, CE 6-2886.

Railroad Cars, Used: Just why you want to buy a second hand railroad car is beyond us, but if you do, Briggs and Turivas, CO 4-1420 will be glad to supply you.

Rent, For: You can rent anything in Chicago from airplanes to sleighs and hayracks and including a wife for the night, but excluding false teeth. Refer to classified book under "Airplanes," "Autos," "Bars," "Bikes," "Dress Suits," "Dresses," "Sleighs."

Secretarial: If you can't stand the puss on the public stenographer in the hotel lobby, and you've got some dictating to do, call FR 2-0180 or else get in touch with A Number One, WE 9-7187 or Business and Professional Men's Bureau, CO 1-0140.

Shopping Service: If you're too busy with the B girls to buy a present for your wife before you return home, call Isabel and Lois Nuckols, AM 2-2599, or Behr, RO 4-0722. Shopper's Escort Company, CE 6-0458 tells you where to get it.

Sightseeing: We wouldn't know about this. Try American, HA 7-8768 or Gray Line, SA 2-4600.

Stags: Personally, we never go to these affairs because we can't stand the food. But if you're in charge of booking one, and don't know where to get the cuties, call Artists Corporation, FR 2-3897, Benn, DE 2-6850 or Kay Jarrett, DE 7-1408.

Sterility Tests: It's always good to know. American, 30 West Washington.

Stockyards: Even if you don't see it, you'll be able to smell it. This is the world's largest concentration point for cattle on the hoof. Some people go to visit it. As far as we're concerned, the stockyards is what "back of the yards" is in back of. This section is one of Chicago's toughest.

Sucker List: Chicago is the mail order center of the world, so it's natural that you can buy lists there giving the names of people who are pushovers for any kind of sales approach. Look under "Mailing lists" in classified phone directory.

Swimming: The Chicago lake front is almost one continuous 26-mile-long beach. They say the prettiest gals go in at Oak Street. So why bother spending your money in a burlesque bar?

Telegraph Office, All Night: If they clean you in a crap game, or the redhead rolls you, you can wire home for money any hour of the day or night from Western Union in the Sherman Hotel.

Theatre Tickets for New York Shows: That's how it is nowadays. Chicago is just a suburb of Broadway. You can buy choice seats for New York hits from Congress, 141 North Clark, CE 6-0600, or from New York Service, 55 East Washington, RA 6-0800.

Venereal Tests: If you didn't take our advice and got too chummy with that taxi drinker or peeler, call National, RA 6-3570 or Lincoln Belmont, WE 5-2277.

Worrier, Professional: While you're waiting for the results, call Frank Teurfs, HA 7-3994 or James Salach, BE 5-1867, who will do your worrying for a fee.

PART FOUR

THE APPENDIX
(*Confidential!*)

A. ANATOMY LESSONS

A *NATION'S* interior geography is important in molding its character. A city, too, is a creature of the way it's laid out.

We are not going to get technical on you by telling you such stuffy facts as the Windy City's longitude and latitude—which we don't know—or delve into its geological underpinning, which we don't know either, or much less care about for that matter.

But the early planners who drafted the first plans of the city, and the subsequent citizens who watched it grow haphazardly along the original lines, are responsible for what's there today, and deserve a bouquet or an indictment, depending on how you look at it.

Roughly speaking (and it's pretty rough) the three sides of the city, North, West and South, are like three spokes of a broken wheel, around a hub which is the Loop, or downtown section.

Legally, State Street, which runs North and South, and Madison, which bisects the city on the East-West line, are the basic dividing lines, and all house numbers begin at these medians.

Sentimentally and practically, however, it's the Chicago River, with its two branches, one jutting southwest and the other northwest, which divides the sides of the town.

Thus everything north and east of the North Branch is North Side. West of the two branches is West Side. Downtown runs from the main stream of the river, at Wacker Drive, south to Roosevelt Road, or 12th Street. All south of that, and east of the South Branch, is South Side.

This is the only geography we are going to give you, but if you're not acquainted with Chicago, it's well to keep it in mind, for the various sides of the town enter into this story frequently, and figure importantly in chapters about crime, society, and naughty gals.

One other physical factor is worth remembering. It's the alley. The alley, which runs through almost every block, even downtown where property is worth tens of thousands a front foot, is extremely important in any consideration of the city's crime and sex habits.

The alleys were planned and are still used for the sensible utilitarian purpose of providing rear exits for the delivery of goods and the removal of waste and garbage.

As such they are of incalculable benefit to the city. But they're poorly lighted and at night make excellent lurking places for footpads, degenerates, and petty gamblers.

At the same time, in the residential sections, they are splendid substitutes for lovers' lanes, being used for romantic purposes not only by car-parkers, but by sweethearts who come afoot and do their love-making on covered ash-cans.

Chicago's uniform house numbering system generally runs 800 numbers to the mile, except in parts of the South Side, and as aforementioned, begins at State and Madison Streets.

Thus, 4800 North Clark Street is exactly six miles north of Madison.

B. CONFIDENTIAL GAZETTEER

(NOTE: Letters in first parentheses refer to direction street runs; numbers and letters in brackets indicate the distance in house-numbers, and the direction east or west of State Street or north or south of Madison Street.)

BROADWAY (N) [600 W] Northside shopping street, with usual quota of horse rooms, taverns, and dope peddlers at principal corners.

BUGHOUSE SQUARE [932 N] Proper name Washington Square, at North Clark and Walton Streets. Haunt of homos, pinkos, nature lovers and nuts. Chicago's version of London's Hyde Park with soap boxers and prosties.

CERMAK ROAD (E-W) [2200 S] As 22nd Street was the Main Lane of the old Levee. Chinatown at Wentworth Avenue.

CLARK STREET (N-S) [100 W] Theatrical, at Randolph, thoroughly commercial in the Loop, bawdy north of the river.

DEARBORN STREET (N-S) [36 W] Cocktail lounges with hookers; horse rooms; lawyers' offices.

DIVERSEY PARKWAY (E-W) [2800 N] Triangle of Diversey, Clark and Broadway is an uptown Tenderloin, with all the fixings.

DIVISION STREET (E-W) [1200 N] Gambling houses, neighborhood gangsters, Negroes, Poles and prostitutes.

FORTY-SEVENTH STREET (E-W) [4700 S] Darktown's chief shopping center, with night clubs, saloons and street walkers.

HALSTED STREET (N-S) [800 W] Sin in any language. The street of many races, beginning with Swedes on the north, then running through Germans, Polish, Italians, Greek, Mexican, Jewish, Negro and Bohemian, with the virtues and vices of all.

HOWARD STREET (E-W) [7600 N] City limits, dry on one side, soaking on the other. More clip artists, whores and reefer salesmen per square foot than anywhere else in Chicago.

JACKSON BOULEVARD (E-W) [300 S] Retail men's apparel shopping center, also musical instruments.

LA SALLE STREET (N-S) [150 W] The Midwest's Bourse, with the Wheat Pit, the local stock exchange and the giant banks. Harvard accents, English tweeds, and old school ties.

LAKE SHORE DRIVE (N-S) [485 E] One of the world's most beautiful, running along Chicago's periphery through and alongside broad acres of parkland and past breathtaking architecture. The goal of every chorine is to end up here as a keptie.

MADISON STREET (E-W) [1 N and S] Median thoroughfare legally dividing the city into North and South. Corner of State is town's busiest. West Madison, town's lousiest.

MICHIGAN AVENUE (N-S) [100 E] One of the world's better known thoroughfares with most expensive shops and broads. This great boulevard, below Randolph Street, was built to what it is now before the 1910's were ended. It's a tip-off to what happened in Chi. The imposing office buildings, clubs and hotels are the solid Chicago constructed by the inspired founders. North of Randolph, the handiwork of a newer generation, is with the exception of a few beautiful modern towers like the Tribune and Wrigley, as hesitant as the era.

THE MIDWAY (E-W) [6000 S] Wide plaisance of the 1893 World's Fair, now the University of Chicago campus. It is the invisible border line between whites and blacks, with Red predominant.

MILWAUKEE AVENUE (diagonal NW) Major shopping street for hundreds of thousands of foreign stock; running through Negro, Italian, Jewish and the largest Polish concentration in the country.

OHIO STREET (E-W) [600 N] A main drag in the new Levee. Assignation hotels and clip dives with call girls.

QUINCY STREET (W) [220 S] Short block between State and the old Post Office. Strolling strumpets.

RANDOLPH STREET (E-W) [150 N] Theatrical,

Tin Pan Alley, politico-legal center. Hookers on the street and B Girls in the "Theatre Bars."

ROOSEVELT ROAD (E-W) [1200 S] Formerly 12th Street. Runs from the Lake and Illinois Central Station through the old Ghetto to Murderer's Row.

RUSH STREET (N-S) [100 E] Deadfall lane, with the plushiest cocktail lounges, the most expensive broads. Once an avenue of fine and aristocratic homes, now sports a pizzeria, tavern, restaurant or intime cabaret every ten feet. Show gals, models and kepties live in the vicinity.

SIXTY-THIRD STREET (E-W) [6300 S] Main Street of Bronzeville's toniest section.

STATE STREET (E-W) [1 E and W] Median thoroughfare dividing the city into East and West. One of the world's great retail shopping streets with more famous department stores per square inch than anywhere in the universe. South State stinks!

STREETERVILLE Eighty million dollars worth of filled-in land, on the near North Side, east of Michigan. Colorful "Cap." Streeter claimed it by squatters' rights. After his dispossess and demise, many of the town's stateliest apartments, hotels and buildings were erected on it.

THIRTY-FIFTH STREET (E-W) [3500 S] Bronzeville's Skid Row, with dope, gambling, and cheap whores at the corner of State.

TOWERTOWN Area surrounding the historic Water Tower at Michigan and Chicago Avenue (800 N.). Generally embraces the pleasanter part of the near North Side, with shops, fine restaurants, rich bohemians and expensive broads.

VAN BUREN STREET (E-W) [400 S] Has small and select Skid Row catering to bums off the Rock Island and New York Central. Marks southern boundary of State Street shopping district. Hookers and homos at State and Van Buren.

WABASH AVENUE (N-S) [45 E] Under the "El" are sporting goods, music and book stores; shops for the upper crust and cafeterias where lonesome stenos dine.

WILSON AVENUE (E-W) [4600 N] Shops, burlesque bars, theatrical rooming houses, pickpockets, pimps and dope peddlers.

C. BACKSTAGE PHONE NUMBERS

Note: For theatres not listed, look up box-office numbers in phone book.

SHUBERT: AN 3-8292.
HARRIS: DE 2-8557.
BLACKSTONE: WE 9-8092.
OPERA HOUSE: DE 2-9210.
SELWYN: DE 2-9058.
CHICAGO (vaudeville): DE 2-9010.
ORIENTAL (vaudeville): DE 2-9255.

D. HEADWAITERS

A nod from one, and you're made. If he fingers you away, you might as well commit suicide.

ALABAM: *Jerry Elsner.*
BLACKHAWK: *"Tully."*
BLACKSTONE HOTEL: *Emile Holiner*
CASINO (South Side): *Paul Small.*
CHEZ PAREE: *"Filler," and Mickey Levin.*
CIRO'S: *Eddie Meyers.*
COLLEGE INN: *"Nick."*
DRAKE HOTEL: *"Frank."*
EDGEWATER BEACH HOTEL: *Paul Janis.*
LA SALLE HOTEL: *Fred Weisman.*
PALMER HOUSE: *Fritz Hagner.*
PUMP ROOM: *"Phil."*
STEVENS HOTEL: *Phil Itta.*

E. GUSTATORY GUIDE

(Listed, but not necessarily guaranteed.)

DINE WITHOUT ORCHESTRAL DIN:

Binyon's, 327 Plymouth (good eats).

Boston Oyster House, Morrison Hotel (famed for fish).

Café de Paris, 1260 N. Dearborn (crepes suzettes to thrill the yokels).

Cameo Room, 116 E. Walton (upper bracket).

Chez Paul, 180 E. Delaware (for them as likes shrimps).

Don the Beachcomber, 101 E. Walton (South Sea food served by a couple of Polynesians named Fritzel & Jacobson).

Fritzel's, State and Lake (swell food in one of the few big time places).

Fred Harvey's in the Union Station and in the Dearborn Station. (Wonderful food, patronized by residents as well as travelers.)

Henrici's, 71 W. Randolph (where the term "Dine Without Orchestral Din" was invented. A Chi landmark).

Imperial House, 30 E. Walton (for them as wants to be chi chi).

Isbell's, 940 N. Rush (moderate prices for good food).

Shangri La, 222 N. State (the Orient was never like this).

Staly's, 127 S. Wells (politicians' hangout).

Tip Top, 111 S. Clark (where they go for steaks and ribs).

INSTRUMENTAL MUSIC, NO DANCING:

Boeuf Sur Le Toit, 1023 N. Dearborn (Frenchy, or did you guess it).

Gibby's, 192 N. Clark (food and hot piano).

Jazz, Ltd., 11 E. Grand Avenue (Dixieland jazz. No food).

Old Heidelberg (main dining room), 14 W. Randolph (mit Wiener waltzes).

Palmer House Chicago Room (gypsy music).

Singapore, 1011 N. Rush (hang-out of show crowd. Piano).

WITH DANCING (And little or no entertainment):

Ambassador Hotel East, Pump Room (snob's paradise).
Ambassador Hotel West, Buttery (intime).
Blackstone Hotel, Balinese Room (chic).
Congress Hotel, Glass Hat (popular).
Drake Hotel, Camellia House (hang-out of the debbies).
Ivanhoe, 3000 N. Clark (novelty spot, with a crazy atmosphere).
La Salle Hotel, Lotus Room (suburbanites' paradise).
Ye Olde Cellar, 322 N. Michigan (swell food, dancing and pretty singers).

WITH FLOOR SHOWS:

Alabam, 747 Rush (hot).
Bismarck Hotel Swiss Chalet (song and dance).
Blackhawk, Randolph and Wabash (popular prices).
Blackstone Hotel Mayfair Room (swank, big name acts).
Chez Paree, 610 Fairbanks Court (stars and babes. One of America's famed clubs).
Ciro's, 816 N. Wabash (intime entertainment).
Edgewater Beach Hotel Marine Dining Room (name bands and big shows).
Old Heidelberg's Rathskeller, 14 W. Randolph (gemuetlich).
Palmer House Empire Room (headliners and ballerinas).
Sherman Hotel College Inn (elaborate shows in famed room).
Stairway to Stars, 16 E. Huron (intimate).
Stevens Hotel Boulevard Room (ice shows usually, name bands).
Vine Gardens, 614 W. North Avenue (shows and bands).

FOR COCKTAILS:

Allerton Hotel (skyview from twenty-third floor).
Balinese Room, Blackstone Hotel (smart).
Chat Room, Parkway Hotel (pretty babes).

Hour Glass, La Salle Hotel (businessmen).

Mich-Boul, south of Bridge (advertising crowd and models).

Pump Room, Ambassador East (the upper crust).

Sheraton Lounge, Sheraton Hotel (pretty gals).

Town and Country, Palmer House (popular Loop meeting place).

F. BARE BABES

Stripping is illegal, said the cop, as he directed us to one of the following Palaces of Peel:

ALOHA, 2443 W. Madison
BACKSTAGE, 935 Wilson
CLUB MAJESTIC, 1658 W. MADISON
EL MOCAMBO, 1519 W. Madison
FLAMINGO, 1359 W. Madison
4811 CLUB, 4811 W. Cermak (Cicero)
FRENCH CASINO, 641 N. Clark
GLASS SHOW LOUNGE, 2950 W. Madison
GAYETY CAFE, 551 N. Clark
L & L CAFE, 1315 W. Madison
McGOVERN'S LIBERTY INN, 661 N. Clark
MUSIC BOX, 932 W. Madison
PLAYHOUSE, 550 N. Clark
PLAYHOUSE, 112 State (Calumet City)
POST TIME, 357 N. Clark
RIO CABANA, 400 N. Wabash
RIPTIDE, 101 State (Calumet City)
RONDAVOO, 100 State (Calumet City)
606 CLUB, 606 S. Wabash
SO-HO, 1124 W. Madison
SPA, Rush at Walton
TALK OF THE TOWN, 1159 N. Clark
TROCADERO, 525 S. State
21 CLUB, 21 State (Calumet City)

G. DINING AROUND THE WORLD

ARABIAN: Mecca, 1806 S. Michigan

BOHEMIAN:

Café Bohemia, 138 S. Clinton
Klas, 5734 W. Cermak
Little Bohemia, 1722 S. Loomis
Little Czechoslovakia, 2609 S. Lawndale
Old Prague, 5828 W. Cermak

CHINESE:

Bamboo Inn, 11 N. Clark
Bamboo Gardens, 202 W. Cermak
Guey Sam's, 2205 S. Wentworth
Hoe Sai Gai, 85 W. Randolph
House of Eng, 106 E. Walton
Ong Luk Yun, 105 N. Dearborn
Tai Dong, 2206 S. Wentworth
Won Kow, 2235 S. Wentworth

ENGLISH: St. Hubert's, 316 S. Federal

FRENCH:

Café De Paris, 1260 N. Dearborn
Chez Paul, 180 E. Delaware
Jacques, 900 N. Michigan
L'Aiglon, 22 E. Ontario

GERMAN:

Berghoff's, 17 W. Adams
Black Forest, 2623 N. Clark
Golden Ox, 1578 Clybourn
Red Star Inn, 1528 N. Clark
Schlogl's, 37 N. Wells

GREEK:

Athens, 530 S. Halsted
Athenian, 228 N. Dearborn
Greek Village, 711 S. Halsted

HAWAIIAN:

Honolulu Harry's Waikiki, N. Broadway near Wilson
Sea Isle, 1149 N. Clark

HUNGARIAN:

Blue Danube, 500 W. North
Epicurean, 316 S. Wabash

ITALIAN:

Adolph's, 1045 N. Rush
Agostino's, 1121 N. State

Bianca, 63rd and California
Boveri's, 20 E. Lake
Corsica, 79th and Western
Mario's, 27 E. Congress
Mona Lisa, 615 N. Wells
Pizzeria, 907 W. Taylor
Riccardo's, 437 N. Rush
Singer's, 100 E. Superior

JAPANESE:
Clark Restaurant, 851 N. Clark
Liberty Inn, 1126 N. Clark
Teapot Inn, 905 E. 43rd
Ted's, 1030 N. Clark

JEWISH:
Carl's, 3211 W. Roosevelt
Gold's, 812 W. Roosevelt
Gwirtz, 3145 W. Roosevelt
Loop Kosher, 10 S. Clark

LITHUANIAN:
Auditorium, 3131 S. Halsted
Universal, 750 W. 31st

MEXICAN AND LATIN AMERICAN:
Chapultepec, 713 S. Blue Island
El Cabron, 920 W. Western
Rancho Grande, 2126 N. Clark
Rio Rita, 1100 S. Halsted

POLISH:
Lenard's, 1307 N. Milwaukee
Warsaw, 820 N. Ashland

RUSSIAN: Yar, 181 E. Lake Shore Drive

SOUTH SEAS:
Don the Beachcomber, 101 E. Walton
Shangri La, 222 N. State
Singapore, 1011 N. Rush

SWEDISH:
Bit of Sweden, 1015 N. Rush
Kungsholm, 631 N. Rush
Sweden House, 157 E. Ohio

VIENNESE: Vienna, 1567 N. Halsted

H. ILLINOIS SEX LAWS

PEEPING TOM: No offense. May be disorderly conduct.

OBSCENITY, WALLS AND FENCES: No offense.

INDECENT EXPOSURE: Fine to $200, imprisonment to one year.

SEDUCTION: $5000 fine and/or one year.

ABDUCTION: One to ten years.

SODOMY: One to ten years.

INCEST: One to ten years.

FORNICATION: $500 fine or one year.

RAPE: One year to life.

STATUTORY RAPE: With consent, under sixteen. One to life.

MISCEGENATION: No offense.

FORCED MARRIAGE: One to ten years.

LEWD AND NOTORIOUS COHABITATION: No offense.

ADULTERY: $500 fine or one year.

BIGAMY: $1000 fine and five years.

ABORTION: One to ten years.

ADVERTISING ABORTION: One to three years, or $1000.

ADVERTISING BIRTH CONTROL: No offense.

LEWD ACTS WITH CHILDREN: One to twenty years.

OPERATING A BAWDY HOUSE: $200 fine and/or one year.

PROCURING: One to ten years.

PIMPING: Up to one year and $1000 fine. One to ten for subsequent offenses.

TRANSPORTING WOMEN FOR IMMORAL PURPOSES: One to ten years. If transportation is across state lines, it becomes a Federal offense.

PROSTITUTION: $200 and/or one year.

PATRONIZING A PROSTITUTE: Same as above.

STRIP-TEASING OR INDECENT EXPOSURE ON STAGE: Up to $200 and one year. (We can show you 200 in one hour!)

GENERAL OBSCENITY: $50 and/or six months.

CHILDREN AS PROSTITUTES: Discretionary with court.

CHILDREN SELLING OBSCENE ARTICLES: $500 and/or six months.

I. LOOP LEXICON

AD: Local underworld term for narcotic addict.

AFT: This afternoon.

"B" GIRL: A female bar-fly employed by saloons to solicit drinks from male customers, on a 50% commission. So called because they put the "bee," "bite" or "buzz" on patrons. See Index.

BEDBUG: Bronzeville's term for Pullman porter.

BEHIND THE LOG: Behind the bar; i.e., a bartender.

BEHIND THE YARDS: Descriptive of something lowdown or cheap.

BOUL-MICH: Chi chi abbreviation for Michigan Boulevard.

BRIDGED: What happens to you when a boat passes through the river, and the bridges go up. Generally a fifteen-minute delay.

CANADIAN: A euphemism for "Jew."

DOLL: Indiscriminate term of greeting between strangers, used similarly to "dear" in New York and "honey" in Hollywood.

DOUBLE CHOCOLATE SODA or SUNDAE (made with chocolate cream and syrup): Where this is called an "All Black," a "Double Chocolate" would be a double portion.

FLAT: Chicago usage for "apartment."

FORMAL: As applied to a gown. Known in the East as an "evening gown."

FRAPPE: A sort of milk shake with ice cream. Elsewhere the word "frappe" is occasionally used to denote a sundae.

FRENCH BASEMENT: Ground floor.

GOLD COAST: Something ritzy.

JABBER: Underworld cant for hypodermic user.

JANITOR: If you called the "super" that in New York, the "superintendent" would go on strike.

JOLIET JOSIE: Jail bait. A female under 18.

JUNK HOG: Localism for opium fiend.

LOG: A bar.

LOOP: Downtown.

MACHINE: Automobile.

MIXERS: See "B" Girls.

MIXESS: A female bartender.

MIXO: Glorified euphemism for bartender.

MIXOLOGIST: A mixo in an ultra place.

PERSONALITY GIRL: Chief "B" girl. A mixer with a following.

PROBATE COURT: Known as "Surrogate's Court" or "Widows and Orphans Court" in some states.

RECEPTION HALL: Foyer.

RED HOTS: Frankfurters or hot dogs.

SHOW-UP: What the police do at the daily prisoners' "Line-Up."

SMECKER: Dope fiend.

SPARROW COPS: Park policemen. Before 1934 there were twenty-two independent police forces patrolling the city's greenswards. Now they've been merged into one force of 700 men.

STATE'S ATTORNEY: Local name for district attorney or county prosecutor.

TAVERN: Legal euphemism for bar or saloon.

THOUSAND ISLAND DRESSING: The same stuff known as Russian dressing elsewhere.

TOOTHPICK ROW: Clark Street near Madison, with its quick lunch-rooms catering to office workers.

26 GIRL: Female who presides over the ever present dice game in nightclubs and saloons. See Index.

WHISKEY: When you ask for "whiskey and soda" in Chi, you get rye. In New York you get Scotch, and in the South or Far West bourbon.

NOTE ON PRONUNCIATIONS

Chicago speaks Middle American, a good, honest speech with vowels given full value, and no lah-de-dah of New England or the East.

Most words spoken as spelled, i.e., Goethe Street is "Gay-the," Desplaines is "Des-planes," Devon is "De-von" and theatre is "the-ay-ter."

INDEX

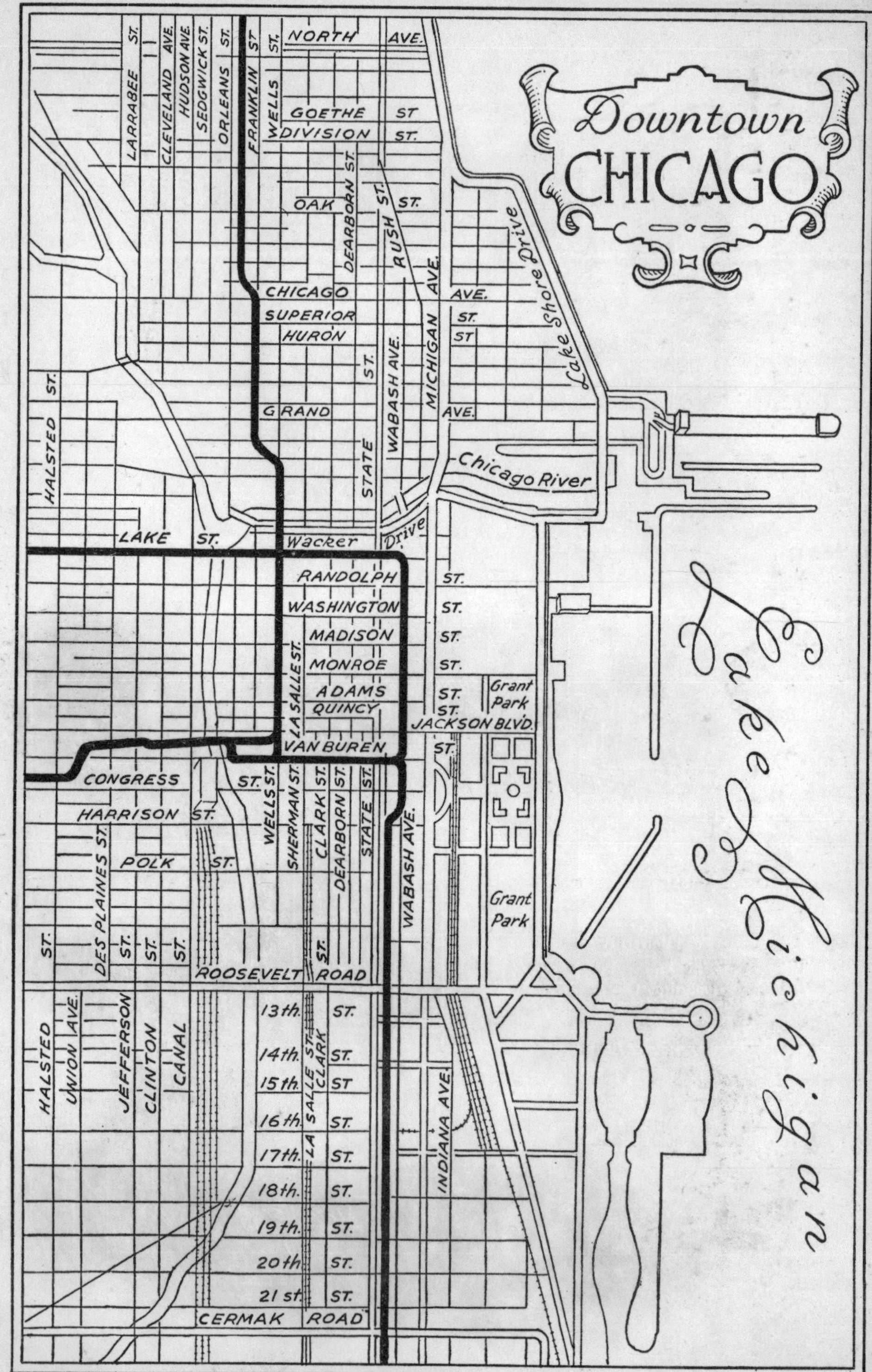
Downtown
CHICAGO
Lake Michigan
NORTH AVE.
GOETHE ST
DIVISION ST.
OAK ST.
CHICAGO AVE.
SUPERIOR ST.
HURON ST
GRAND AVE.
Chicago River
LAKE ST.
Wacker Drive
RANDOLPH ST.
WASHINGTON ST.
MADISON ST.
MONROE ST.
ADAMS ST.
QUINCY ST.
JACKSON BLVD.
VAN BUREN ST.
CONGRESS ST.
HARRISON ST.
POLK ST.
ROOSEVELT ROAD
13th. ST.
14th. ST.
15th. ST
16th. ST.
17th. ST.
18th. ST.
19th. ST.
20th. ST.
21 st. ST.
CERMAK ROAD
LARRABEE ST.
CLEVELAND AVE.
HUDSON AVE.
SEDGWICK ST.
ORLEANS ST.
FRANKLIN ST
WELLS ST.
DEARBORN ST.
RUSH ST.
STATE ST.
WABASH AVE.
MICHIGAN AVE.
Lake Shore Drive
HALSTED ST.
LA SALLE ST.
WELLS ST.
SHERMAN ST.
CLARK ST.
DEARBORN ST.
STATE ST.
WABASH AVE.
DES PLAINES ST.
ST.
ST.
ST.
ST.
Grant Park
Grant Park
HALSTED
UNION AVE.
JEFFERSON
CLINTON
CANAL
LA SALLE ST.
CLARK
INDIANA AVE.